FEMINISM ENCHANTED

FEMINISM
ENCHANTED

YANBING ER

Columbia University Press   *New York*

Columbia University Press
Publishers Since 1893
New York   Chichester, West Sussex

Library of Congress Cataloging-in-Publication Data

Names: Er, Yanbing, author.
Title: Feminism enchanted / Yanbing Er.
Description: New York : Columbia University Press, [2025] |
Includes bibliographical references and index.
Identifiers: LCCN 2025008888 (print) | LCCN 2025008889 (ebook) |
ISBN 9780231213202 (hardback) | ISBN 9780231213219 (trade paperback) |
ISBN 9780231559775 (ebook)
Subjects: LCSH: Feminism.
Classification: LCC HQ1155 .E72 2025 (print) | LCC HQ1155 (ebook) |
DDC 305.42—dc23/eng/20250606

Cover design: Milenda Nan Ok Lee

Cover art: Ellen Gallagher, *Blubber* (2000). Ink, pencil, and paper on linen,
120 x 192 inches (304.8 x 487.7 cm). © Ellen Gallagher.
Courtesy of the artist and Gagosian

GPSR Authorized Representative: Easy Access System Europe, Mustamäe tee 50,
10621 Tallinn, Estonia, gpsr.requests@easproject.com

In memory of my grandfather
Woon Wei Tuck

CONTENTS

ACKNOWLEDGMENTS

Feminism Enchanted emerged out of the supportive presence of many people, without whom it simply could not have come into being. Not unlike the strange and irreducible force of enchantment that I detail in the pages that follow, each of them embodies a special kind of magic that has made manifest this book. First and foremost, I am grateful to Elizabeth Grosz for all she has done for me. In our conversations, many of which have transpired in times of uncertainty and doubt, Liz has never stopped reminding me of the value of my work and, indeed, my own self. Over and again, Liz has shown me that an ethical imperative must guide not only the words that we write but also—and perhaps, more importantly— the ways that we act in this world. I may not ever be able to repay her kindness, but I am determined to pay it forward.

My thanks also go to Robyn Wiegman: there is no one else whose thinking and writing has been more transformative for my own. It is a rare gift to have had my work read by Robyn with such care, precision, and rigor; it is the unparalleled capacity of her intellectual vision that demanded a better, and much more reflexive, version of the original manuscript. Robyn's feedback, per the exceptional scholarship that she has produced, has taught me that the difficult but necessary practice of staying with our own critical turns of thought will also be an endlessly rewarding one. I hope I have done some justice to our shared objects of study in this book.

Wendy Lochner's belief in this project was invigorating from the very beginning. Wendy's support for my work never once waned throughout this journey, which could so easily have been a grueling and brutal one otherwise. Over the last few years, it has been a joy and a constant reassurance to receive multiple, enthusiastic emails from Wendy with the exact same subject line "Good news!"—emails detailing both the most major and the most minor milestones of this book. Working with Wendy has been wonderful experience, and I thank her for her patience and steadfast commitment to my work.

My undergraduate education at Nanyang Technological University (NTU) in Singapore was a formative and thoroughly enjoyable one. At NTU, Wernmei Yong Ade and Neil Murphy encouraged me to attend graduate school, and nurtured my early interests and ambitions. Perhaps the first intimations of *Feminism Enchanted* were formed during my time as a graduate student at the Department of English and Scottish Literature at the University of Edinburgh. With her fierce spirit and gentle humor, Carole Jones taught me how to become a more open-hearted academic and a better person. Lynne Pearce has been an unwavering source of support ever since. From the program, I will always treasure the warmth and solidarity of my friends Sarah Arens, Sarah Bernstein, Peter Cherry, Dave Coates, and Muireann Crowley.

I have had the great privilege of spending time at various institutions in the United States and United Kingdom where the writing of this book began in earnest. At Brown University, the Pembroke Center for Teaching and Research on Women offered a focused and generative space to think further and more expansively about questions of feminist theory. I am especially thankful to Bonnie Honig, Leela Gandhi, Anjuli Gunaratne, Anna Thomas, and Ron Wilson for engaging my work. I spent a whirlwind summer at the Department of Gender Studies at the London School of Economics, where Clare Hemmings and Sadie Wearing took time to speak with me about my ideas on enchantment. My very first, electrifying trip to the United States was in fact to the Feminist Theory Workshop at Duke University as a graduate student, and I was fortunate to be given the opportunity to return to the Department of Gender, Sexuality, and Feminist Studies some years later. At Duke, I must thank Elizabeth Grosz, Robyn Wiegman, Logan O'Laughlin, David Morgan, Sarah Wilbur, and M. D. Murtagh. I also want to acknowledge the tireless work of the administrative staff at each of these places, the people who facilitated my travel and stay: Donna Goodnow, the late Hazel Johnstone, and Julie Wynmor. An Overseas Postdoctoral Fellowship from the National University of Singapore (NUS) made all this possible for me.

At NUS, I have had the absolute pleasure of teaching smart and engaged students who have kept me excited about the work that I do. In particular, thank you to Yi Feng Choo, Melvin Ong, Alex Tan, and Ying Hu—all of whom will be happy to see that my book has finally materialized. My colleagues Heather Brink-Roby and Beryl Pong have listened and offered advice with the right measure of wisdom and compassion. I am so lucky to be able to call the both of you my friends, and I cannot wait to celebrate more of our achievements together.

This was a book written in the company of many friends, some of whom read and commented on earlier portions of the manuscript, and all of whom helped me to cross the finish line. Thank you, my brilliant friend Sarah Bernstein: words cannot express how much I cherish our ongoing correspondence on all manner of things. I will forever be on your speed dial and I am honored to be on yours. Anjuli Gunaratne and I wrote our books together over many hours and in the midst of many upheavals. I am so glad that we have become each other's biggest supporters in work and in life. Heather Brink-Roby was there for me during those times it mattered the most—from her I have learned what it means to be a true friend. I miss hanging out in Durham with Logan O'Laughlin, who has never failed to cheer me up whenever things feel down. Many thanks also to Hayun Cho, Claire Gullander-Drolet, Jin Yao Kwan, Jenny Morris, and Jerrine Tan, who have encouraged me in each of their distinct and irreplaceable ways. My friends outside of academia remind me of a life beyond writing that is also worth living: Priscilla Gan, Wanting Huang, Yifang Huang, Tiffany Seow, and Li Rong Wee.

The excellent team at Columbia University Press shepherded *Feminism Enchanted* smoothly and swiftly to publication: thank you to the superb Alyssa M. Napier for all other editorial support, and Kathryn Jorge for expertly handling the production process; my gratitude also goes to Zachary Friedman, Meredith Howard, Milenda Lee, and Zubin Meer. Paula Durbin-Westby built the comprehensive index, and Alex Tan provided invaluable assistance with a final round of proofreading. Costica Bradatan made things shift for me when they appeared utterly immovable; I will never forget his readiness to extend help. Thank you to the incomparable Claire Colebrook for taking the time and effort to read my manuscript—it is a dream to have my work engaged by a thinker like you. A Faculty of Arts and Social Sciences (FASS) Book Grant Scheme from NUS furnished the funds for indexing and other production costs. I am also grateful to Thomas Lay at Fordham University Press for taking a chance on this project, and the readers he secured who provided helpful and constructive reports.

Thank you to my family, who have given me the freedom to go my own way, and provided a soft place to come home to. They are the reason I look forward to my every next adventure in life, because I know I will always have their unconditional love and support. *Feminism Enchanted* is dedicated to the memory of my grandfather, who never hesitated to buy me all the books that I asked for. He would certainly have been proud of this one. Finally, this is a book that was written—in every sense of the word—alongside Irving Goh, who has not only been with me every step of the way, but has also reminded me that it never hurts to have faith in things vital and mysterious that endure beyond the limits of my own imagination. If this book is an accomplishment, then it is both his and mine.

Sections of this manuscript have appeared elsewhere, as follows: chapter 1: "Underwater with the Feminist Waves: Black Gender and Oceanic Lifeworlds in Rivers Solomon's *The Deep*," *Diacritics* 51, no. 4 (2023): 60–77; chapter 2: "Anticipations, Afterlives: On the Temporal and Affective Reorientations of Sexual Difference," *Feminist Theory* 19, no. 3 (2018): 369–86; chapter 4: "A Commons Beyond the Human," *Environmental Humanities* 15, no. 2 (2023): 162–80. Thank you to the editors of these journals and the readers of these earlier versions of my work.

FEMINISM
ENCHANTED

INTRODUCTION

A Literary Mode of Enchantment

This is a book that is animated by the possibilities enfolded in a seemingly impossible question: What happens when feminist scholarship is untethered from a narrative of feminist political progress? The impossibility that marks this question stems from an underlying premise that the idea of progress is inseparable from the story of modern feminism. Indeed, one could safely say that feminism and its attendant movements have generally, and not without good reason, been perceived as coextensive with a steadfast desire for progress. But *Feminism Enchanted* opens with the provocation that while this alliance may certainly have advanced many of the more pragmatic efforts of feminism, it has also diminished the very political and intellectual dexterity of feminist thinking. By this I mean that feminism's unwavering eye on political progress, no matter how indispensable for repealing the hierarchies of gender discrimination in civil, legal, and socioeconomic domains, has engendered an ideological stance that has too narrowly constrained the objectives of feminist politics and more insidiously, too, the frames of reference used to justify their aspiration. In other words, so much of what feminism currently stands for, and why its constitutive modes of analysis are mobilized, has been established on the unyielding bedrock of progress. And this universal axiom of progress has largely foreclosed what feminism is and can do. Taking this impasse as its point of departure, this book asks after those other possibilities for feminism that might come into being when feminism is imagined over and against the decree of progress. On this account, it challenges existing forms of feminist critique for their abiding commitment to progress and its exclusionary means of operation. At stake is another kind of feminist imaginary that might be gleaned from alternative modes of feminist inquiry, an expansive and far more supple understanding of feminism than that which has paradoxically been held back by an irrepressible obligation to progress.

Feminism Enchanted is therefore a book about thinking and knowing feminism differently. It introduces what I call a *literary mode of enchantment* for this exact purpose, and examines how this heuristic might fundamentally transform how we engage feminist critique today. Enchantment, in this vein, is understood to be as much a way of reading as it is a state of being. It allows us to encounter both feminism and the world anew. I will shortly be clarifying the literary crux of the mode—that is, how literature singularly makes possible this work of enchantment. But at the outset, *Feminism Enchanted* invokes the conceptual power of enchantment for its refusal of the logic of progress that has so completely enveloped our structures of existence. This might itself be regarded as a counterprogressive move, given the alleged disenchantment of the West in the wake of liberal modernity. Fraught with backward connotations of animism and the supernatural, enchantment was deemed entirely oppositional to civilization and the modern sensibility. In light of this history, enchantment is an anachronistic idiom that this book resurrects, and more precisely reclaims, as a vital analytic for recalibrating the progressive coordinates of so much contemporary feminist scholarship. It is the unruly tendencies of enchantment that I draw on as the basis for this recuperation: that which was indiscriminately banished, excluded, or oppressed in the name of progressive reason. The mode of enchantment illuminates the presence of those forms of life incommensurate with the relentless march of progress, hence countering the discursive and material violence that has ensured their invalidation as such. In the process, it evokes a feminist imaginary that pays heed to the dissonant genealogies of feminism, one that bears witness to the unevenly distributed lifeworlds of feminism that we collectively inhabit and will continue to create.

If enchantment constitutes another kind of feminist critical practice in this book, it is only because the imperative of literature ensures its requisite agency as such. To some degree, literature certainly embodies an aesthetic medium that inspires the feeling of being enchanted—an affective phenomenon that I will later unpack as part of the reason for my engagement with the literary as the main site of textual analysis for this project.[1] But by raising the question of literature in the present context of feminist studies, *Feminism Enchanted* also tracks a more overarching line of inquiry: What value does the literary imagination hold now for contemporary feminist thought? To ask what literature can do for feminist theory at this time is to signal a certain retrograde endeavor, not unlike the aforementioned retrieval of enchantment, for the insistence that literary criticism is key to thinking and knowing feminism is not new, after all. The elucidatory potential of literary analysis was a leading force behind a substantial proportion of feminist scholarship that emerged in the 1970s and 1980s. As both a textual practice and a suggestive way of understanding the world, literary studies then constituted a major source of feminist knowledge production. Yet, moving into the 1990s, and amid the ubiquity of poststructuralist forms of critique, the conceptual interests of feminist theory began to diverge from literature, with the priority of the literary considerably waning at the close of the twentieth century.[2] Never again would literature and literary criticism hold the same intellectual sway in the wider field of feminist studies.

In a historically recursive gesture, *Feminism Enchanted* harkens back to the earlier significance of literature for feminist studies so as to reveal what potentialities its endorsement might bring to the current moment. This is an act of return that does not simply involve some nostalgic retreat to a former time. Instead, it designates an anachronism reflective of the present juncture at which feminism in the public sphere appears to have fallen completely out of sync with a forward trajectory of progress. I write this amid a slew of seemingly unending attacks against gender equality that have caused the undoing of feminism's historic social and political gains. In the United States alone, the Dobbs Supreme Court decision overturned *Roe v. Wade* in 2022 after almost five decades of precedents and removed the constitutional right to abortion. A mounting number of antitransgender legislations is also being filed across the country, which includes the restriction of or exhaustive ban on gender-affirming care for transgender youth. All these are indicative of a global trend of gender conservatism fueled by the rise of authoritarian right-wing ideologies, which has seen the rollback of women's and minority rights across Europe, Latin America, and various parts of Asia and Africa. They represent a concerted effort to impose violence on minority others on the basis of gender, sexuality, and race, and their pernicious strategy to dissolve hard-earned effects of feminist advocacy has shown unmistakable signs of succeeding. In many ways, we live in a time when history looks to be moving backward for feminism, when so much is lapsing into a more reactionary past. This is a temporal state that can no longer be indexed by a framework of progressive reason.

To be sure, the resurrection of the literary for feminist studies that this book undertakes is not merely a passing allusion to the current state of feminism. Its reaching back in time is more crucially motivated by the belief that literature can in fact help feminist theory make better sense of such a plight, that under these present circumstances, literature still has much to teach the scholarly project of feminism that has transacted primarily in the methodological conventions of social and political progress. In essence, literary inquiry offers a pivotal means to reckon with what is newly at stake for feminist critical practice. I make this case once again in the long shadow of a progress narrative that has not only directed the political investments of feminism but also structured the discursive habits of the movement's accompanying scholarship.[3] Prevailing forms of feminist theory have assumed this progressive stance because, as various scholars have since observed, what we want most from feminism tends to influence the very knowledge that we produce about it.[4] Put another way, the acts of feminist thinking that we privilege are those that might best satiate our political desires. But if this is a paradigm of knowledge-making beholden to such emancipatory ideals, then its analytical power is foreclosed, too, by these terms. By acknowledging the limits of this given function, especially in a social order that relentlessly confounds our hopes for political change, my project mounts a defense of the literary as an instrumental approach of thinking with and about feminism today. Literature's ability to guard questions without forcing them into a premature validation of (progressive) paradigms of thinking, to paraphrase Barbara Johnson here, presents an occasion for how feminist studies might begin to train a different way of knowing.[5]

Feminism Enchanted takes the above capacity of literature as the grounds to study what is gained when we loosen our grip on feminist methods that are underpinned by the notion of progress. It draws concurrently on the overtones of enchantment to examine how a literary mode of enchantment might fulfill such a task. This mode of enchantment encompasses both an affective state and an incantatory act—it is at once a being and a doing. And it is deeply attuned to literature and the literary in a manner that undergirds these twinned valences of its definition. If enchantment names a certain state of enraptured being, then it can often be located at the event of a literary encounter when one becomes momentarily transfixed by the act of reading, rendered spellbound in and by the presence of a text.[6] The aesthetic experience of enchantment prompts a state of suspension, this phenomenon more broadly characterized by the interruption of linear time and the arrest of all bodily movement and rational consciousness. To be immersed in the world of a literary text is therefore to concede to a form of sensory captivation, during which familiar logics of reality cease to operate. This is a condition not reducible to mere paralysis or debilitation. Instead, enchantment initiates a reflexive pause in the established order of things, which in turn heightens a mood more receptive to ways of living and knowing altogether incongruous with our own.[7] This critical hold of enchantment, here construed as an affective and hermeneutic response to the elemental call of literature, sets a stage for the possibility of unexpected meaning to emerge.

It is this interpretive stance of enchantment that orients how this project approaches feminism as an intellectual object of study. This is not to say that I read feminism as a kind of literary text in what follows, but rather that I allude to the literary trappings of enchantment as the basis for attending to a feminist undertaking that might amount to something other than a progressive political agenda. By drawing on the phenomenological comportment of the literary, this book parses the structure of such an encounter with feminism, especially insofar as it comes to clarify a way of being that is positioned, and that lingers, in the space between feminist knowing and doing.[8] At the moment of this encounter, enchantment suspends normative methods of feminist knowledge production secured by the desires and expectations that undergird our struggle for political progress. It invites us to stay with the epistemological tensions that imbue our every meeting with academic feminism, and dwell in the uneasy truth that the feminist modes of thinking that we devise are never obliged to come save us. To this end, the modality of enchantment compels what Robyn Wiegman would call an "inhabitation" of the critical project of feminism.[9] This entails a commitment to the difficulty inherent to our ongoing practices of thinking and knowing feminism, a receptiveness to the fact that these practices can, and indeed should, sometimes be incommensurable with the labor of social and political justice. Throughout this book, then, enchantment suffuses the scene of such an inhabitation and ultimately recasts our existing relation to the given field of feminist studies.

The literary mode of enchantment is also underscored by its incantatory power—that is, its supernatural ability to bring something into being. At the heart of this account of enchantment is its inextricable association with magic and its verbal manifestation as charm. The English word *charm* originates from the Latin *carmen*, meaning "song" or "verse," and finds further specificity as a chant that can produce magical results.[10] Here, enchantment, in terms of its otherworldly potential that is often realized only in the utterance of a magic spell, yet again discloses an affinity with literature. It goes without saying that it is poetry, of course, that is most closely aligned with the spoken formula of charm. There is arguably no literary genre that better embodies a charm's formal configurations of musicality, sound, and rhythm.[11] The sonorous impulse that abounds in forms of poetry that are akin to charms is not randomly modulated, therefore, but organized by what Northrop Frye has identified as "coincidences of the sound-pattern."[12] In other words, what orders such poems is the auditory structure of repetition that shores up their incantatory quality. And whether issued in the devices of rhyme, alliteration, assonance, or more, central to such patterns of repetition is the hypnotic effect that they have on sensory experience. These recurring sounds are intended to bewitch the imagination, which leads either to the compulsion toward a particular course of action or to the cessation of such action altogether.[13] At all times, and never to be forgotten, the numinous presence of enchantment lies beneath the delivery of every incantation, the invariable power of its magic conjuring the otherwise unimaginable into existence.[14]

With this resonance between charm and poetry in mind, the literary mode of enchantment is similarly contingent upon the structure and function of repetition. A conscious technique of repetition animates my task in reading and interpreting feminism, as it revisits well-trodden histories and reassesses widely held beliefs, if only to generate new circuits of feminist knowledge.[15] This is what I term enchantment's *recantatory force*, a reflexive counterpart to that of its incantatory power. To be sure, the iterative nature of recantation does not suggest a superficial process of replication, nor a complete renunciation of the past.[16] Rather, it constitutes a subversive tactic that is itself a transformative critical practice.[17]

This is an argument that I put forth in view of Sara Ahmed's claim that "repetition is the scene of a feminist instruction."[18] To illustrate what she means, Ahmed intentionally enacts the repetition of certain words that persist as value-laden concepts, thereby allowing them to acquire novel meaning when juxtaposed against different contexts.[19] She then tracks the theoretical and material resonances that echo in the wake of this act, which serve as her foundation, or the revelatory event of instruction, from which new and surprising ideas about feminism can be garnered. Following Ahmed, I use the recantatory tendencies of enchantment as a strategy for illuminating the residues of what has hitherto gone unnoticed and unheard in more authoritative narratives of feminism. This is less an exercise in historical excavation than a circling back to certain entrenched, and often contentious, feminist knowledges and turning them over for fresh insights. Against the instinctive rush to move on from these pasts, I seek to extend their historical import into the varied contexts of this feminist present. Once more, it is the linear and sequential logic of progress that is disavowed by this approach, a defiance of teleological reason, for these temporal loops of enchantment account for prior knowledge not as an immutable or expendable piece of evidence but, instead, as something infinitely apprehensible in new light. The reprise of enchantment urges us to read, and indeed to commit to, the edifying practice of rereading the intellectual archive of feminism for the unpredictable array of meaning that can only be yielded in this way. By summoning these alternative forms of knowledge, what enchantment offers in consequence is a glimpse of a more capacious horizon of feminist politics.

In the final analysis, it is the question of literature to which we return. For it is literature that ultimately permits this complex magic of enchantment, particularly through the speculative environment that it provides for the above pursuits of feminist thought. The tangible proof of enchantment's work can therefore be found in the literary texts that I will go on to discuss in this book. More to the point, *Feminism Enchanted* harnesses the power of enchantment for the unfolding of what I identify as textual lifeworlds in the imaginative environment of literature, lifeworlds that take shape in the works that I examine, lifeworlds that we will come to dwell in as readers. In each of the chapters that follow, the literary mode of enchantment develops and sustains the fictional infrastructure of a distinct textual lifeworld.[20] These discursive worlds crystallize what it means for feminism to comprise nonidentical, but also relational, expressions of political and aesthetic knowledge: one that might be conceived of through a Black and queer perspective of the ocean, for example, or else be forged in an Indigenous Igbo cosmology; one that might be refracted by the minoritarian histories and geographies of the transpacific zone in one instance, or be centered on an Aboriginal Australian point of view in another. Collectively, then, the textual lifeworlds assembled in this book will cultivate the inhabitation of an immersive feminist imaginary, which—in both its constitution and its practice—is testament to a feminism thoroughly invigorated by the affordances of enchantment.

AN UNRULY VERNACULAR OF ENCHANTMENT

To take the concept of enchantment as the catalyst for another kind of feminist thinking is in many ways to tread into somewhat perilous waters. My use of such metaphorical language here is no coincidence: Most commonly glossed as a state of intoxication and rapture, enchantment occupies a special place in the history of the Western imagination because of its association with the malevolent presence of the Sirens in Homer's epic poem *The Odyssey*. These mythical beings are the leading actors in a classical scene of seduction, where their irresistible song would lure unsuspecting seafarers to their inevitable deaths on the rocky shoreline. It is the sorceress Circe who forewarns the hero Odysseus ahead of his journey home that he will soon meet the Sirens—part-bird, part-woman creatures who are legendary for their otherworldly ability to "bewitch all passersby."[21] Circe draws his attention to the fatal aftermath of their song by describing the innumerable bodies of perished mariners that now lie all around the Sirens in "great heaps . . . , flesh rotting from their bones, / their skin all shriveled up."[22] This is the wretched fate that befalls those who have become spellbound by their enchanting refrain. As the story goes, Odysseus is nevertheless determined to listen to the fateful song of the Sirens. On Circe's counsel, then, he orders his sailors to plug their ears with her gift of beeswax, and to also bind him tightly to the mast of the ship, which ensures their safe passage past the island from where the deadly call of the Sirens emanates.

This Homeric episode is but one example in the wide-ranging, transhistorical scope of Western literature and culture that has assigned the seductive force of enchantment to a specifically gendered mode of operation, one that has been rendered even more pernicious by the sexual politics of desire.[23] In just the above scene, enchantment signifies the confluence of multiple intensities of transgressive power that have governed the asymmetrical relations of gender. It represents a formidable threat to the sanctity of a masculine, and therefore rational and transcendent, consciousness that, when dissolved, leads to danger and imminent death. Moreover, the wild and unruly qualities of enchantment gesture not only to the alarming loss of a self-contained psychic interiority that its experience will instigate. They also allude to the Sirens themselves in their written portrayal as monstrous, trans-species beings, which trouble the norms that have long upheld the existent hierarchies of Man.[24] Enchantment is further bound up in the problematic of sexuality, particularly when discerned in terms of its centrality to the mechanisms of desire. The siren song, as itself an evocative turn of phrase, has come to encapsulate some of the anxieties surrounding the pleasures and perils of female sexuality; it is an enduring reference to the myth that allegedly set the stage for these ideological tensions more recently thrown into relief.[25] All this is to say that the notion of enchantment has come to embody a vexed and ambivalent locus of feminist thinking. After all, if the subversive and uncontainable properties of enchantment might undermine a dominant order of identity predicated on enclosure and classification, they have too often been exhorted in the same breath as its damaging cultural stereotypes, which have been weaponized to further reinforce the denigration of the already subordinate category of femininity. The insurgent potential of enchantment, in other words, has historically figured as a double-edged sword for feminism. But even as this book acknowledges the gendered fallout from one of enchantment's most well-known origin stories, it does not provide a feminist genealogy of the term. Rather, *Feminism Enchanted* seeks to reclaim the disorderly trace of enchantment by leveraging its errant states of being, which have stood at complete odds to the stability of prevailing epistemic regimes.

In its underlying motivation to reclaim the concept of enchantment, this is also a project conceived in view of Max Weber's famous 1917 declaration that "[t]he fate of our times is characterized by rationalization and intellectualization and, above all, by the 'disenchantment of the world.'"[26] Weber's lament reveals what to him was an undeniable loss that had begun in the seventeenth and eighteenth centuries, and which became only more apparent in the late nineteenth century. As he observed, the ascendant apparatus of modernity, notably influenced by Enlightenment values of science and reason, had eclipsed a former conception of a world that had once been suffused with the inexplicable mysteries of animism and magic.[27] Weber detailed the rise of modernity as one thus concomitant with the encroaching forces of secular reason and evidential logic, forces that were indispensable for the scientific, political, and economic developments of the time. But this had inevitably led to an instrumental and calculated ordering of both the world and its formative condition of humanity, which was administered at the expense of spiritual convictions. Weber expressed a deep regret about this state of affairs, elsewhere describing it as a metaphorical entrapment in an "iron cage."[28]

This Weberian archetype of Western modernity has since generated a substantial amount of scholarship over the question of whether enchantment had truly retreated from modern life, and how best to locate or to reinstate its presence if so.[29] This involves several divergent lines of inquiry, none of which this book will be pursuing at length. By narrating yet another prominent story that has been circulated about enchantment—at least by way of its companion event of disenchantment—I am less interested in adjudicating its currency than in following its script to identify what modes of knowledge, and which forms of existence, had been banished by modernity as an age underscored by the systematic processes of rationality and demystification. Indeed, the account of modernity that Weber provides is largely dependent not on the eradication of enchantment per se, but on the management of its otherness as that which was perceived to be incompatible with its overall epistemological and ideological vision. With this in mind, my attention is directed to what was lost, bracketed out, or undermined in this endeavor of establishing the dominant referent of the modern world as such: the lingering underside to its consolidation. It is this maleficent vernacular of enchantment that the book draws on for the articulation of its feminist imaginary, one that is correspondingly given expression by those marginal lifeworlds relegated by the modern historical imagination.

As a key and rather literal instance of this subordination, the fearful connotation of enchantment was projected onto a kind of nefarious, and specifically feminine, practice of witchcraft in early modern Europe. Central to this assumption was the portrayal of witches in possession of diabolical powers as blasphemous women who represented a sinister, encircling threat to those governing social, political, and religious institutions of patriarchy at the time.[30] The imminent danger posed by female sexuality and its hallmarks of recalcitrance and waywardness was weaponized against women accused of practicing witchcraft.[31] But as Silvia Federici has argued from a Marxist perspective, the brutal histories of gendered violence that marked this period, distilled in the great witch-hunts enacted primarily in sixteenth- and seventeenth-century Europe, should also be read as coterminous with the ascendance of the capitalist order and the development of the modern proletariat.[32] The figure of the witch, as she describes, was "the embodiment of the world of female subjects that capitalism had to destroy: the heretic, the healer, the disobedient wife, the women who dared to live alone, the obeah woman who poisoned the master's food and inspired the slaves to revolt."[33] For Federici, the persecution of such condemned women prompted monumental shifts in broader political and socioeconomic structures, which eventually culminated in the rule of capitalist patriarchy. In this sense, the removal of certain powers of enchantment was a strategy of ossifying a modern social order that hinged on the oppression of a distinctly gendered other.

At work in the consecration of the modern world as disenchanted is also a process of colonialism that was carried out in the name of the Enlightenment vision of humanism. The constitution of a liberal and secular ideal of the human lay at the center of this universalizing project, which required the abrogation of forms of life and ways of thinking that were regarded as antithetical to its eminence and sovereignty.[34] Accordingly, the progressive narrative of modernity and its supposed claim to disenchantment was premised on a retreat from a premodern other deemed as savage, primitive, and uncivilized. I present these adjectives assembled not by coincidence, nor merely in their similarity to enchantment as translated in the supposedly regressive beliefs in witchcraft and ritual practice. Rather, I parse their backward nuances alongside the interminable histories of colonialism and imperialism that have actively exploited their prevalence to more easily justify systemic modes of dehumanization and violence. If the trajectory of modernization seemed to eclipse a broad swathe of enchantments that materialized in various phenomena of mysticism and superstition, it did so only under the guise of a Western colonial ideology that sought to elide their seething presence.[35] It is in this sense that the self-fashioning of Enlightenment humanism as an integral aspect of Western modernity can be seen as coeval with the dispossessions created by European colonialism.[36] For Sylvia Wynter, these endeavors have circumscribed what she calls "the coloniality of being," which reified a category of humanness that has come to disproportionately announce—if not entirely define—the social and political epistemes of the present. This hyperbolic description of Man was produced by various stratifications

of existence that had in turn been enforced by specific mechanisms of colonial power. As she writes, its invention as a philosophical and scientific paragon of modernity was made possible
"only on the basis of the dynamics of a colonizer/colonized relation that the West was to discursively constitute and empirically
institutionalize on the islands of the Caribbean and, later, on
the mainlands of the Americas."[37] Enchantment has thus
become entangled with the realities of lifeworlds that have long
existed, and even once flourished, at the peripheries of Western
modernity. And its pejorative overtones continue to be wielded
as a force of destruction against such communities, resulting in
the catastrophic decline of Indigenous populations around the
world, for instance, as an illustration of the indiscriminate reach
of this permanent colonial logic.

This risky terrain of enchantment, which covers multiple
forms of debased otherness, contextualizes the backdrop that
my project navigates in its search for new configurations of
feminist meaning. This is to say that the feminist imaginary
that coalesces in what follows is bound not only by the recognition but also the reclamation of enchantment as a radically
intransigent state of being. This is a state of being cast in the
brutal and unending circumstances of particular gendered and
racialized histories. In many ways, then, this book channels
what Weber had once called the "mysterious incalculable forces"
of enchantment to participate in a wider recuperation of the
concept that has come to span several disciplines in recent
years.[38] These reassessments of enchantment do not invoke an
impossible return to the past, or a revival of certain sacralized
histories or traditions. Instead, and as demonstrated by scholars
such as Jane Bennett, Akeel Bilgrami, Rita Felski, David Morgan, and many others, enchantment has been restored as a useful and productive analytic for responding to various social,

political, aesthetic, and environmental crises at the forefront of the contemporary consciousness.[39] For instance, enchantment has been considered to present a more ethical way of relating to beings and things in the world around us, for which its affective undercurrents initiate a greater receptiveness to diverse forms of alterity and difference.[40] Enchantment has accordingly emerged as a profoundly generative source from which more expansive modes of existence might be conceived.

FEELING FOR ANOTHER WAY OF READING

But as already discussed, my interest in enchantment rests also on its designation as a different way of reading. In contrast to those who have sought to rehabilitate the tarnished state of enchantment as a diminished and excluded state of being, I draw on its potential as a heuristic for thinking and knowing feminism. For this reason, I find it helpful to position my formulation of the mode of enchantment alongside several thinkers who have since conceived of the notion of wonder in a comparable way. *Wonder* is a far-reaching term that has concerned philosophers from Aristotle to Plato, from René Descartes to Luce Irigaray, and others; indeed, it warrants a separate chapter in the annals of Western thought—much less non-Western cultures—that lies beyond the scope of this book.[41] To put it briefly, however, I understand wonder as a proximate but discrete phenomenon to enchantment, which entails a separate etymological lineage, and therefore also its own intellectual baggage.[42] For one, wonder does not unequivocally allude to the ruthless detractions of gender and race in the ways that I have shown enchantment to do.[43] Neither does it explicitly denote the intensities of an otherworldly and oftentimes willful magic that might summon alternative lifeworlds of possibility into being. But its descriptive resonances with enchantment are nevertheless unmistakable: Wonder also enfolds an experience of surprise, joyfulness, and delight; it is an emotion that is likewise excited by an encounter with the marvelous, the extraordinary, or the inexplicable.[44] On these grounds, the ethical openness to otherness that wonder comes to share with the disposition of enchantment is to me a fruitful point of reference for further clarifying the latter as a critical practice.

More precisely still, it is the reflexive curiosity appending the occasion of wonder that further sharpens my theorization of enchantment for this book. I had earlier emphasized that the mode of enchantment on which my project depends persistently interrogates the facade of the already given for latent and unpredictable insight. This is an exercise that fundamentally resists the closure of teleological meaning. And it is in this sense that enchantment might be seen as consonant with the critical practice of wonder already employed by several scholars. In her examination of the geographies of Black Canada, for instance, Katherine McKittrick observes the presence of Blackness as something that provokes the feeling of surprise, insofar as the actuality of Black existence persistently unsettles the dominant social and historical narratives of racial production that have been told about Canada. But perhaps more significantly, Blackness is also surprising because it reveals the exact forms of hegemonic knowledge production that have afforded the surprise of Blackness as such. That is, the element of surprise turns our attention to the racial and colonial structures of knowing that have at the outset enabled its affective manifestation upon an encounter with Blackness. For McKittrick, the feeling of surprise preceding wonder and curiosity is a concerted response that then "invites new avenues for exploration that are both unexpected and underacknowledged and call into question the contexts that produce surprise and wonder in the first place."[45] In other words, wonder prompts a reassessment of those regulating patterns of intelligibility that since have delimited the notion of Blackness, just as it also opens up new and unprecedented frameworks of thinking.[46]

Sara Ahmed makes a similar point elsewhere about feminist wonder and its reflexive power.[47] While the surprise of wonder seems initially predicated on a confrontation with the unknown as a kind of irreducible difference, Ahmed reorients its force inward and on to those prevailing ideological and epistemological arrangements that have so indelibly enclosed our modes of living.[48] And this for her applies to the construct of feminism itself—as she writes: "What is striking about feminist wonder is that the critical gaze is not simply directed outside; rather, feminist wonder becomes wonder about the very forms of feminism that have emerged here or there."[49] Feminist wonder is therefore a sensibility that estranges us from what we already know about feminism, essentially rendering it other to itself. It defamiliarizes what we have assumed the underlying endeavors of feminist historiography and politics should do or even be, thereby inaugurating new openings for their thinking. As an echo of the stance that my own project adopts toward feminism through the adjacent modality of enchantment, then, Ahmed's conception of wonder acknowledges that "nothing in the world can be taken for granted, which includes the very political movements to which we are attached."[50]

By suggesting that the problematic of wonder might yield more reflexive bearings for perceiving feminism, Ahmed provides a segue into what Jennifer Nash has identified as the recent "introspective turn" in women's studies.[51] This is a turn exemplified by feminist and queer thinkers such as Clare Hemmings, Victoria Hesford, Robyn Wiegman, and Nash, one that has involved a closer examination of the discursive politics that have shaped the dominant theoretical and historiographic knowledges of feminism.[52] Their work has accordingly cast an interrogative light on the attachments, investments, and desires that have hewn the scholarly discipline of feminism. As previously mentioned, *Feminism Enchanted* joins this conversation through its broader critique of the cornerstone of progress upon which much of feminist scholarship has been based; it seeks to move against and beyond the constraints of progressive reason instantiated in what Hemmings has termed the "political grammar" of dominant paradigms of feminist thought.[53] By rewiring this political grammar through an intervention predicated on the overlooked possibilities of literary inquiry, this book offers a response to the ongoing reckoning in feminist studies with its constitutive habits and commitments.

It is against this same backdrop that I mobilize the mode of enchantment for its explicit acknowledgment of the affective pull that feminism, as a transformative political endeavor, has inevitably had on our collective consciousness. If the fact remains that we are enchanted by feminism itself—ineluctably drawn to its promises of social change—then my reflexive engagement of this state of enchantment itself is intended to make more visible the affective life of feminist knowledge production, to urge closer notice to what Wiegman describes as the "impulses that keep us enthralled" by our fields of identity study.[54] But my project takes this affective orientation of enchantment beyond a mere relation of attachment. It further repurposes enchantment into something that can be harnessed, not unlike the notion of wonder, as an approach of critical estrangement. On the one hand, then, enchantment openly clarifies our affective stakes in the emancipatory ideals of feminism; it signals our perennial hope for its movement to deliver a more just world. On the other, enchantment expresses a way of reading and engaging feminism as an object of study, one that becomes placed under the rigor of constant scrutiny. Enchantment extends a kind of interpretive attention that undermines the certitude of well-established feminist histories and knowledges. After its repudiation by the liberal Western episteme, more specifically, enchantment historicizes these dominant accounts of feminism through marginal perspectives of gender and race, and in turn stories them anew.[55] This process of rendering feminism strange, of persistently calling into question its prevailing constructs and assumptions, is not at all an attenuation of our enduring attachments to the political and intellectual force of feminism. It is by contrast an affirmation—for only if we truly believed in what feminism can still do, as this line of argument goes, would we care enough to critique its existing knowledges for the sake of those that it will henceforth produce.

By defining enchantment as a way of reading, *Feminism Enchanted* also appears to share a critical vocabulary with recent developments in literary studies that have urged the uptake of alternative frameworks of reading. Indeed, this book's theorization of enchantment is in a partial dialogue with the work of Rita Felski, whose phenomenological focus on the "thick descriptions of experiential states," as the site for devising new modes of critique, leads her to spell out enchantment as a useful concept for reimagining how literary criticism might be performed.[56] Felski's focus on enchantment as a literary phenomenon is in line with current scholarly interest in its ethical potential. She argues that as an absorptive aesthetic effect, enchantment simulates an experience of being taken "out of ourselves," which then allows for a perspective of generosity and open-mindedness to be fostered.[57]

This claim for a less parochial approach to literature and literary criticism can be located in a broader field of study: Felski's writing on enchantment has been considered part of what is now known as the postcritical turn in literary studies.[58] Alongside her, advocates of postcritique have resisted what they view as a historically dominant stance of academic literary criticism. This is a stance that has privileged a rational and objective detachment from the text, just as it has rewarded a skeptical and mistrustful lens of analysis.[59] With this in mind, scholars have collectively canvased for other reading practices and interpretive methods that might more expansively elucidate our encounter with a literary text, which would then open it to a greater possibility of meanings.[60]

Despite my emphasis on the affective dimensions of enchantment as key to its critical practice, this is not a project that participates in academic discourse on postcritique, however conceived.[61] In contrast, my approach to the works of literature in the following chapters can best be described as close textual analysis, guided by the question of how these texts come to open new ways of knowing feminism differently.[62] This is why the mode of enchantment presents a way of reading feminism rather than a way of reading literature.

That being said, a tangible fact of literariness remains central to enchantment's use as a feminist method. This working relationship once more clarifies my project's aim to rejuvenate some of the historically convergent interests of feminist and literary studies. I earlier touched on the rising tide of poststructuralist thought that has been held chiefly responsible for the critical attenuation that occurred between the two fields. Poststructuralist claims on the constructedness of gendered identity had the polarizing effect of troubling a coherent account of "woman," which then caused an existential crisis of the feminist imagination. This predicament was exacerbated by what Susan Gubar, in particular, named as the supposed threat of "racialized identity politics" wielded by feminist scholars of race, class, and gender.[63] For Gubar, this preoccupation with the intersecting histories and politics of lived experience irretrievably fractured the conceit of a unified category of women, eventually undermining its primacy as the foremost subject of feminist literary criticism. In this context, Gubar's professed grief over the loss of the literary bastion of feminist studies at the time can be glossed as a lamentation for a white feminist epistemic privilege that could no longer remain standing.[64]

This book is no elegy for the historical heyday of feminist literary criticism. In fact, and if this is a literary object that has since been marked with certain racist, universalizing, and essentialist undertones, then there should be no mourning for its disappearance in the feminist theory of decades past, only a reevaluation of its scholarly significance at this time. But to do this is nonetheless to attempt a retrieval of the "bad object" of literature, as Naomi Schor would term it—which is representative of an ethically suspect time in feminist studies and, more specifically, a tarnished scholarly artifact that continues to evoke feelings of apprehension and misgiving.[65] This present work enacts a rewriting of this more insular understanding of the literary by turning toward rather than away from these bad feelings.[66] In the process, it shows how literature's transitive acts of storytelling might instead make manifest an ensemble of lifeworlds shaped by particular, minoritarian histories and ideologies.[67] The literary emerges in this project as constitutive of marginal ways of feminist living and being; it refuses claim to any illusion of deracinated existence. In a more overarching sense, I am guided by what Schor asks after she observes the vanishing of the literary: "Will a *new* feminist literary criticism arise that will take literariness seriously while maintaining its vital ideological edge?"[68] What I draft here is therefore an allusive response to Schor's meditation, not so much by devising a new practice of feminist literary criticism but by affirming that literature and literary inquiry might still serve as an indispensable engine of current feminist scholarship. *Feminism Enchanted* takes "literariness" seriously enough to contend that the ideological edge of ongoing feminist theorizing can and must be extended by the capacity of literature. It revives a feminist use of literature, albeit one that tracks a radically different agenda from before.[69]

TEXTUAL INHABITATIONS

The dual dynamic that underpins the mode of enchantment— that is, both its recantatory and incantatory vectors—informs the structure and logic of the chapters in this book. On this basis, every chapter will attest to the work of enchantment. Beginning with a critical reconsideration of a conceptual object or idea that holds particular significance for feminist thought, each chapter will then open into a discrete and singular life-world that is produced by a close reading of a literary text. In a sense, these latter sections are validated by the worldbuilding elements of fiction: the ability for its narratives to unfold other possible versions of reality. But I also see my interpretation of the literary texts assembled in this book as generating what Paul Ricoeur has identified as a *"proposed world* which I could inhabit and wherein I could project one of my ownmost possibilities. That is what I call the world of the text, the world proper to *this* unique text."[70] Ricoeur writes of the world proposed by a text as one that constitutes a "distanciation" from empirical reality; it is an alternative world that reconfigures the familiar bearings of the reader's existence into something that is quite distinct.[71] To me, what is key about Ricoeur's conception of the hermeneutic experience of literature is less the manifestation of this textual world per se, and more the nature of the relation that the reader comes to establish with it. For when the reader is invited to inhabit a different world proposed by a text, they are not simply called on to fully submit to the terms of this other world. Instead, the reader is driven to enact a shift in their given perspectives through the act of textual inhabitation. This is the effect of the alternative textual world illuminating not only other, potential forms of being but also new and imaginative possibilities that in turn become "opened up within everyday reality."[72] It is the reader's understanding of the very world in which they belong that becomes utterly transformed by this brief inhabitation of another.[73]

If this book had earlier raised the question of inhabitation with regard to feminism and feminist theory, then Ricoeur's delineation of the hermeneutic function imputes the term with added literary nuance at this juncture.[74] What the literary thus introduces is another dimension to the idea of inhabitation as a critical condition of being. In this vein, the textual lifeworlds enclosed within the chapters that follow will invite their inhabitation in a manner that shifts the parameters of what we have come to know and expect of the intellectual project of feminism.

The first chapter, "Underwater with the Feminist Waves," harnesses the recantatory force of enchantment to reimagine one of the most influential metaphors for narrating feminism: that of its progressive waves. What enchantment prompts is a sensory disorientation that shifts our dominant ways of thinking toward—and indeed, into—the sea. In the process, it critically estranges the discursive legacy of the feminist waves by inflecting it with certain historicizing undercurrents of racial capitalism. Instead of the familiar image of surface waves, the chapter examines what it would mean to consider the oblique, underwater presence of the *internal wave* as a renewed paradigm for understanding feminism, especially as an oceanic manifestation that has long evaded the grasp of human perception. By taking the physical and environmental properties of this subsurface wave as an interpretive frame, it turns to a reading of Rivers Solomon's 2019 novella, *The Deep*, to show how this conceptual submergence of the wave metaphor displaces frames of knowing predicated on human exceptionalism. The novella tells of the impossible existence of a civilization of water-breathing descendants of drowned, pregnant African women thrown overboard from slave ships crossing the Atlantic. Drawing on this alternative feminist genealogy, the mode of enchantment conjures a speculative lifeworld of Black and queer forms of being fully acculturated to the depths of the sea. It shores up an archive of Black gender that is steeped in the living environment of the ocean.

Chapter 2, "A Demonic Afterlife of Sexual Difference," takes up another prominent intellectual artifact that has preoccupied the feminist scholarly imagination: the concept of sexual difference. Animated once more in this chapter is enchantment's recantatory impulse, which is trained on sexual difference as one of the most polarizing imports of what has come to be known as French feminist theory. If allegations of racism and essentialism have become synonymous with the very mention of sexual difference, I enact an anachronistic retrieval of the term to juxtapose its significance with exactly those marginal perspectives that it has been accused of overlooking. By tracking the gesture toward the unknowable future that forms the conceptual basis of sexual difference, the chapter positions the work of the feminist philosopher Luce Irigaray alongside that of the Afro-Caribbean thinker and cultural theorist Sylvia Wynter. I show how Wynter's Black feminist project of undoing the overrepresented idea of Man, particularly as expressed through her formulation of the "demonic," finds affinity with, but more urgently expands, the insular future that marks Irigaray's proposed revolution of sexual difference. The chapter then turns to an analysis of Akwaeke Emezi's novel *Freshwater* (2018) to navigate the representational politics of sexual difference as mediated by the racialized terms of the demonic. My reading of the novel examines how its rendering of this afterlife of sexual difference through an Igbo cosmology imbues the concept with a newfound relevance for feminist discourse.

Chapter 3, "Feminist Revolutions: Inscrutable, Out of Reach," moves on to examine how the form and meaning of a feminist revolution might be transformed by the mode of enchantment. While the previous chapters tarried with the remainder of some conceptual objects of feminist scholarship, this one marks a shift to a broader critique of models of thinking premised upon the desires and expectations for (feminist) political progress. In contrast to the conventional understanding of a feminist revolution that plots a teleological arc of emancipation for women and demands the realization of tangible change, this chapter charts a revolutionary event that instead remains inscrutable. I ascribe an ethical function to this expression of inscrutability, insofar as it refuses appropriation by the logics of liberal feminist progress, concurrently safeguarding the irreducibility of minoritized difference. Inscrutability thus exemplifies a strategy for theorizing a revolution in a different way, especially as attuned to the politics of transnational feminist knowledge production. The chapter examines how an inscrutable feminist revolution might be made legible in Ruth Ozeki's 2013 novel, *A Tale for the Time Being*. My reading draws on the novel's traversal of the time and space of the transpacific zone, and presents an account of revolution that is characterized by its multiple vanishing points. More precisely, I trace the transcultural fragments of a Japanese feminism at the turn of the twentieth century, which hold together a revolution in the text that cannot be contained by the histories of the transpacific imaginary, even as it is indelibly shaped by its memory. It is written both into and out of existence, fundamentally beyond reach in its true eventfulness.

The fourth chapter, "A Commons Beyond the Human," tests the reflexive power of enchantment on a term that has of late been widely endorsed for its potential to bring into being a better future: *the commons*. In the process, this final chapter of the book also demonstrates an extended use for the mode of enchantment that has found its initial bearings in, but now moves beyond, the domain of feminist inquiry. By exposing current theories of the commons as having been produced and sustained by human-centered paradigms of intellectual reasoning, the chapter develops what I call a *commons beyond the human*. This is an attempt to rethink the commons concept beyond its regulating logics of liberal humanism, a radical reconsideration of the kinds of politics it should and might still enable beyond the lure of progressive reason. Through a reading of Alexis Wright's novel *The Swan Book* (2013), I show how a commons beyond the human gathers in the text through the more-than-human existence that is engendered between a young Aboriginal girl, Oblivia, and a flock of black swans. The novel presents neither the disavowal of the inherited knowledges of the commons nor a concrete policy to herald its appearance in a conjectural future, but rather a critical expansion of its transitive acts of worlding. This is made feasible by its insistence on upholding an Indigenous Australian ontological reality as the structuring provision for its narratives—one that has long stressed its dissonance from dominant Western genres of thinking and being.

If each of these chapters invokes a discursive conception of feminism that must be experienced and inhabited in completely different ways, then this book does not arrive at any conclusive definition of the purpose and meaning of the wider feminist imaginary. Its literary mode of enchantment has simply presented a more introspective practice for understanding feminism's pasts, for encountering its present, and for imagining its futures. In this sense, what *Feminism Enchanted* takes is the first, and arguably most crucial, step of cultivating better strategies of thinking and knowing in the pursuit of more livable ways of being. In the coda of the book, I offer some brief reflections on the subversive power of the literary that feminist critique must now enlist to not so readily be captured by counterfeminist movements that are rapidly proliferating around the world. This is to issue a final call for us to ensure that feminist scholarship does not continue to be held back—or even diminished—by what we already wish for it to do; that its power might eventually come to exceed the limits of what we have ascribed to its capacity to act in this world. *Feminism Enchanted* ultimately makes known that the key to unlocking these possibilities now lies in the imperative of literature.

1

UNDERWATER WITH THE FEMINIST WAVES

In an early scene of William Shakespeare's *The Tempest*, the airy spirit Ariel embodies a kind of invisible Siren figure when he first sings to the shipwrecked Ferdinand, son of King Alonso of Naples: "Come unto these yellow sands, / And then take hands."[1] Ariel's enchanting appeal is part of an elaborate ploy by the exiled magician Prospero, whose strategy to recover his usurped dukedom involves uniting his daughter Miranda with the prince Ferdinand in marriage. Ferdinand's ill-fated arrival on the island is marked by deep sorrow, as he mistakenly believes his lost father to have drowned at sea. In some of the most famous lines of the play, Ariel confirms the fact of Alonso's watery demise: "Full fathom five thy father lies; / Of his bones are coral made; / Those are pearls that were his eyes: / Nothing of him that doth fade, / But doth suffer a sea-change / Into something rich and strange."[2] It is at this same time that Ariel leads the grieving Ferdinand to Miranda through the mesmerizing refrain of a song. In its constitutive sound patterns and rhythm as well as through the overall outcome it produces, Ariel's song is a spell, which in the most fundamental sense is cast to drive the main plot forward.[3]

As it turns out, Ariel's above narration of Alonso's death is a complete fabrication, for the latter has in fact washed up alive on another part of the island. Yet this imaginary event that Ariel presents to Ferdinand is precisely that which offers a point of departure for this chapter. In this alternative reality, Alonso's body lies in the depths of the ocean and has become utterly changed by the living environment in which it is submerged. What Ariel recounts in detail are the nonhuman forces of the sea laying claim to an ostensibly decaying corpse. But, in the process, some of the most recognizable features of Alonso's human corporeality have not merely decomposed into imperceptible matter. They have instead been reclaimed and further made anew by various forms of marine life.[4] Indeed, it is through this transformative power of the ocean that Alonso has undergone a "sea-change / Into something rich and strange."[5]

Ariel's lyric, originally sung under Prospero's command to bewitch the unsuspecting Ferdinand, holds a different implication for the omniscient reader. In describing Alonso's body, Ariel displaces human selfhood and singularity by invoking the nonhuman capacity of the sea. But he does not simply refer to the ocean as a profound force of nature. Rather, Ariel compels us to consider how the particular conditions of its materiality might be suggestive of a different mode of thinking—one that lies beyond the order of the human.[6] He first underscores the liquid abyss of the ocean: "Full fathom five" below the surface is where Alonso's body has come to rest.[7] In so doing, Ariel's utterance does not only manifest as a charm that artfully captivates Ferdinand. It also initiates a process of sensory disorientation that attunes us readers to the ontological status of the sea, thereby estranging us from our familiar ways of being and doing.[8] More to the point, it is our assumptions about what it means to be human, here reflected in certain anthropocentric truths about life and death, that are upended. Ariel refuses the logic of finitude that marks human processes of death and dying by conjuring the unsettling image of a body whose parts have been reconfigured by the transgressive presence of sea creatures. This is an image that disavows the sovereignty of human identity and existence in favor of a multispecies ecology that is now thriving underwater. But the figure of the human has neither disappeared nor been destroyed; after all, Ariel tells us that there is "nothing of [Alonso] that doth fade."[9] Rather, it has acquired new and unexpected meaning that can only be generated by thinking with or, perhaps more accurately, through the sea. Ariel's song moreover demonstrates the radical effect of adopting such an oceanic perspective, for what was presumed dead has in fact taken on another kind of otherworldly, subaquatic life. If Ariel has cast a spell to irrevocably alter the course of Fernando's actions, then he has also delivered an incantation that remembers and raises the dead through the elemental specificities of the sea.

Following Ariel, what richer and stranger things abound when our dominant human paradigms of knowing and knowledge-making are plunged into the depths of the sea? What surprising, and more expansive, forms of meaning might such an ontological immersion summon forth? The first chapter of *Feminism Enchanted* examines the possibilities held open by these questions by taking on one of the most influential stories that has been imparted about feminism: that of its consecutive waves. This is a story that has accounted for the rise of the women's movement in the United States and beyond; it is one that has become synonymous with the emergence of feminism in the West.[10] Needless to say, such a bold claim to universality can only be the result of various historiographic acts of reduction and erasure. And it is along these very lines that the ubiquitous metaphor of the wave has since been extensively interrogated as an approach of feminist historiography. These critiques have exposed the inability of the canonical wave narrative to fully capture the complex political, ideological, and cultural histories of feminist social change. They have further revealed how its extensive influence as a critical framework has inadvertently come to perpetuate an exclusionary myth of feminism, a myth largely founded on the privilege of a white and middle-class agenda.

Nevertheless, the story of feminism's consecutive waves has irrevocably overrun the wider public consciousness. It also continues to spark fierce debate in the field of feminist studies.[11] In spite of the well-documented shortcomings of the wave as a foundational paradigm for understanding feminism, then, what Jo Reger has termed its "discursive legacy" still inflects the narration of feminist histories, if only as a vexed inheritance that must first be acknowledged before it can later be disavowed.[12] Its staying power, in other words, is undeniable, and its afterlife enduring; the presiding story of the feminist waves simply cannot be dispelled from the collective imagination. How exactly might we then grapple with its problematic heritage? I am less interested in detailing the epistemic inadequacies of the wave narrative as we know it—or conversely, in defending its interpretive merit—than in expanding the figurative potential of its central metaphor for theorizing feminism. To this end, I take both its tenuous expression and abiding legacy as the premise of this chapter and ask: How do we continue living with a story that has proven so formative to how we have come to know feminism, when what counts as livable demands an urgent and radical revisioning of its existing meaning?

With this in mind, this chapter will extend the conversation about the conceptual relevance of the wave metaphor for thinking feminism today. It does so by engaging the literary mode of enchantment to reread the prevailing story of the feminist waves in order to narrate it anew. This marks the first act of recantation that I conduct in this book, in which I recursively gloss this familiar feminist script that we know so that its existing meaning becomes critically estranged. In contrast to corrective strategies that have sought to move on from, or to refute, the classic story of the feminist waves, I argue that it is paradoxically by staying with its organizing metaphor as a key storytelling device for narrating feminism that feminist history might be imagined differently. This presents a more overarching attempt to undermine conventional methods of feminist historiography, an exploration of how to write feminism's histories and its futures otherwise. By harnessing the recantatory force of enchantment, the chapter performs a reflexive endeavor of dwelling in the wake of the cresting accounts of feminist revolution it has told, and of reckoning with the tangible fact of its watery materiality. More precisely, it mediates the symbolic currency of the wave metaphor through an oceanic perspective that is historicized in relation to distinct racial, colonial, and environmental modalities. This mediation is framed by what Joshua Bennett has called a "Black hydropoetics": a way of thinking located at the convergence of Black studies, animal studies, and ecocriticism, which is theorized through the ecologies of the ocean to articulate new and other possibilities for Black life.[13] If another possible story of the feminist waves is unfolded in this chapter, then, it is one that features a Black and queer lifeworld as its narrative cornerstone.

Instead of the ubiquitous image of surface waves crashing on the shore, this chapter will focus on the underwater phenomenon of the *internal wave* to propose a revised understanding of the existing metaphorical construct.[14] In essence, internal waves are propagated by the differences in density that mark the stratified layers of the ocean.[15] These waves are immense and far-reaching, yet have proven difficult to observe due to their relative invisibility from above the surface of the sea; they circulate in the recesses of the ocean in ways that are almost imperceptible to the terrestrial human eye. Here, I am taking up Ariel's above invitation to immerse the seemingly indelible ways we have come to make sense of this world into the alien environment of the sea. My interest in the internal wave thus involves not only a turning toward the tangible nature of the wave metaphor, but also a submergence of its conventional definition. By alluding to the physical and ecological properties of this subsurface wave, I examine what it would mean to consider its oblique presence as a renewed paradigm for narrating feminism, especially as an oceanic manifestation that has evaded the grasp of human perception.

The chapter will finally turn to a close reading of Rivers Solomon's 2019 novella *The Deep* to show how this submergence of the wave metaphor displaces our frames of seeing and knowing that have been predicated on human exceptionalism. The immersion of the metaphor has the effect of illuminating what lurks beneath—and indeed, what lies beyond—the otherwise sweeping view of colonial modernity as all that we have been trained to see. My approach to the text is further driven by the incantatory power of enchantment, which carries out a speculative task of worldbuilding that altogether spurns the disciplinary limits of history. It is a task occasioned by the imaginative disposition of literature. Accordingly, my reading of *The Deep* centers on its portrayal of a mythic, errant civilization brought to life by the fluid conditions of the ocean. By pursuing the conceptual possibilities of a metaphor now attuned to its material specificities, my analysis will trace another account of the feminist waves: one that arises from a gathering of Black and queer forms of being acculturated to the depths of the sea.

WAVE WORK, WAKE WORK

It goes without saying that there can be no exhaustive or unbiased overview of the historical events that the feminist waves have been called on to encompass. But the gist of the story goes something like this: The first wave of feminism tracks the battle for suffrage in the United States that began in the late nineteenth century, second-wave feminism is most closely associated with the women's liberation movement in the 1960s and early 1970s, and third-wave feminism emerged in the 1990s amid calls for greater attention to intersectional identity from queer feminists and feminist of color. What subtends this narrative of the waves is not only the progressive arc of historical time. This is also a story that has been institutionalized as one of continuous advancement for the feminist movement as a whole. It has painted a linear and sequential picture of each wave as having surpassed the last, especially in terms of its growing inclusion of standpoints of race, class, gender, and sexuality. As Nancy A. Hewitt writes, "The propagation of new waves was not simply a means to recognize distinct eruptions of activism across time. Feminists in each wave saw themselves as improving on, not just building on, the wave(s) that preceded them."[16] An unmistakable logic of progress thus indexes this emblematic piece of feminist knowledge, marking both the temporal and interpretive scene of its articulation.

Numerous scholars have since addressed the historical inaccuracies in the above story of the feminist waves, along with the ethical issues of its presentation as such.[17] Taken together, their work has better identified the obscured actors who were in fact playing major roles in the feminist movement; it has held in more generative tension the asymmetries of a falsely unifying chain of events. Indeed, these projects have provided a more complete portrayal of the feminist histories that can now be categorized under the rubric of the waves. But this chapter does not simply make visible those perspectives still rendered marginal to the dominant feminist archive; neither does it seek to invalidate, correct, or even complicate the original iteration of the wave narrative. Rather, it is guided by the belief that to truly think the feminist waves anew, a critical intervention must be staged at the existing means of its disclosure.[18]

By glossing the origin story of the feminist waves as one primarily of progress, I think through and with the wave metaphor against its conditioning of progressive reason on two intersecting levels. The first is a refusal to adhere to the common wisdom of writing history progressively and teleologically, a rejection of the critical feminist habits that have given rise to the authoritative narrative of the waves. On this account, I justify the engagement with literature that follows and explain how a speculative mode of fiction in particular tells a countergenealogy of feminism dislocated from the regulating norms of historiography. The second task involves a resistance against moving on from the metaphor of the wave entirely, against dismissing its current relevance for understanding feminism altogether. I stay with the metaphor on this basis and, with its most recognizable reference to the sea, examine the stories about feminism it might continue to reveal at this time. In a reflection of the analytic that Christina Sharpe has called "wake work," this is a methodological imperative for narrating another story of the waves that focalizes a uniquely Black and queer feminist perspective.[19] Even as this narrative is steeped in an oceanic imagination that embodies a protracted history of racial, capitalist, gendered, and environmental brutality, then, its literary expression demonstrates the audacity to conjure other, alternative futures out of this aftermath.

If the wave metaphor necessarily eludes the capture of progressive conventions of feminist historiography in this chapter, it initiates a story that is predicated upon what Saidiya Hartman has deemed "impossible," for the ways that it defies and exceeds existing limits of knowledge production.[20] In other words, the very impossibility of its telling must be understood as the immediate consequence of ways of knowing that are, by definition, fundamentally violent.[21] In its refusal of organized reasoning, temporal causality, and teleological progression, this narrative of the feminist waves circumvents the enclosure of a feminist historiography that has only been able to catalogue the events of a developmental arc of history as well as those forms of living that have readily adhered to its premise. It retrieves and affirms a lifeworld of feminism that has been obfuscated by the discursive and material taxonomy of its own archive. This is an archive that Patrice Douglass has diagnosed as "structurally anti-black," insofar as it has been conceived within the epistemic order of Western modernity.[22]

Against such insidious logics of archival production, this chapter draws on the lens of Afrofuturism to enact its own practice of the impossible.[23] My analysis of Solomon's *The Deep* will later demonstrate the vitality of the literary medium for reimagining the story of the feminist waves. This is a counternarrative dependent on the fictional conjectures of the text for evoking a different future for Black life, even as it contends with the ongoing realities of social death and the legacies of intergenerational trauma. In this sense, I identify the Afrofuturist mode in the text as exacting what Kodwo Eshun has called a "chronopolitical intervention": a disruption of the colonial apparatus that has enforced a linear, chronological unravelling of the future on its own predictable terms of violence.[24] By interrupting and transcending governing principles of knowing and knowledge-making forged in the cradle of colonialism, the text suspends racist and capitalist visions of futurity contingent on the historical persecution of Black life.

There is a second recursive valence to my engagement of the wave metaphor in this chapter. In many ways, it is already evident in my circling back to the origin story of the feminist waves instead of simply moving on. But unlike other scholars who have modeled their analyses around other, more oblique definitions of the wave metaphor as connoting that of a radio frequency, for example, I moreover remain with arguably its most predictable reference to the sea as the basis for my inquiry here.[25] In so doing, I concede to the unwavering impression that the prevailing story has cast on our collective consciousness, and acknowledge how the incoming tides of the ocean have been used as its most identifiable template. My intention is not to debate the usefulness of different invocations of the wave metaphor that have each been attuned to the symbolic potential of the ocean, nor to isolate still another aspect of its meaning from which to justify its continued relevance. Instead, I stay close to its perceptible allusion to the sea precisely because of the enduring narrative about feminism that it has correspondingly established.

This is a reflexive decision on my part: to tarry with the wave narrative as a vexed object of feminist knowledge rather than simply letting go of its troublesome legacy, as though such a process of moving on could be taken as a desirable or even viable possibility in the first place, anyway. What would it mean if we resisted the immediate imperative to consign this story to the intellectual backwaters of feminist history?[26] What new and different insights about feminism might be gleaned from lingering in the long shadow of its narrative event? These questions revolve around a more encompassing concern of this chapter, which asks what to do with those stories about feminism that have so irrevocably shaped our ways of thinking and knowing that the option of renouncing or leaving behind their conceptual significance cannot, and perhaps should not, necessarily be seen as a progressive epistemological maneuver. This is not to excuse the numerous failings of these stories, but to show how their shortcomings might in fact be tempered by the very refusal to move too hastily, or too easily, on.

For how it concurrently stays with, yet also calls into question, the constitutive terms of feminist history, this practice of retelling the story of the feminist waves is resonant with what Christina Sharpe has defined as wake work: "a mode of inhabiting *and* rupturing this episteme with our known lived and un/imaginable lives."[27] On the one hand, wake work is articulated through its consciousness of the unfinished time of slavery, its occupation of the reality of Black subjection that has structured the entirety of this world.[28] On the other, wake work comes up against this invariable present despite its persistence as such; it insists on another horizon of Black life that might be envisioned out of the inevitability of history. In this chapter I think alongside Sharpe's analytic of wake work by remaining in the wake of the feminist waves. This amounts to a critical exercise that I enact with a heightened awareness of the exclusionary history of feminism, which must be rewritten from an ontological standpoint for it to be more ethically recast at all. From this process, I present a counternarrative that troubles the ceaseless reproduction of the same history of erasure through its animation of other forms of living and knowing. If Katherine McKittrick has elsewhere described a story as something that "prompts," insofar as it "demands representation outside itself," then the revised story of the feminist waves that I tell in what follows not only holds feminism more accountable to its own occluded histories.[29] It also prompts the possibility for Black and queer lifeworlds to be reimagined—and indeed, to flourish—beyond their ongoing subjugation in the present.

A METAPHOR IN ITS ELEMENT

What might it mean to take seriously the materiality of the wave metaphor not simply as a figurative model for feminist historiography but also as a literal one? To parse the continued significance of the wave metaphor for feminist thinking, this chapter argues that it is crucial to consider the physical medium immanent to its etymology, its tangible nature as beholden to the sea. This is my attempt at centering a vital oceanic perspective that lies in plain sight of a formative account of feminism, one that has oddly been overlooked in the ways it has thus far been conceived.[30] By alluding once more to the sensory disorientation triggered by Ariel's charm, I ask how a methodological submergence of the wave metaphor might fundamentally displace our prevailing modes of understanding. In other words, and if much of what we know about the feminist waves has ironically been cast in what Melody Jue has diagnosed as a "terrestrial bias," then this chapter is interested in what other forms of meaning they might hold when this bias is exposed and overturned in favor of the sea.[31]

In a broader sense, I engage the elemental specificities of the ocean in view of a burgeoning, interdisciplinary conversation that has of late come to be organized under the developing field of critical ocean studies.[32] Scholarly attention on the oceanic imaginary is, of course, nothing quite so new; in particular, the immense and far-reaching geopolitical tensions of the twentieth century, coupled with newfound critical attention to the transnational ebbs and flows of global capital, empire, and the slave trade, have collectively established the space of the ocean as a vast, aqueous receptacle from which to track the uneven exchange of peoples, objects, and knowledges across wider expanses of time and space.[33] More recently, however, twenty-first-century studies on the ocean have shifted their focus to critically examine its onto-epistemological capacities amid profound upheavals of thought precipitated by the advent of the Anthropocene. By this latter term, I refer not only to the acute and compounding effects of anthropogenic climate change on the ocean itself—including the looming threats of global sea-level rise and ocean acidification—but also to the ways that it might invite us to explore methods of knowing and living beyond the exemplary logics of the human. Taking the "wet ontology" proposed by Philip Steinberg and Kimberley Peters as one of the major catalysts for this undertaking, such work has evaluated the ontological agency of the ocean as shaped by non-Western, particularly Indigenous, practices of being in the world, alongside its material and conceptual force for theorizing more-than-human entanglements underwater.[34] This is an endeavor that has aspired to unsettle the ruse of objectivity in dominant paradigms of anthropocentric knowledge through the strange and alienating context of the sea.[35]

Keeping in mind the familiar story of the feminist waves, I consider the manifest presence of the ocean as what Jue has termed an "environment for thought," where its unique materiality and physical conditions pose a key vantage point from which to productively deform the assumptions of our already given realities.[36] The point here is not merely to excavate what further knowledge the ocean might offer up to us. It is rather to implement a technique that Jue calls "conceptual displacement," through which the immersive potential of the sea is employed to confront the implicit biases surrounding what and how we know, such that they might then become transformed.[37] This chapter accordingly enacts a conceptual displacement of the wave metaphor as it has conventionally been used as a framework for feminist historiography. I do this insofar as the narratives about feminism that the metaphor has thus far uncovered— through the critical habits of history that it has mobilized— have largely omitted the agentic properties of the sea. To conceptually displace the metaphor in the context of the ocean, then, is to seek another register of its significance that can only be realized underwater; it is to tell a counternarrative of feminism that can only emerge from being submerged in the aquatic environment that lies below the surface of the sea. By transposing a question that Jue puts forth into the more specific context of this essay, I ask: How would ways of speaking about the feminist waves change when its metaphorical crux is plunged into the environmental context of the ocean?[38]

Of course, the depths of the ocean cannot be understood as some ahistorical chasm of nothingness. If the crosscurrents of its surfaces have figured as a stage for the transoceanic expansion of capital and empire, then its depths have become a preserve of the historical memory wrought by these violent projects of modernity. The oceanic terrain through which I reconceive the wave metaphor is more explicitly steeped in the material histories of the transatlantic slave trade: it constitutes a literal, aquatic graveyard of the human wreckage from the oceanic crossings of the Middle Passage. I am therefore guided not only by the physical milieu of the ocean, but also by its tangible claim to the embodied archive of Black life and death. This is a perspective sharpened by Omise'eke Natasha Tinsley's queer reading of the Black Atlantic, where she critiques the maritime metaphors that have been invoked to theorize its imagination.[39] What Tinsley observes is that because these metaphors all too often obscure the materiality of the Black and queer experience in their abstraction, they squander the embodied, erotic potential of Black queerness as a site for radical resistance.[40] Her response to this predicament—which has in many ways motivated my own retention of the wave metaphor for feminist thinking—is not to do away with such metaphors altogether, but to "return to the materiality of water to make its metaphors mean more complexly."[41] Here, Tinsley issues a call to restore the elemental specificities of the ocean back into the metaphors that have contended with its social, political, and historical meaning. And perhaps most crucially, she entrusts this materiality to the corporeal matter of Black and queer lifeworlds that the ocean suspends.[42]

For the above reasons, this chapter takes the oceanic phenomenon of the internal wave as the metaphorical construct that prompts its renewed story of the feminist waves. Internal waves are typically formed, as their name would suggest, *within* the sea and, more precisely, along the interface between two different layers of the oceanic water column marked by varying levels of density.[43] This stands in contrast to the waves that occur on the surface of the ocean, which are most frequently caused by wind blowing across the sea or, in other words, by friction at the interface between the atmosphere and the ocean. Surface waves are a familiar sight on the horizon: their crests are highly visible across the open ocean and on the shoreline. For all their ubiquity, then, it is the generic image of the surface wave that immediately comes to mind when the idea of the feminist waves is invoked.

And it is indeed the undulating dynamics of the surface wave to which scholars have most often gestured to explain the historical and political momentum of the women's movement. By turning instead to the internal wave as the central metaphor from which a counternarrative about feminism might be imagined, I am submerging the dominant understanding of the wave underwater. This is a categorical displacement of the wave metaphor into the sea, for, after all, internal waves surge in the depths of the ocean rather than at its surface. Internal waves are in fact a global phenomenon and can commonly be found in oceans and other bodies of water all over the world.[44] But even as they often feature colossal wavelengths of hundreds of feet, they appear on the surface of the sea only as subtle ridges of smoother and rougher bands of water.[45] This is why Thomas Peacock has described internal waves as the "lumbering giants of the ocean," where their elusive appearance from above the water belies the fact of their tremendous size and power below.[46]

In what follows, two key aspects of the internal wave will direct my reading of Solomon's *The Deep*, both of which I think, and conceptually extend, through the lived histories of a Black and queer imaginary. Each of these attributes serve as distinct points of departure for transforming how the existing narrative of the feminist waves has been known and understood. The first relates to the indiscernibility of internal waves from the oceanic surface, quite simply because of their manifestation underwater. As earlier explained, the primary reason why internal waves are relatively invisible to the untrained human eye is because they form along the interface of different layers of the ocean, stratified as such by differences in density. They move only within the fluid medium of the sea. The undersea presence of the internal wave is therefore most often observed on satellite imagery that can record its imprint on the water surface, or by scientific instruments like echo sounders that measure the depth and density of the ocean through sound waves. But for the most part, internal waves are effectively hidden in the depths of the sea.

To train our attention on their manifestation is thus to acknowledge the existence of what might reside unseen and unknown in the dark recesses of the ocean. It is moreover to be attuned to the power of what might lie in such a watery abyss where light cannot penetrate, and to be receptive to the possibilities of that which evades our limited fields of vision. By this I refer not only to what might literally be occluded from our sight, but also to that which cannot be registered by, and therefore exceeds, our presiding frames of reference. In the latter sense, then, I rely on the speculative mode of *The Deep* to illuminate a deep-sea lifeworld of the otherwise unimaginable. What the text conjures into being is a civilization composed of the descendants of drowned, pregnant African slaves who were forced overboard during the Middle Passage. Their impossible existence clarifies a form of Black temporality suspended by the liquid memory of the sea, one that eludes the capture of progressive modernity. This is an anachronism of time that I argue pries open another dimension to narrating feminist history that centers and reclaims the Black experience over and against the unspeakable loss of slavery.

Internal waves are also known to play a crucial role in maintaining the ocean ecosystem. Their biological impact cannot be understated: Internal waves supply nutrient-rich water closer to coral reefs nearer the coastline, for instance, and transport marine life like zooplankton around the water column as the precondition of wider ecological processes.[47] Cetaceans such as humpback and pilot whales have also been observed to forage by following behind an internal wave, insofar as the physical forces of the latter carry the potential to draw in prey in the form of small fish and squid.[48] Internal waves can therefore be said to be part of a complex, nonhuman web of multispecies interactions in the ocean. This is the second characteristic of the phenomenon from which I extrapolate to frame my analysis of the literary text. I trace how the kinship of a queer, nonhuman genealogy, once more saturated by the embodied materiality of the sea, comes to sustain the oceanic lifeworld in the text. More to the point, *The Deep* rejects the hegemonic definition of the human as a transcendent and discretely bounded subject in favor of the openness and fluidity of the ocean; it populates its narrative with amphibious beings that are inextricably enmeshed in a more-than-human underwater ecology. The novel ultimately illustrates what an account of feminist history might resemble if its dominant forms of narration are displaced from the epistemological inventories of the human.

TIME SUBMERGED, SUSPENDED

If the literary mode of enchantment has compelled an undersea reorientation of our existing ideas surrounding the wave metaphor, it now constructs a textual lifeworld through Rivers Solomon's novella *The Deep*, a lifeworld that us readers are invited to inhabit. This process of inhabitation, a state of being immersed in the imaginative terrain of the text, is what enables us to envision another, different story about feminism. *The Deep* tells of the mythical existence of the water-breathing wajinru, a deepsea civilization founded in the horrors that laid the oceanic burial ground of the transatlantic slave trade. Plumbing the depths of this tragedy, the text envisages other potentialities for Black experience beyond the death sentence of slavery; its narratives perform an act of radical revisioning that births this submarine afterlife out of the brutal realities marking the Black diaspora. The text intervenes at the rupture and irretrievable extinguishing of one world to summon the redemptive beginnings of another.

This speculative lifeworld assembled by the literary text is one that coheres around an origin story first conceived by the enigmatic Detroit electronic music duo Drexciya. Indeed, the sea creatures of *The Deep* that inhabit the mysterious abyss of the Atlantic as a figural resistance against the bloodshed and cruelty of the Middle Passage were once created as the mutant Drexciyans who had rewritten the script of an inevitable demise. Their impossible history was initially canonized in the liner notes of the duo's 1997 compilation album *The Quest*:

> Could it be possible for humans to breathe underwater? A fetus in its mother's womb is certainly alive in an aquatic environment. During the greatest holocaust the world has ever known, pregnant America-bound African slaves were thrown overboard by the thousands during labor for being sick and disruptive cargo. Is it possible that they could have given birth at sea to babies that never needed air? [. . .] Are Drexciyans water breathing, aquatically mutated descendants of those unfortunate victims of human greed? Have they been spared by God to teach us or terrorize us?[49]

Here, Drexciya introduces the fantastic existence of these water-breathing dwellers who have made a seamless, if implausible, transition from the womb to the sea. The storyline of Solomon's novella can thus be traced back to the duo's sonic fiction, whose overall musical project ultimately offers less of a cogent, fully fledged exposition than the opportunity to effectively disorient its listeners through the futuristic and alienating soundscape that they produced.[50] Drexciya's musical gesture to such an audacious survival has become an opening to other ways of imagining the unending devastation of the slave trade.[51]

Building on this imaginative infrastructure, what *The Deep* further explores is the question of memory as an embodied vehicle for historical trauma. It is one that the text both inhabits and turns over in the course of its narrative, parsed through the sustained aftermath of the violence of slavery. There is no simplistic trajectory of progress that the text therefore charts for the existence of the wajinru, even as it draws on the provocations of Afrofuturist thought. Instead, *The Deep* fleshes out the visceral cost of the wajinru's triumphant evolution into aquatic beings: the traumatic legacy that inevitably follows from being "born of the dead."[52] It introduces as its central protagonist the character of Yetu, who has been appointed the historian of the wajinru, tasked to bear the painful weight of their collective ancestral memory. It is a "sickness of remembering"—both physically excruciating and mentally draining—that she must endure as the medium for the wajinru's harrowing beginnings.[53] By contrast, the rest of her community are biologically predisposed to forgetfulness and therefore spared from this onerous burden of remembering the past. But the blissful ignorance granted by the absence of such memories also amounts to a kind of empty, meaningless existence that eventually wears thin. As Yetu's mother Amaba remarks: "One can only go for so long without asking who am I? . . . Without answers, there is only a hole, a hole where a history should be that takes the shape of an endless longing."[54] To alleviate their yearning for the past, the wajinru convene at an annual ceremony called The Remembrance, where Yetu shares stories of a history that she has collected with the others before taking possession of them again.

In the throes of its most recent event, however, it dawns on Yetu that to continue with her responsibilities as historian would mean for her mind and body to soon be crushed by the unbearable pressure of the memories she is obliged to keep. She chooses then to flee the wajinru and ascend to the surface of the sea.

What Yetu escapes here are the watery confines of the ocean, which have long served as an agentic preserve of the gravity of colonial histories.[55] Indeed, it is these pervasive, structuring conditions of the sea that the wajinru more ostensibly inhabit in *The Deep*, even as they are at the same time portrayed as having somehow averted the watery fate of a preordained slaughter. To this end, the text underscores the ocean less as a space of open-ended, utopian possibility—as its aquatic terrain has commonly figured in Afrofuturist descriptions—and more as an immersive memorial to the slow decay that marks the atrocities of the slave trade.[56] If the ocean constitutes the encompassing environment of the narrative, in other words, it is one that is thoroughly saturated with the remains of the dead.

This is the unsettling, haunting milieu in which the wajinru are destined to abide, which Yetu most acutely senses as an occupational hazard of being the historian. Yetu must perpetually suffer the intrusions of the ocean as the only one conscious of the trauma that it holds. The ocean has come to render her body "a wound" against which the constant sting of its individual salt crystals press; she is able to "parse each granule . . . of the flaky white mineral [that] scraped against her."[57] This terrible onslaught is the physical manifestation of the memories belonging to the wajinru's enslaved ancestors, the totalizing atmosphere of anti-Black violence that had once enveloped their being.[58] And as M. Jacqui Alexander elsewhere writes of such waters overflowing with the memories of slavery: the dead "do not like to be forgotten."[59] Yetu, who is cursed with hypersensitive electroreceptors that had ironically characterized her disposition as suitable to be historian in the first place, experiences these tangible afflictions of the sea on an intense and all-consuming level. Unlike the rest of the wajinru, Yetu is aware that their current, tranquil flourishing should not be seen as a given inheritance, but rather the consequence of a long, racialized archive of abjection and cruelty. She feels the ripples of these historical arcs of anguish still circulating around her, reminding her that the wajinru continue to live in the permanent time of slavery extending even into their reimagined future.

As earlier detailed, then, this all proves too much for Yetu, who decides she has had enough of all this, and escapes upwards into open air. But even as she is now released from those memories that had caused her such immeasurable hurt and pain, Yetu feels utterly "unmoored" in her newfound encounter with this freedom.[60] The text likewise clarifies her experience in a literal, physical sense: If the liquid surroundings of the ocean had earlier overwhelmed her being, the more terrestrial environment of the rockpool where Yetu washes up is equally debilitating. As an amphibious creature, Yetu does not quite struggle to breathe above the surface, but the mere function of having to draw breath on land reveals itself to be a "new, uncomfortable feeling, and her lungs felt unsatisfied."[61] And in these superficial waters devoid of the tactile pressure and feedback of the ocean, the light "was so unbearable" that she soon begins to pine for home, paradoxically "coveting the deep sea, its blanket of cold and dark."[62]

Fully displaced from the depths of the ocean, Yetu is not only removed from the collective presence of her wajinru kin, but also from the memories of her ancestors that have long steeped in the shadowy waters. And it is only in this underwater realm that the new beginnings of the wajinru could have emerged in the first place. As Yetu realizes, "Absent the rememberings,

who was she but a woman *cast away?*"[63] Yetu has fled the ocean
in a purposeful alienation of herself from the wajinru, but this
process has also brought her back to a primordial occasion of
death by being thrown off a slave ship. Cast away from her
water-dwelling society, she is also cast off from a temporal fault
line that had opened a speculative counterfuture for the conception of the wajinru, and cast back into an oppressive history of
enslavement. Yetu's departure to land has figured as a return to
a wretched time of colonial modernity. The ocean cannot simply
be construed as a more comfortable abode for Yetu; it is also the
paradigmatic space of a newly fashioned possibility of survival
in and out of the wake of slavery to which she has now been
barred access. What Yetu longs for in the more overarching
sense, therefore, is being "a part of not just the sea, but the
whole world. Without the History, she felt out of place and out
of time. She missed being connected to all."[64] After all, it is the
ocean that had once conjured up, and now composes, the entire
lifeworld of the wajinru. It has encompassed their alternative
cradle of civilization, complete with its own radical vectors of
time and space that have otherwise been foreclosed by the violent, racialized logics of a progressive history.

My designation of the wajinru as inhabitants of this other
measure of oceanic time is in part an extension of Hortense
Spillers's provocative claim that those "African persons in 'Middle Passage' were literally suspended in the 'oceanic.'"[65] Here,
Spillers transposes the Freudian psychoanalytic inclination of
oceanic feeling—an originary state of undifferentiated identity—
into the specific context of the transatlantic slave trade.[66] In this
regard, her articulation of the "oceanic" becomes historicized in
line with how the enslaved were "removed from the indigenous
land and culture, not-yet 'American' either, these captive persons, without names that their captors would recognize, were in

movement across the Atlantic, but they were also *nowhere* at all."[67] The ocean is this way set as the elemental scene of Black death, the site of an unimaginable violation and dissolution of Black identity at which the enslaved have become what Spillers calls the "culturally 'unmade.'"[68] In this rendering of oceanic space, they are excised from an identifiable category of the human, which traps them in a position of stasis, a state of suspension that accordingly compels their displacement from the temporal flow of history.[69] Having been dispossessed of all signifiers of personhood and humanity, which underwrite particular orientations to space and time, the enslaved are altogether forced out of a temporal formation that has come to track the developmental narrative of colonial modernity. They are made lost from a world that has coerced their exile.

But the banishing of the enslaved from familiar historical and spatial coordinates in this manner also generates a condition of possibility for envisioning alternative forms of temporality.[70] It inscribes a plurality of counterhistories and futures of modernity that serves to puncture the telos of racial capitalism. On one level, the inertia that is embodied by these Black subjects expunged from time presents an immediate critique of the velocity of progressive history. This is what Habiba Ibrahim would describe as their "untimeliness" as such, a temporal inhabitation incommensurable with the configuration of colonial modernity, which cannot be parsed in its prevailing codes of intelligibility.[71] This itself constitutes a fracture of the seamless perpetuation of dominant time, a refusal of its totalizing regime. But on yet another level, Spillers also intimates the transformative capacity of this process of "unmaking" that, at the advent of the Middle Passage, has become so foundational to the nature of Black existence.[72] More precisely, it is the event of this unmaking that ultimately calls forth the speculative reimagination of Black life underwater. It is only against the backdrop of this brutal unmaking that such alternative acts of remaking paradoxically come to be made viable, those that find their true bearings in the watery depths of the sea. To put simply, then, the ocean offers Blackness another beginning.[73] This radical juncture of possibility marks the point of departure taken by the narrative of *The Deep*: The text exploits the oceanic suspension provoked by the crossings of the transatlantic slave trade to bring into being other temporalities of a Black lifeworld now held by the sea. If the waters of the ocean have long suspended the embodied trauma of slavery, then they, too, have sustained the precipitate of a different kind of future for Black life.

BREATHING UNDERWATER

The Deep continues to position the ocean as fundamental to its reimagination of Black life. Yetu explicitly identifies the ocean as the original entity that ensured the survival of the wajinru; she describes its waters as "the progenitor of all life."[74] Through this description, the text underscores its submarine lifeworld as conceived beyond the definition of the human as a transcendent, exceptional, and discretely bounded subject. *The Deep* rejects the proprietary nature of the human in favor of the openness and fluidity that the ocean represents, populating its narrative with amphibious beings that are inextricably enmeshed in a more-than-human underwater ecology.[75] The elements of the ocean have not only given life to the wajinru, but also continue to flow through their bodies, literally circulating in the very breaths that they take. And furthermore, it is the giant whales of the deep that have rescued some of the earliest wajinru pups in a gesture of queer, multispecies care. But if it is revealed that the wajinru are the descendants of enslaved victims of the Middle Passage, who were forcibly denied their humanity at the advent of Western modernity, then their remarkable animation is also emphasized as the defiant continuation of this specific register of life beyond the human. In this light, the existence of the wajinru must not only be read as an acknowledgment of their transcorporeal entanglements with the sea, which indeed discloses the nonhuman incursions of their genesis.[76] It must further be traced against the racialized logics of liberal humanism that have privileged the sanctity of the human as such. What the text ultimately presents is a countergenealogy of Black and queer life that altogether refuses this hegemonic lineage of the human.

In many ways, this idea of an errant genealogy is explicitly dramatized in *The Deep*; by drawing on the original Drexciyan mythology, which centered on the afterlives of pregnant slaves who drowned during the Middle Passage, its narrative is deeply invested in the transformative arc of their submarine evolution into the extraordinary figures of the wajinru. This is a wayward—if impossible—genealogy that the text pursues, one that defies its initial severance to extend its momentum underwater. For the wajinru, who are born from these bodies fallen into the liquid depths of the sea, it is the ocean that had first given "all of itself to [them], giving the wajinru the spark of life, showing them that if only they knew how, water could be breathed."[77] Here, the ocean comes to acquire an unmistakably maternal quality, assuming the role of an unlikely custodian serendipitously assumed in the wake of the tragic incapacitation of slavery. It is the gestational capacity of its waters, not quite so different from the amniotic fluid that surrounds and protects an unborn fetus in the womb, that sustains the otherworldly forms of life manifesting as the wajinru. If the text is invested in disclosing the ancestral lineage of the wajinru, it stresses its deviation from normative filiations of the human. In one sense, then, its narrative underscores the origins of the wajinru as decidedly strange, and as founded on the renunciation of the familiar, terrestrial biases of being human. These water-breathing beings have taken up an alternative line of descent that ensues from the derangement of human pedigree; they occupy a speculative condition of being otherwise. But in another sense, what the narrative clarifies is also an oceanic origin story that in fact subtends the material conception of what has come to be known as the human altogether.

To make this argument, I draw on the work of Rachel Carson, who has characterized the sea as "the great mother of life" from which all animate beings on the Earth originated millions of years ago.[78] While the precise scientific alchemy of oceanic conditions for this emergence of life remains unclear, Carson observes that "the sea produced the mysterious and wonderful stuff called protoplasm": such stuff that now flows through both its briny waters and the biochemical makeup of all animals that now exist on the planet.[79] As she continues, "Each of us carries in our veins a salty stream in which the elements sodium, potassium, and calcium are combined in almost the same proportions as sea water."[80] And this fact is perhaps made most plain in the "miniature oceans" of amniotic fluid that we all have inhabited at one point in our lives.[81] Carson draws our attention to the overlooked universality of all living bodies as implicated in and by the ocean.[82] She accordingly exposes the dominant understanding of the human as a self-enclosed, insular, and autonomous individual to be the stuff of mere fiction, explicating instead its perennial and inescapable entanglement with more-than-human forces of existence. Carson in this way establishes such a definition of the human to have been derived from and upheld by anthropocentric modes of thinking and knowing. In turn, *The Deep* extends from her claims to convey that this same definition of human exceptionalism must also be seen as inseparable from the violent apparatus of colonial modernity.

It is from this key premise that the text unfolds its countergenealogy of Black life, one that reckons with the legacies of racial capitalism that have authorized such a consolidation of the human. And its critique of such paradigms—or, as Yetu puts differently in the narrative, its disavowal of those "specific ways of classifying the world that [she] didn't like"—is further exemplified by the multispecies kinship that the wajinru have come to assemble underwater.[83] If the very first mothers of the wajinru have been destined to death by drowning, then their offspring released into the wide expanse of the ocean ultimately live "only by the graciousness of the second mothers, the giant water beasts . . . whales."[84] It is these immense creatures of the deep who more explicitly become the wajinru's "only kin"; the marine mammals feed the newborn wajinru who would otherwise have died of starvation, bond with them, and guide them away from the surface of the sea and down into safety.[85]

In its designation of these whales as such nonhuman guardians of the wajinru, *The Deep* invokes the radical politics of what might be deemed a queer ecology that coalesces between them underwater. Broadly speaking, I mean by *queer ecology* an emergent critical praxis that seeks to unravel prevailing assumptions surrounding sexuality and nature, betraying their articulation as entrenched in heterosexist frameworks of knowledge production.[86] The conceptual terrain of queer ecology is therefore primed for the reimagination of what has thus far constituted the "natural," especially in its convergence with multiple discourses of sexuality, race, and ecology. Queer ecological forms of resistance have challenged normative accounts of evolutionary theory and biological reproduction to gesture toward alternative potentialities of kinship beyond the human. The otherworldly phenomenon of the aquatic wajinru, then, as already the aberration of conventional processes of human evolution, becomes further compounded by their vital affinity with the whales as cetaceans that have long traversed the expanse of the ocean.[87] If the wajinru are said to inhabit a "world beyond this world," then it is one in which the hierarchical demarcations between humans and other beings are dissolved in favor of distinctively queer, relational possibilities of existence.[88]

The text further inflects this existence through the material histories of the wajinru, in which the queer ecology that gathers in its narrative is one that is steeped in the racialized politics of Blackness now plunged into the sea. Aside from attending to the neonatal demands of the wajinru, *The Deep* goes on to describe how the sonic presence of the whales also figures as a kind of connective tissue that affirms the relations between their disparate forms of life. During a close encounter with a looming blue whale, one of the first wajinru prepares themselves for a certain demise. But the whale opens its mouth only to reveal pups that it has thus far kept safe and well-fed, miniature versions of the wajinru that it has now intentionally reunited in recognition that they all are "one kind."[89] And while their attempts to converse with the whale are fraught with some level of incomprehension—where the sounds that it makes lie "beyond the most rudimentary levels of communication"—the wajinru nevertheless construe the proximity of the immense creature as an expression of radical, interspecies care.[90] More precisely, it is the sorrowful hums of the whale, "thunderous and sad," that register the immeasurable grief surrounding both the fate of the wajinru's ancestors and the other wajinru offspring who have not been so lucky to survive.[91] The cries of the whale as a response to these deaths are interminable, and the acute "pang of loss" that is crystallized in their reverberations comes to resonate with the wajinru in a manner that transcends the seemingly unsurpassable language barrier between each of their constitutive lifeworlds.[92]

This mourning of the whale for its newfound wajinru kin is yet another transgression of boundaries that are necessarily troubled by a queer ecological modality. Its familiar anguish eclipses the inheritance of trauma by a singular human species, gesturing instead to the violent repercussions of colonial modernity that can be felt on more sweeping, planetary scales of time and space. It is in this overarching sense that the calls of the whale can thus be perceived as a sonic remembrance of those lost to the ongoing histories and present of slavery. For Alexis Pauline Gumbs, who suggests that emergent strategies of a Black and queer feminist theorizing might be drawn from the life lessons of marine mammals, the calling of blue whales connotes this exact historical meaning. As she writes, "We are all living in the long water prayer of the blue whales, that meditative sound that travels hundreds of miles underwater. With one breath they send sound across entire oceans, envelop the planet in far-reaching chant."[93] The enfolding lament of these whales not only serves as an infinite and unforgettable testament to slavery in the holding environment of the ocean.[94] It is also a ceaseless benediction for the dead, which is "still blessing our water selves now" in its monumental significance.[95] In this sense, the text shows how its queer ecology composed under the auspices of the ocean resists the structural dimensions of history, illuminating other possibilities of living and living on that might be located only in such speculative, ungovernable terrains beyond the human. The alternative story about feminism that it tells cannot be contained by accompanying systems of knowing and understanding predicated on the temporal and spatial limits of liberal humanism.

At its heart, what *The Deep* offers is a suggestive opening for the storying of feminist history in a way that departs from its conventional methods of historiography. That the text tells of the transformative potentialities of Black and queer forms of life in the wake of colonial modernity is a productive consequence of the submergence of the wave metaphor into the embodied materiality of the sea, a conceptual displacement of the heuristic device we have so closely associated with our understanding of feminism. If another story of feminist waves can be located here, then, it is one that has evidently drifted from its most well-known version, swept away by the forces of a reconceived metaphor that roils within the ocean instead of at its surface. It is a story not intended to replace what we already know—as if this could realistically be achieved, in any case—but rather to demonstrate how feminism might be known differently, and indeed, so much more richly and strangely, through a reflexive intervention of multiple configurations of progressive logic. This has altogether been the effect of the literary mode of enchantment, which in this chapter has been harnessed for its capacity to provide a new kind of sensory experience that more critically attunes our perspectives to the sea, and to further build an imaginative, textual lifeworld on the bearings of such a reoriented existence.

2

A DEMONIC AFTERLIFE OF
SEXUAL DIFFERENCE

In her introduction to *écriture féminine*, which was published in a 1981 special section of *Feminist Studies* under the title "The French Connection," Ann Rosalind Jones surveys the writings of four theorists—Julia Kristeva, Luce Irigaray, Hélène Cixous, and Monique Wittig—as indicative of an emerging body of feminist work that has come to be widely known as "French feminism."[1] Jones was writing at a time when feminist literary criticism in the US academy saw a proliferation of perspectives marked by a distinctively psychoanalytic focus on language, the unconscious, and sexual difference.[2] In contrast to the primary goals of Anglo-American feminist literary criticism that had historically been concerned with building a female literary tradition, then, scholars of French feminism would shift the conversation away from the biological sex of the author to the question of language as a structuring condition of reality.[3]

But in a strange turn of events, the tale that is most often told of French feminism and its impact on the feminist imagination is one completely antithetical to this account. French feminism—itself a reductive term that typically characterizes only the work of Cixous, Irigaray, and Kristeva in Anglo-American academic feminism—has since become inextricably tied to accusations of biological essentialism. Jones is one key critic who fueled this claim, writing that because French feminist theorists believed Western thought to have been founded on the systemic repression of women's experience, their critique depended on a "bedrock female nature" from which to assert their claims for the deconstruction of patriarchal frameworks of knowledge.[4] And biological essentialism was not the only offence that French feminism had egregiously committed. Jones argued that French feminism failed to acknowledge the social differences between women: its methods were ignorant of the identity categories that distinguished women in their lived existences, and were thus universalizing in their nature.[5] As she asks in this vein: "What about variations in race, class, and culture among women?"[6]

The effect of such allegations by scholars like Jones has been entrenched in the academic feminist imaginary. At this time, the reputation of French feminism is one irretrievably tainted: It has come to be most widely known as a school of feminist thought that is both essentialist and universalizing, and often invoked as a fraught historical moment from which academic feminism has long progressed in its necessary search for greater inclusivity and diversity.[7] If there has been an institutional avoidance, or even a disparagement, of French feminism in the field of feminist studies, in other words, it has largely been driven by anxieties over its incriminatory referent. The mere mention of any of the main theorists of French feminism, for instance, or the deployment of its key concepts such as sexual difference, continues to shore up unease over old specters of a regressive feminist past.[8] But by bringing up the damaging narrative that has been told about French feminism, my point in this chapter is not to rechart its genealogy, or to provide a fuller and perhaps more rigorous picture of its definition.[9] I am not interested in adjudicating the disagreements that have been centered on the twinned problematics of essentialism and universalism and their relation to French feminism, nor in offering more evidence to support or overturn our assumptions about French feminism. Rather, and in line with the methodological turn of the preceding chapter, I treat the problematic legacy of French feminism as a point of departure for thinking and theorizing feminism in a different way. What would it mean to resist the tendency to turn away from French feminism as an ethical smoke screen of feminist progress, and instead reckon with its difficult remainder in the feminist imagination?[10] What new and other kinds of insight might be gleaned from such an approach that refuses the progressive bearings of feminist knowledge production?

Acting with the broader aims of this book in mind, this chapter applies the recantatory force of enchantment to the specific concept of sexual difference as one of the philosophical cornerstones of French feminist inquiry. This is the second act of recantation that *Feminism Enchanted* performs, which involves a reflexive return to the feminist potential that I believe to still inhere in the critical premise of sexual difference in order to uncover the surprising insight it might articulate at this time. Once more, my objective is not to offer a corrective account of the term with an intention of directly assuaging the charge of its ethical limitations, but instead to retrieve it through an alternative critical practice that is this book's mode of enchantment.[11] This anachronistic treatment of sexual difference will place it in an intertextual dialogue with certain valences of race, embodiment, and gender that had originally provoked the anxieties surrounding French feminism as a wider body of work; it entails a juxtaposition of the ideological significance of sexual difference with precisely those marginal perspectives that it has historically been accused of overlooking. It is less of an attempt to remediate the long-held afflictions of sexual difference, therefore, and more an exploration of how a particular understanding of the concept resonates in unexpected ways with seemingly disparate paradigms of race and colonialism. I will show how this reading of sexual difference, which stays with its speculative possibilities rather than simply moves on from its troubled history in feminist studies, makes legible another afterlife of the concept.

In what follows, I take the feminist philosopher Luce Irigaray's conceptual proposition of sexual difference for the specific purposes of this endeavor. Interpretations of the exact meaning of *sexual difference*, and even the naming of the term itself, have shifted in response to Irigaray's own changing philosophical preoccupations throughout the course of her career.[12] But for the context of this chapter, I focus on the gesture of sexual difference toward a future of the resolutely unknowable, insofar as this definition is crucial for disrupting our binding knowledge of feminism as a narrative of progress. I trace the scene of wonder that marks this paradigm of sexual difference, underscoring how its impetus for the indeterminable and unforeseen might be parsed in more ethical terms. To this end, I read Irigaray's notion of sexual difference alongside the Afro-Caribbean philosopher and cultural theorist Sylvia Wynter's sweeping undertaking to fundamentally rethink the category of the human. Wynter's project of undoing—and indeed, imagining beyond— the overrepresented idea of Man, particularly as expressed through her formulation of the "demonic," is one that finds affinity with, but more urgently expands, the insular future that marks Irigaray's proposed revolution of sexual difference. The chapter ends with a close reading of the Nigerian writer Akwaeke Emezi's debut novel *Freshwater* (2018) to navigate the representational implications of sexual difference now mediated by the fundamentally racialized terms of the demonic. In other words, if the expression of the demonic calls for a mode of representation that defies and eludes dominant frames of knowledge, then I clarify how literature might accommodate its ethical demand. My reading examines how Emezi's rendering of the textual lifeworld of *Freshwater* through a distinctively Indigenous cosmology might amount to a literary allusion toward the critical possibilities of the demonic.

THE WONDER OF SEXUAL DIFFERENCE

To fully understand Irigaray's theory of sexual difference, it is first necessary to trace how the concept emerged from the undercurrents of some of her earliest work. Irigaray's psychoanalytic negotiations in *Speculum of the Other Woman* (1985) and *This Sex Which Is Not One* (1985) are largely predicated on her critique of the history of Western philosophy as being mired in, and thus perpetuating, a falsely neutral logic of singularity. In essence, Irigaray's project is an attempt to rehabilitate the impoverished reflection of feminine difference, an act of retrieving and writing from this othered perspective that has invariably been occluded by the existing patriarchal order.[13] Irigaray undertakes this task by recognizing that the feminine, which encapsulates the irreducible difference of "Woman" that cannot be expressed in the terms of existing knowledge, has solely been understood within the binary opposition that privileges the hegemonic economy of the masculine. Accordingly, she suggests that all forms of feminine subjectivity that now circulate have simply been disappointing renditions of the same and, moreover, "the inverse, indeed the underside, of the masculine."[14] As she writes, *"sexual indifference"* is that which *"underlies the truth of any science, the logic of every discourse,"* and our epistemological standpoints have been derived entirely from the interests that serve patriarchal domination.[15] Irigaray's framework of sexual difference finds its origins in uncovering and affirming the categorical otherness of a devalued feminine subjectivity that has always been suppressed by the ideal model of the masculine, as the representation and proliferation of the masculine subject. This methodical undoing of Western thought and reason is the conceptual provenance for the feminist "revolution" of sexual difference that she will later come to seek.

Irigaray's *An Ethics of Sexual Difference* builds on the groundwork of these earlier writings. It expands on the recovery of the feminine in a quest for further-reaching, and potentially more radical, implications for feminism. In a formative statement, she explains what it would take for sexual difference to eventually come into being:

> A revolution in thought and ethics is needed if the work of sexual difference is to take place. We need to reinterpret everything concerning the relations between the subject and discourse, the subject and the world, the subject and the cosmic, the microcosmic and the macrocosmic. Everything, beginning with the way in which the subject has always been written in the masculine form, as *man*, even when it claimed to be universal or neutral.[16]

While Irigaray certainly begins with reassessing the notion of psychoanalytic subjectivity as the underpinning task of sexual difference, then, she extrapolates from this narrower premise to contest more pervasive beliefs that are implicit in larger systems of knowledge. Irigaray's exposure and dismantling of the masculine subject has the effect of rendering existing epistemologies inherently unstable, insofar as they too have been authorized by this uncontested, masculine stance. The implications of this for feminist thought are extraordinary: Irigaray suggests that with the advent of sexual difference, in its instantiation of the irreducible difference of the feminine, new openings in discourse might consequently be discovered, ones with a crucial feminist emphasis. When she calls for us to "reinterpret everything," Irigaray hints at the overturning of all discourse as also having validated a solely masculine view.[17] Her observation of existing paradigms of knowledge as having only been reflective of the masculine instills in the processes of sexual difference a subversive feminist power when it is invoked to challenge the universality of patriarchal knowledge.

What Irigaray foregrounds in her conception of sexual difference is therefore its suggestive capacity for summoning feminist perspectives yet unthought. It is this conjecture of sexual difference that compels new and alternative forms of feminist knowledge. But herein also lies a paradox inherent to its imperative: While Irigaray alludes to the anticipatory inclinations of sexual difference as an unrealized horizon for feminist thought, she simultaneously emphasizes its utterly unrecognizable configuration in the masculine discourses of the present, which have always masqueraded as an objective and neutral totality. In this sense, sexual difference enfolds a vital otherness that effectively displaces its expression from all orders of thinking and knowing. If sexual difference is to truly be revolutionary in the way that Irigaray intends, then the very condition of its possibility lies in its failure to conform to our present structures of existence; its articulation cannot be conceived along any terms of the already given.

In this vein, Judith Butler suggests that Irigarayan sexual difference might best be inferred as "a question that prompts a feminist inquiry, it is something that cannot quite be stated, that troubles the grammar of the statement, and that remains, more or less permanently, to interrogate."[18] As Butler further observes, the idea of sexual difference "does not assume the form of facts and structures but persists as that which makes us *wonder*, which remains not fully explained and not fully explicable."[19] I will later return to this scene of wonder as an affective inclination that, when critically reconceived, urges an ethical expansion of the possibilities of the concept for theorizing feminism. But first, what Butler points out is that while sexual difference might manifest as a question, it is not one that can or should be answered. Instead, sexual difference displays a curious tendency to agitate even greater forms of uncertainty; it makes precarious all current modes of discourse as having only been wrought through masculine frames of reference. In the process, sexual difference enacts a disconcerting but crucial disjuncture from the more immediate concerns of the feminist agenda, such that feminism itself might eventually come to see its project as radically unbound from the confines of long-established realities. By defying the limits of the known and the knowable, it holds open a space for feminist thought to be expressed in the speculative intimations of an uncontainable future, one that Irigaray writes is therefore "still and always open."[20]

This coming-into-being of sexual difference has led Elizabeth Grosz to argue that the only time of its existence "is that of the future."[21] And it is precisely in this regard that sexual difference has come to inform several discussions, especially as outlined at the turn of the new millennium, on how feminism should more reflexively attend to the emergence of its possible futures.[22] Sexual difference for Grosz, insofar as it engenders an encounter with the indeterminable and the unknowable, is a prism through which an unprecedented feminist future might be envisioned. This stands in opposition to the limitations of a more constrained future that only accommodates a deterministic end to its goals. The invitation that sexual difference extends for the future of feminism finds no premise in its pasts and present; it cannot be predicted by the finite and often teleological bounds of the existing feminist imagination. Grosz explains that such a future involves the instantiation of a truly radical feminist politics, which demands an "investment in the power of the leap, by which the actual emerges and produces itself from its virtual resources, that generates the new, in both politics and theory."[23] In this sense, the anticipatory tendencies of sexual difference not only beckon another, alternative vision of a feminist future that does not follow from the immediacies of the past and present. It also comes to herald a new and different kind of feminism altogether, complete with concomitant forms of politics that have not yet been, and in fact may never fully be, conceived.

Fully invested in the unknowability of the future, such a feminism does not offer any reassuring panacea for the wrongs of patriarchal discourse. It cannot provide any direct or satisfactory response to the more practical axioms of the feminist movement. In this sense, it is a feminism that Robyn Wiegman posits as "nonidentical": one that "will not be efficient; it will not have the clarity of productive order; it will not guarantee that feminist struggle culminates in a present that is without waste to the future."[24] In a corresponding manner, the politics of such a feminism cannot be foreclosed by the realities of a tangible past and present, insofar as it operates only in the horizon of a future detached from their aims. To be clear, this is not a feminism that threatens the dissolution of the lived political praxis of feminism itself. It simply uncovers an intrinsic counternarrative that clarifies the elements of the provisional and the unpredictable that coexist within feminism's critical edifice.[25]

My point in delineating the tenets of this other kind of feminism is to draw attention to how its defiant inhabitation of the speculative has once more animated certain anxieties over its emphasis on the unknown. But in contrast to before, I want to now read these anxieties as a constructive occasion for thinking and theorizing feminism.[26] If sexual difference, as a markedly French feminist concept, had earlier triggered anxieties from within feminism over its propensity for essentialism and universalism, then this conceptual proposition of Irigarayan sexual difference sparks curiously similar feelings, although this time over its gesture to a feminism that resides only in a future that cannot be anticipated. These latter anxieties are provoked by concerns over the inability of such a feminism to capture any working definition of progress, over its refusal to address the political urgencies faced by feminism in its currently recognizable form. And as touched on earlier in this book, such affective intensities should be seen as coextensive with the discursive politics of feminism. Because there is no discernible trajectory of progress that can be plotted by this alternative conception of feminism, it instigates a condition of epistemological paralysis in hegemonic modes of feminist historiographic narration. The feminist desire to uphold a linear and straightforward ideal of a progressive future, and to consequently profess a triumphant story about its political agency, becomes undone by this difficult confrontation with a future that cannot yet be imagined in the now.[27]

In line with the overarching concerns of *Feminism Enchanted*, then, sexual difference incites a productive attenuation of feminism's commitment to political progress. Its ever-perplexing construct sustains new and discontinuous forms of feminism, in and for a future that does not merely resemble the past. But there is an ethical risk that accompanies the valorization of such a future. As Sara Ahmed observes, a feminist philosophy of futurity, in its gravitation toward the allure of the new, is tethered to a perilous embrace of an abstract and universal otherness itself. She warns that the "collapse of otherness with the future promised by narratives of becoming can work to leave the past for dead."[28] What Ahmed reveals is that the unchecked privileging of a future of feminism that is resolutely new and unknowable, as effectively "the time of and for otherness," relegates the particular histories of its pasts and present to utter insignificance.[29] For such a future hinges on the precondition of absolute alterity, and operates on the basis that the pasts of feminism are completely spent and should thereby be left behind. Instead of an overriding appeal to this future of abstract otherness, then, Ahmed suggests that "it is through attending to the multiplicity of the pasts that are never simply behind us, through the traces they leave in the encounters we have in the present, that we can open up the promise of the 'not yet.'"[30] If there is a radically unanticipated future for feminism to endorse, then it must be mediated by the unfinished potential of its pasts that present modes of feminist thinking should ceaselessly strive to apprehend. Feminism must first reckon with the enduring presence of its pasts for a truly revolutionary future to be had.

At this point, I want to circle back to the pertinent moment of wonder that Butler had earlier associated with sexual difference in order to examine its potential as a disposition that might precisely compel this more ethical stance urged by Ahmed. Sexual difference, as Butler notes, "makes us wonder"; its conceptual refrain to the speculative and the unknown sparks an affective stance that corresponds to its articulation as such.[31] Butler borrows this term from Irigaray, who had originally called for a return to wonder as an ideal of René Descartes's first and primary passion.[32] Irigaray writes that wonder, as a "feeling of surprise, astonishment," is a necessary element "in the face of the unknow-able" as it allows for a relationship of alterity to exist between the sexes to constitute an ethics of sexual difference.[33] Wonder is thus evoked in the presence of the new, a feeling aroused by an encounter with the unexpected that sexual difference incites; it is the disposition that most clearly orients our existing ways of knowing and being to the unprecedented future that sexual dif-ference invites.[34] But in line with Ahmed's ethical insistence for more attention to be paid to the significance that lies latent in feminist pasts, how might this same phenomenon of wonder be activated for such a purpose? How might wonder simultane-ously be mobilized to identify new patterns of meaning in the assumed familiarity of the pasts that would otherwise remain imperceptible and unseen?[35] What might wonder be able to teach us about the encompassing pasts and present of feminism, if only to not reproduce a future of the same? A satisfactory response to these questions entails an expansion of the impera-tive of wonder as an affect synonymous with the advent of sex-ual difference, a reflexive embodying of its experience for the unfolding of more ethical futures.

EXIT SIGN OF THE DEMONIC

To think further about this instructive capacity of wonder, I turn to the work of Sylvia Wynter, for whom the scene of wonder can-not be glossed as a mere expression of affect. Rather, Wynter calls for the exploration of wonder as a phenomenon that arises as a specific consequence of modes of cultural and historical repre-sentation.[36] Wonder must not be perceived as an abstract, singu-lar, or transcendental experience that is devoid of prior meaning, but as always already embedded in the varying social, political, and ideological contexts that have produced its very being. The instigation of wonder should therefore be taken as a generative starting point for more closely examining how it has come to be in the first place; wonder should be parsed as reflective of those dominant modes of knowing and knowledge production that have structured its manifestation as such. And by calling attention to the underlying epistemological bearings of its expression, wonder throws their purported legitimacy into crisis, thereby creating new openings for thinking. Here, Wynter's explication of wonder introduces an interrogative register to its manifestation, which when considered alongside the event of sexual difference, comes to expose the universality of the latter's philosophical gesture to a radically unknowable future. On which, or indeed on whose, epistemic terms of the unknowable can sexual difference cast its claim to such a futurity? This line of inquiry lays bare which other epistemologies may also lie beyond the present horizon of knowledge. Such an impetus for wonder might be understood less as an ushering in of an enigmatic otherness, and more a disentangling of what has remained unthinkable in the past and present in order for the conditions of such a future to even be made possible. If there is an alternative future to be imagined, and to be beheld in such wonder, then such a future can only come into existence from the active undoing of hegemonic frameworks of living and being that are currently in obstruction of its eventual emergence.

By bringing Wynter into the conversation at this juncture, my intention is not at all to conflate her own expansive and far-reaching project with that of Irigaray's. Where Irigaray seeks to dismantle the patriarchal underpinnings of Western philosophy from a largely psychoanalytic standpoint, Wynter's work traverses a critical genealogy of Western humanism and outlines the material and discursive ways that its central archetype of Man has come to be organized and established. Alert to the colonial logics of Western modernity, Wynter traces an origin story of how a certain exclusionary model of humanness— namely white and bourgeois—was not only invented but also became the "descriptive statement" for the human altogether.[37] It became sanctioned as the only legitimate figure of the human at the expense of those beings and lifeworlds deemed inferior to its representation as such. What Wynter presents is a critique of this ascendant conception of Man as falsely universal and, in her terms, entirely "overrepresented" in its contemporaneous worldview. She argues that "the struggle of our new millennium will be one between the ongoing imperative of securing the well-being of our present ethnoclass (i.e., Western bourgeois) conception of the human, Man, which overrepresents itself as if it were the human itself, and that of securing the well-being, and therefore the full cognitive and behavioral autonomy of the human species itself/ourselves."[38]

Wynter calls for a movement away from the singular, totalizing referent of the human that has been naturalized as Man, toward multiple "genres of being human."[39] But there is no alternative placeholder for this largely liberal humanist subject of Man, only the sustained unravelling of its hierarchical structures of representation as the very strategy that locates the possibility of new and other collective ways of being in the world.[40] By rewiring our presiding circuits of knowledge production, she traces what viable forms of meaning the human might then acquire when it is emancipated from the sovereign constitution of Man. In short, then, what lies at the heart of Wynter's intervention is an ontological rethinking of the human, an attempt to breach the epistemic legacies of Man that have so irrevocably fashioned our current orientations of thinking, knowing, and living.

All this has led Katherine McKittrick to suggest that Wynter poses the question of "how we might give humanness a different future."[41] It is from this exact perspective that Wynter's transformative endeavor is, to me, compelled by a radically open-ended tendency toward a different future. It is buoyed by the potential of futures still unspoken, upheld by the insistent possibility that such an unthinkable futurity in the now might be imagined through the work of abolishing the colonial truths of Man. In the context of this chapter, Wynter's encompassing gesture to futures yet to come thus finds affinity with Irigaray's conceptual provocation of sexual difference. Both Irigaray and Wynter are instigating a search for the prospect of a future that is unbound by the dominant grammars of the present, a future that must not materialize from a ceaseless repetition of the violence inherent to existing frames of reference. But because the stakes of this future for Wynter rest on the reconfiguration of humanness, it is the systematic overhaul of the epistemological ground on which we stand that precedes its cue. Wynter stresses the rewriting of narratives that have instituted the genre of Man such that the future might in turn elude the containment of present systems of thought. In other words, what she places the most pressure on is the knowledge of the already given as well as the historical, discursive, and material dynamics that have thus far ensured its presumed infallibility. If there is a palpable sensibility of wonder that imbues Wynter's project, as well, then it is not so much driven by the unknowability of the future in itself, than it is focused on how this unknowability has come to be engendered by prevailing modes of knowledge production.[42]

Here, my key objective is to consider how Wynter's emphasis on rewriting the scripts of permissible social realities, when read in conjunction with Irigaray's speculative revolution of sexual difference, can assign an urgent epistemological history to the more abstract terms of the latter's intimation of a feminist future yet to come. Bringing these two seemingly dissonant theorists together introduces new inflections of meaning to their work. To this end, and despite the ethical shortcomings of the future advanced by Irigaray's notion of sexual difference, I wager that a categorical dismissal of Irigaray's insights is far less constructive than a discursive expansion of their original premise through such a juxtaposition with Wynter's instruction.

My reluctance to entirely abandon the concept of sexual difference tracks my engagement with the metaphor of the feminist waves in the preceding chapter. Of course, it stems from a fundamental belief that sexual difference continues to be a generative premise for thinking through some of the complexities of feminist futurity. But I stay with sexual difference also as an allusion to the overarching refusal of progressive logic that this book underscores: I argue that casting aside the concept at this time would amount to the act of turning away from French feminism that has occurred in the feminist academic imagination. To spurn sexual difference for its ethical inadequacies would be to set it up once more as something to be avoided and from which to be immediately advanced, to again denounce it as evidence of the political failures of the feminist movement and therefore an object of inquiry that deserves no further attention. By dwelling with the potential of sexual difference for feminist thought, therefore, I do not mean to also absolve its pitfalls. Rather, I ask how these apparent blind spots might still be addressed, but through a different path that stems from an intertextual dialogue with Wynter's onto-epistemological reckoning with the dominant genre of Man. In a sense, this is also a confrontation of the anxieties that have swirled around sexual difference as an identifiable part of the French feminist body of work, and now also around its gesture to an unknowable feminist future. Instead of alleviating these uncomfortable feelings by falling back on a convenient habit of moving on, I confront them to chart another afterlife of sexual difference.

To continue to trace this afterlife of sexual difference, I look to Wynter's well-known conception of the "demonic" to examine how its demand for another perspective of thinking—one that must be conceived as altogether extrinsic to Western frames of knowing and knowledge-making—conditions a "new science of human discourse, of human 'life' beyond the 'master discourse' of our governing 'privileged text', and its sub/versions."[43] In light of its opening to this new and other lifeworld, I posit that the demonic fundamentally constitutes an exit sign to a different future.[44] The expression of the demonic agitates the foundations of the knowable present to offer a radical alternative to its perpetuation. In her essay, Wynter describes what she more specifically terms the "demonic ground" as the space "outside of our present governing system of meaning, or theory/ontology."[45] It is that which cannot be represented by existing paradigms of knowledge. The demonic ground is not merely some obscure presupposition but, rather, is marked by the "ontological absence" of Black female subjectivity, which Wynter identifies as the primary lack to the epistemic hallmarks of Western reasoning.[46] Explicit in Wynter's formulation of the demonic ground is thus also a critique of the hegemonic Western discourse of feminism, which has arranged its political and epistemological coordinates around a universal form of patriarchal oppression. What she reveals is that the variable "race," as the primal category of difference on which all our modern conventions of meaning rests, troubles the exclusionary analyses of gender undertaken by Eurocentric modes of feminism.[47]

I am most interested in Wynter's idea of the demonic in its capacity for overturning prevailing discourses of feminism. As the basis for her inquiry into the absent nexus of racialized gender, Wynter draws on the demonic model as it has originally been employed in scientific experimentation, which poses "a vantage point outside the space-time orientation of the humuncular observer."[48] The demonic model cannot be forged from within the limits of the knowable, in other words, but through the inception of an altogether extrinsic perspective of analysis from which the totality of structuring reality can accordingly be surveyed. By leveraging the articulation of the demonic, then, Wynter suggests that one "is able to take these designs of the measuring rod and their 'privileged texts' *as the object* of our now conscious rather than reactive processes of cognition."[49] This is to say that the demonic model casts off any epistemological dependence on privileged systems of meaning; it does not make use of those frames of reference that have made legible our governing systems of knowledge and therefore will not propose a straightforward alternative that continues to corroborate their being. Instead, what Wynter underscores is that the demonic renders their precedent our very object of analysis. In its refusal to conform to existing patterns of intelligibility, the demonic serves as a critical heuristic that unsettles the terms of the already given, if only to then flag an exit sign to another, different horizon of a future to come.[50] To return the discussion to the concept of sexual difference as earlier defined by Butler, then, the demonic likewise prompts a question for which the dominant episteme simply cannot provide an answer key. Beginning with Irigaray's formulation of sexual difference and then extending into the crux of Wynter's insistence on the recalibration of all knowledge on the basis of its ontological forgetting of race, what both of these concepts collectively ask after is an elsewhere of future possibility that might tentatively be envisioned and ultimately inhabited beyond the enclosures of the present.

A LITERARY MEETING GROUND

Given the ontological predicament that the demonic presents, how might its operative strategy be accommodated in the present? Which modes of representation might better orient us to take up its necessarily estranged perspective? I raise these questions with the acknowledgment that the "demonic ground" to which Wynter gestures does not have a cartography that can or should be fully traced; its speculative terrain cannot be mapped out by the epistemological instruments that we now possess. Nevertheless, and if the demonic essentially instigates another way of organizing reality beyond the dominant Western worldview, it remains key for these other realities to be cultivated and made legible. Gloria E. Anzaldúa writes of this necessity for rendering a different reality into being: "If reality is only a description of a particular world, when a shift of awareness happens we must create a new description of what's perceived—in other words, create a new reality."[51] With this in mind, I trace how a specifically literary imperative might allow us to begin composing such a new reality.[52]

More precisely, I argue that literature serves as a bridging apparatus for validating what Wynter would designate as the demonic ground and the perspectival shift that it demands. The space of a literary text offers what Daniel Wright has defined as a "meeting ground," which is able to sustain multiple kinds of existence and therefore different forms of reality.[53] Wright explains his use of the metaphor of the novel as a meeting ground in two ways: the first as an interplay between fictionality and actuality, and the second as the convergence, or at least the proximity, of "incommensurate ontological frameworks, each with its own vocabulary for describing metaphysical foundations."[54] In the latter description, the text serves as an interstitial terrain for the expression of competing realities, realities that are constituted by discrete, and oftentimes contrasting, ontological points of reference. Read in the context of this chapter, the metaphor of the meeting ground lends particular significance to the articulation of the demonic not because it makes manifest the demonic per se, but because it altogether rejects any universal or singular occupation of reality. By presenting a domain for plural ontological realities, a literary text enacts the persistent troubling of any given worldview that its reader might possess, and accordingly establishes the figurative exit signs indicative of a demonic elsewhere that always abounds. It is this provocation of the literary meeting ground that I find most constructive, insofar as it dramatizes the ethical function of the demonic.

This metaphorical structure of the meeting ground forms the basis, and constitutes another example, of what *Feminism Enchanted* has referred to as a textual lifeworld, which will in this chapter unfold in my analysis of Akwaeke Emezi's 2018 novel *Freshwater*. This is a novel that is saturated with the malevolent presence of Igbo spirits, their supernatural bearing compelling the narratives of the text to conspicuously deviate from the recognizable configurations of our structuring reality. Its narratives test the bounds of the already given, positioning themselves across those territories of itinerant worlds that willfully transgress the limits of the explicable. In the initial sense, I am indeed making the rather obvious point that the spiritual presence that *Freshwater* harbors implies the immanent workings of the demonic both literally and figuratively; these malevolent spirits embody an incontrovertible existence that is not of this world, and they in turn demand an ontological reckoning with the structuring realities of what we know. At the outset, then, the novel orients us toward a displaced worldview of the demonic by trafficking in the mode of the supernatural, and ensures that its readers are fully conscious of having entered a world of a strange and different kind.

But the text refuses to fully be defined by its supernatural themes and instead exploits the conventions of the genre to interrogate our assumptions about the nature of our given reality. *Freshwater* must be acknowledged for its self-professed semi-autobiographical portrayal of Emezi's own life, and as deeply conditioned by the spiritual and cultural truths of Indigenous Igbo cosmology.[55] Emezi is resolute in building the infrastructure of their novel around the metaphysical traditions of Igbo lore; they have stressed how its "non-human center" serves as the catalyst for the unspooling of its otherworldly episodes.[56]

Freshwater lays bare its metaphorical meeting ground in this manner, where the collision of multiple and irreducible realities ensures the constant unsettling of its reader's prevailing ways of knowing. This is to say that Emezi is not so much creating an imaginary world where malignant spirits might be thought to straddle the bounds of the living and the dead, than they are validating the concrete terms of its already existent reality. To this end, the narrative premise of the novel is contingent upon the interpretive prism of an Indigenous Igbo ontology that is wholly other to liberal, Western humanism, which forms the indisputable basis for its paranormal turns of events. By staking this claim of historical and political certitude, *Freshwater* urges its readers not only to become more attuned to such a marginalized worldview, but also—and perhaps more crucially—to acknowledge the legitimacy of its attendant modes of existence. Emezi thus performs an act of poetic reclamation of a way of being in the world that has long been deemed primitive and implausible in the eyes of liberal humanistic progress. By insisting on the straightforward fact of Indigenous beliefs that have been relegated as inferior and unsound in the aftermath of colonial modernity, and by purposefully shifting the status of this othered perspective from a forsaken periphery to the center, the novel ultimately calls into question certain dominant frameworks of knowing and the objects of knowledge that they create. In what follows, I focus on the conceit of gender as such an object of knowledge that can be found in the novel. I more closely examine how the meaning of gendered identity and expression becomes irrevocably refracted by its lens of Igbo religion and culture, which then extends a critique of Western discourses of feminism that have long been upheld as objective and universal.

ABERRATIONS OF GENDERED EXISTENCE

Freshwater is a novel that makes use of the deceptively familiar genre of the Bildungsroman to narrate the tumultuous story of its main protagonist Ada, tracing her journey from girlhood in southeastern Nigeria to life in North America as a college student in Virginia. While the text can indeed be observed to plot a trajectory of Ada's cumulative rites of passage into becoming an adult, it otherwise wreaks havoc on our readerly expectations of how a normal life can and should unfold, bending the conventions of what might initially have been considered a coming-of-age narrative beyond all recognition. This is not entirely unexpected for as the novel clarifies, Ada is no ordinary being—she is a spirit child, otherwise known as an ogbanje in the context of Igbo cosmology, and therefore an individual who always has "one foot on the other side."[57] In the traditional sense, ogbanje are devious, trickster spirits born into the human world only to be fated to die early in an endless cycle, this way embodying a vector of suffering and torment for their biological families.[58] As Christie C. Achebe explains in this vein, the "literal meaning of an ogbanje is . . . one who comes repeatedly or one who dies and comes again."[59] Generally speaking, ogbanje tend to die as children or adolescents, which already designates a tragic and inauspicious end to a full and normal passage of life. But the vindictive process of birth, premature death, and rebirth, in which these part-human and part-spirit beings continually partake, is one that more precisely scorns the Igbo philosophical and religious belief in the cycle of reincarnation.[60] For one, the ogbanje are a symbolic affront to the more benevolent purpose of reincarnation in their ruthless desire for vengeance. And insofar as their demonic presence perpetually shuttles between the bounds of the real and the spiritual, the ogbanje further represent an utter aberration of human lineage, an unwelcome force of disturbance in the natural sequence of things.[61] As Achebe observes, they are believed instead to have a "mysterious and supernatural etiology . . . not altogether within total human understanding," and for this reason are considered as "elusive, mysterious, and incomprehensible."[62] It is around these perverse mythological bearings of the ogbanje phenomenon that Emezi creates and populates the multiple realities of their novel, which come to illuminate the unsettling fabric of a lifeworld hostile to any dominant configuration of knowing or living.[63]

This is a lifeworld that takes shape in the text through its chorus of ogbanje characters. The multiple, alternating perspectives in the novel are a direct reflection of the polyphony of spiritual entities that reside within Ada. *Freshwater* discloses the grave, cosmic error that occurred when Ada enters the world by being birthed to her human mother Saatchi, the very same day that the ogbanje also "died and were born" in line with their own ungodly arrangements of space and time.[64] The ogbanje do not end up fully integrating with Ada into a seamless agent per the usual process of their combined inception. Instead, in a strange and potentially cataclysmic subversion of the destinies of both Ada and the ogbanje, the gates to the underworld are left open when they were meant to be closed upon birth, leading the spirits to be summoned as "a distinct we instead of being fully and just her."[65] As these malignant spirit voices declare in the first-person collective "We" that marks several chapters in the novel: "[Ada] was contaminated with us, a godly parasite with many heads, roaring inside the marble room of her mind."[66] Ada does not come into being as an autonomous person, therefore, but as an embodied human host to multiple and competing spiritual selves. These spirits have in turn found themselves forsaken in a purgatory of "unexpected limbo," sentenced to "those yawning gates between worlds, left wild, growing in all directions but closed."[67] In this sense, the ogbanje are recalcitrant beings that cannot be contained by ontological limits of the living and the dead; their capricious animation reveals them as dismissive of, and ungovernable by, the laws of humanity. Moreover, the early demise of the ogbanje has been preordained by nature. They accordingly treat Ada as an impermanent abode of flesh, her life a "placeholder, an interlude" in the short time before they will die once more.[68] It is by this monstrous logic, entirely removed from human orders of existence, that these spirits wield their otherworldly sovereignty at the expense of Ada's physical and psychological well-being.

What ensues in the text is a litany of incidents that detail Ada's troubles with depression, self-harm, disordered eating, and suicidal ideation. These disturbing episodes arrive as a kind of existential given in light of Ada's traumatic life events, which include the separation of her parents as a young girl, and multiple instances of violent sexual assault that plague her as a child and into adulthood. Against this backdrop of unspeakable trauma, Ada is initially determined to consult psychiatric help that might best treat her afflictions, despite her awareness of the snarl of evil spirits within that may in fact be held culpable for the chaos inflicted on her mind and body. Asughara, one of the more authoritative spirits of the narrative's profusion of ogbanje, explains Ada's need to diagnose her symptoms via this medical route: "Ada wanted a reason, a better explanation. We were not enough, we were too strange. . . . So instead she read lists of diagnostic criteria, things like disruption of identity, self-damaging impulsivity, emotional instability and mood swings, self-mutilating behavior and recurrent suicidal behavior. I could have told her it was all me, even that last one. Especially that last one."[69] What Ada seeks out are explanatory frameworks for her spectrum of conditions that might be explained by conventions of human behavior, frameworks that are far more reassuring to her insofar as they are grounded in Western medical practices. But there are no prognoses that lie there for her to heed, no comforting solutions that might alleviate her distress. For Ada's madness has not originated from this world, and cannot be treated by any means that obey its epistemological limits.

Instead, Ada's various conditions carry a markedly paranormal origin; they simply cannot be parsed in human modes of knowledge.[70] In their assessment of Ada, the ogbanje admit that "when we said she went mad, we lied. She has always been sane. . . . Everyone knows the stories of hungry gods, bitter, scorned, and vengeful gods. First duty, feed your gods. If they live (like we do) inside your body, find a way, get creative show them the red of your faith, of your flesh; quiet the voices with the lullaby of the altar. It's not like you can escape us—where would you run to?"[71] The mayhem that plays out on the enclosed terrain of Ada's human corporeality, in other words, can essentially be attributed to the caprices of reckless spirits, who know nothing of, and moreover want nothing to do with, the quotidian rules of human existence. If Ada reflects a discernible plurality of mental disorders, then the narrative expresses them as only an incidental revelation of supernatural maleficence. Accordingly, she might best be construed as "a question wrapped in a breath," as the ogbanje repeatedly suggest in the text: "How do you survive when they place a god inside your body? We said before that it was like shoveling the sun into a bag of skin, so it should be no surprise that her skin would split or her mind would break."[72]

In this vein, the ogbanje compel us readers to adopt a stance of perpetual questioning, which is animated by the otherworldly coordinates of the novel's lifeworld. Once more, this is a lifeworld that reveals itself to be the site of competing ontologies, and accordingly one that disallows any one position of conclusive belief from being held. I take the novel's representation of Ada's gendered identity as the evidence of this claim, examining how it effectively attenuates the production of colonial constructs of gender. On a more overarching level, what it ultimately comes to disturb are the dominant ideological underpinnings of feminism itself, insofar as they likewise have been conceived, organized, and upheld by colonial logics of modernity. If the novel relays an account of Ada's protracted struggle with gender dysphoria and her eventual decision to transition, it does so in a manner that is cloaked by the wrath of the ogbanje at finding themselves imprisoned in an embodied, human form.[73] Ada's refusal to abide by gendered norms can thus be given meaning only in the context of Igbo spirituality.

As a child, Ada is often mistaken for a boy, an oversight that she welcomes for its ready accommodation of her transgressive nature. The ogbanje reflect on how she feels "like a trickster" with this ability to effortlessly "move between boy and girl, which was a freedom, for her and for us."[74] The spirits find comfort in being housed in Ada's early physicality, for its liberty to exceed the corporeal limits of gender. But this changes when Ada reaches puberty, in an inevitable event where "hormones redid her body, remaking it without consent from us or [her]. We were distressed at this re-forming of our vessel . . . because it was nothing other than a reminder that we were now flesh, that we could not control our form, that we were in a cage that obeyed other laws, human laws."[75] The adolescent transformation of Ada's body not only solidifies its position in the restricted domain of a single gender. As an extension of the fleshly confinement in a particular gendered category, it also serves as a harrowing reminder to the ogbanje of the violent decree of humanity that they should not have to be subjected to. For these reasons, they commence an elaborate plan to recast Ada's body through surgical means, letting "a masked man take a knife lavishly to the flesh of her chest, mutilating it better and deeper than we ever could, all the way to righteousness. After such carvings, how could one human matter?"[76] This drastic alteration of Ada's body is the result of the ogbanje's quest to deform those corporeal aspects that visibly accord her the semblance of being human; it is part of their plan to ravage those markers of humanity that refute their belonging in another world, which involves tailoring a physical receptacle that might better suit the unruliness of their supernatural existence. The spiritual beings explain their seemingly anarchic actions: "To make the vessel look a little more like us—that was the extent of our intent. We have understood what we are, the places we are suspended in, between the inaccurate concepts of male and female, between the us and the brothersisters slavering on the other side."[77]

There are, of course, human frames of reference that can explain the "carving plan" that Ada undergoes.[78] These multiple procedures can otherwise be defined by medical terminology like "gender reassignment, transitioning," as the ogbanje note with mild interest.[79] But in the broader Igbo scheme of things, all this remains an insignificant afterthought to how the spirits knew "what we were planning was right."[80] The ogbanje are acting in view of a wholly different metaphysics of being, and in accordance with an otherworldly logic that they do not cede to human ways of thinking and living. Even as Ada's reconfiguration of her gendered body in the novel might correspond to medical processes of gender transitioning, therefore, the novel stresses how her decisions have instead been motivated by the ogbanje's complete disregard not only of strict demarcations of gender, but also of the prevailing concept of gender altogether.

This is only a reflection of their inherent spiritual disposition, as Misty Bastian explains further, for "to be an ogbaanje is to be characterized other—and to bring alterity home in a way that transcends the more ordinary, bifurcated 'otherness' of gender."[81] What Bastian illuminates here is that these deviant spiritual entities constitute a kind of alterity that allows them neither to be categorized as male or female. But she suggests in her statement, too, that the ogbanje cannot be encapsulated by human divisions of gendered identity, even if the spectrum of gender itself might further expand with political, historical, or ideological developments. This is because such matters simply lie beyond the ontological interests of these spirits. It would be a gross misreading to designate their presence in the novel as exhibiting a queer or transgender model of existence, at least as projected by dominant archetypes of feminist thought. Although the actions of the ogbanje, through their human conduit of Ada, may indeed resonate with her character as grappling with such gendered complexities, in other words, these spirits are ultimately foregrounded in their intrinsic otherness to the human world altogether. This is not to say that the novel deems these questions of sex and gender as unimportant or trivial per se, but rather that it lays bare once more its narrative center as anchored by Igbo cosmology, around which such human minutiae must inevitably fall away.

If *Freshwater* professes a kind of disregard for gender as an organizing principle of liberal, human existence, then implicit in this gesture is also a more perceptive critique aimed at the universality of Western discourses of feminism. More to the point, what the novel comes to disabuse us of is the presiding authority of feminism as a pervasive mode of knowing and knowledge-making, a feminism that has been sanctioned as such by material and discursive forces of colonial modernity predicated on an exclusionary concept of the human. It is a brutal exercise of doubled colonization that Western frameworks of gender are unthinkingly applied to other, more peripheral lifeworlds, ones that have never conformed to a human epistemology that has animated the modern problematic of gender in the first place, and that moreover have historically been oppressed on this very basis. Writing in the specific context of African studies, scholars such as Oyeronke Oyewumi have observed that "historically and currently, the creation, constitution, and production of knowledge have remained the privilege of the West."[82] And this unequivocal superiority of Western paradigms of intellectual production must be perceived as an extension of the literal project of European colonization that was carried out on African territories from the late nineteenth century onwards. That Western concepts of feminism and gender continue to be imposed on African societies to apprehend the latter's experiences and ways of being is a seamless perpetuation of such acts of conquest and imperialism.[83]

The novel's invocation of the ogbanje, then, as more-than-human entities that defiantly reject dominant structures of feminist understanding is its attempt to elude being read through, and therefore being colonized by, this hegemonic system of knowledge. The textual presence of these evil spirits represents both a revelation of, and a retaliation against, the broader notion of feminism as unquestionably founded in the tenets of colonial modernity. Fashioned as what this chapter has earlier designated as figurative exit signs of the demonic, the ogbanje lure the readers of the novel away from the familiar scope of dominant perspectives; they dare us to see how different the world would be if only we were better attuned to other subjugated existences that continue to trespass on our reality, and that might simply be hidden in plain sight. For after all, the residues of these dispossessed lifeworlds still endure in the form of those "godly stowaways that came along when the corrupters stole our people, what the swollen hulls carried over the bellied seas, the masks, the skin on the inside of the drum, the words under the words, the water in the water."[84] The novel asks after these fugitive ways of knowing and being, tracing their remainder in the protracted wake of colonial violence.[85] In response, it suggests how the cultivation of a more reflexive orientation toward these liminal ontologies might disrupt the unyielding arrangements of our own ontologies, for the sake of another possibility of life and living.

But at the end of the day, there is no vision of a utopian future that *Freshwater* anticipates, no promise of a better tomorrow that it makes. In fact, and if there is any horizon of futurity to which its narratives gesture, it is one that can only come into view after the shedding of the old skins of humanity. If a different future is to be upheld as a possibility, there must first be an interruption of the continuity that has thus far guaranteed the passing down of human paragons of knowledge, a casting away of this unquestioned inheritance. As Ada declares nearing the close of the novel: "I did not come from a human lineage and I will not leave one behind."[86] This is a statement that encapsulates her decision to exist alongside the multiple ogbanje that reside within her, such that they might together pave the way for an escape from the violent grasp of human descent. "I am my others," as Ada thus concludes, "we are one and we are many."[87] It is only when Ada no longer denies her identity as an otherworldly being, who has always straddled the planes of multiple realities, that she finds herself closer to becoming liberated from the boundaries of human existence, and therefore from living by the terms of its brutality. Ada is able to reach this conclusion only because she realizes that she must let go of being human to join hands with the ogbanje instead of trying in vain to battle against their spiritual propensities, so as to ensure their collective survival forward. This survival is in turn hinged on her unadulterated belief in a different kind of lifeworld, a belief that gathers in the text through the force of other, irreducible ways of knowing and being. As the ogbanje speak of Ada's increasing conviction in the Igbo ontology from which they came forth: "And so we were strengthened, because belief, for beings like us, is the colostrum of existence."[88]

3

FEMINIST REVOLUTIONS

Inscrutable, Out of Reach

F ranny Choi's "Orientalism (Part I)" is a poem that opens
on the defensive, with a question that betrays an innate
desire to belong: "What wouldn't you do / to be held?"[1]
The speaker dangles the promise of being loved and cherished as
a human being, of being held by others with whom they might
find close affinity. But there are high stakes involved in this
manner of inclusion—the negative contraction that lies within
the question implies that what the speaker would do to be held
knows no bounds. Indeed, and as the poem continues, the
speaker describes the extreme ends they would go to just so they
might belong: "Don't tell me / you've never taped shut / your
own mouth."[2] This deliberate silencing of oneself is an exercise
in restraint and submission, carried out in recognition of certain
codes of existence that have deemed some lives more worthy of
acceptance than others. The speaker's question is hereby revealed
to be premised as much on the necessity for survival as it is on
the hope of inclusion. If their act of effacement has been performed as a precondition for the possibility of belonging, then it
has likewise been undertaken as a tactic of self-preservation. For
what such an act might increase are the odds of staying alive in
a world entirely hostile to marginal forms of humanity, of being

held—in another sense—together in the face of its relentless environment of violence and coercion.

Through the title of her poem, Choi invites us to think about the symbolic repercussions of this diminished orientation of existence. She identifies this way of being, one that is predicated on the assiduous erasure of the self as a vital means of survival, to have become a major contributing factor to the Orientalist stereotype of the figure of the Asian. This is a figure distinguished by its inscrutable nature: a racialized trope that has been produced and calcified by various social, cultural, and historical representations of Asian subjectivity as the devalued other to Western ideals of modernity. The inscrutable Oriental both does not speak and is difficult to read. They are engulfed in an air of mystery and unknowability, a pernicious abstraction that renders their particulars, as Vivian L. Huang has observed, as "flattened, homogenized, and objectified . . . appearing as surface that can or cannot be penetrated."[3] Against this background, the speaker's claim to the strategy of diffidence and self-censure, initially devised to foster normative relations of the social, and to better their chance of enduring oppression, has ultimately backfired. It has paradoxically reified the logic of exclusion that the speaker had originally aspired to overcome. There is a perverse rationale behind this logic that has effectively been substantiated by the speaker's own actions: that which reduces the figure of the Asian to a mute and passive object, thus relegating it to a status less than human.

In the precise context of Choi's poem, this figure is made manifest in the literal object of a vase. As the first two lines of the second stanza read: "There are many ways to hold water / without being called a vase."[4] This concrete image of the vase immediately summons the material life of Chinese porcelain, which tracks multiple, overlapping histories of aesthetic production, global trade, and colonial capture. Anne Anlin Cheng has else-where pointed out that the ornamental character of porcelain has given rise to a conception of Asiatic femininity that is inscribed with fragile, delicate, and insensate qualities.[5] It is an association that once more shores up the disingenuous coupling of persons and things rife in Orientalist modes of knowing. For these rea-sons, the speaker compels a departure from the vase as the repre-sentative holding container for water, insofar as its significance as such has come to be intertwined with, and moreover to validate, only a recessive form of Asian subjectivity. But they do not merely prompt a more expansive consideration of the kinds of vessels that might be used to hold water. Rather, the speaker also draws our attention to what it means to "hold water" in the first place: to hold validity as a statement or theory, and to secure legiti-mate personhood along these lines. In the process, the speaker registers the fact that there are, and must be, other ways to mat-ter without having to conform to essentialist notions of racial-ized identity.[6]

The final lines of the poem recall again the speaker's yearn-ing for recognition, but this time as mediated through an insa-tiable thirst to establish their profile on the basis of irreducible difference: "To drink all the history / until it is your only song."[7] Following from the speaker's earlier conclusion, it is not so much that their want for validation has since disappeared, rather that they have come to more perceptively interrogate the terms by which this validation should be defined. To quench this reas-sessed need, the speaker asks after the very minoritized history that had designated them as other, seeking to grapple with the alterity of their selfhood in this manner. What they uncover is that to be beholden to all the history that has led up to, and still saturates, the entirety of their being is to exemplify a subject that simply cannot be assigned a fixed label. For it is the liquid disposition of this history that must be reckoned with, which in its fluid capacity defies the colonial vision of Orientalism to homogenize and discriminate. It is a history that eludes the grasp of universalizing frames of comprehension—in this sense, it is one that stays persistently out of reach, one that cannot in fact be held. There is no one way to fully know or represent this history, in other words, only the reflexive admission of its provenance to be fraught and nonidentical, and for its articulation to take shape in diverse but equally valid forms. The speaker finally clarifies for us the singular experience of such a history, parsed in the utterance of an "only song" that cannot be suppressed.[8] At the close of the poem, it is this impossibility of containment that stands in contrast to the self-imposed silence that has for so long typecast the figure of the Asian. What was once held back can no longer be held in.

This chapter of *Feminism Enchanted* anchors its argumentative crux in the scene of inscrutability that plays out in my above reading of "Orientalism (Part I)." Choi's poem rightly exposes the risks of embodying any aspect of inscrutability, which can so easily reinforce damaging Orientalist stereotypes of Asian existence. But what if inscrutability might itself be mobilized as a strategy against misplaced fantasies of inclusion, assimilation, and equal participation in social life? This is a provocation that I rehearse in view of recent scholarship on Asian and Asian American modes of existence that have employed political, aesthetic, and affective expressions of inscrutability to refuse the encompassing narrative of liberal, multicultural progress.[9] These works have reclaimed inscrutability as a key approach of Asian resistance and endurance, and in the process occasioned new minoritarian lifeworlds of possibility. In many ways, "Orientalism (Part I)" similarly alludes to this subversive potential of inscrutability; it shows how inscrutability might bypass the threat of containment, which circles invariably as a problem of epistemological mastery. The poem underscores the fluidity of a marginal history that cannot be contained by dominant paradigms of interpretation: a history that remains willfully inscrutable in the face of the insistence on transparency and legibility, and therefore one that "holds water" in this further sense of being able to withstand such scrutiny.[10] It is this critical intervention of inscrutability that allows for the particular lived histories of minoritarian subjects not to be registered by prevailing forms of knowing and hence evade the colonial tendency for possession and appropriation.

In the pages that follow, I transpose this ethical function of inscrutability into the context of transnational feminist knowledge production, exploring how it might open up another way to think and theorize a feminist revolution. I situate my study in the wider intellectual imaginary of transnational feminism not to advance a new mode of its analysis, but rather to offer a response to the politics and ethics of knowledge production that have oriented the methodological locus of much of transnational feminist theory. Broadly speaking, the transnational now inflects a branch of feminist critique that, through its indexing of the asymmetries of race, class, sexuality, ethnicity, and nationality, challenges the hegemonic construct of feminism itself as centered on a white and middle-class female subjectivity.[11] It altogether rejects the formula of a seemingly inclusive feminism deduced from what M. Jacqui Alexander and Chandra Talpade Mohanty have observed as an "often unspecified liberal episteme."[12] If the critical practices of transnational feminism are committed to acknowledging the unevenly distributed histories and material realities of women across the world, then they must make no assumption of shared experience, nor deduce any abstraction of a universal feminist politics.[13] Guided by this aim of transnational feminist theory, I argue that the expression of inscrutability can be engaged as a productive strategy against efforts of mainstream feminist discourse to elide the trace of otherness in the name of a common struggle. The intractable gesture of inscrutability works against the epistemic structures of domination inherent to such discursive production; it safeguards the sign of difference from totalizing enclosures of knowledge.

The chapter examines how such a dynamic of inscrutability might more specifically transform how we perceive and make sense of a feminist revolution. To this end, it continues to draw on this book's mode of enchantment to reimagine the form and meaning of a feminist revolution, especially as attuned to the ethical demands of transnational feminist knowledge production.[14] What enchantment enacts is a recantation of the paradigmatic model of a feminist revolution, which has historically been endorsed by, and sought to fulfill, a teleological narrative of advancement for women.[15] But this is a narrative of progress that has been conjured by a hegemonic feminist imagination; it is founded in Eurocentric determinations of liberalism and democracy that are too often presumed to be universally desirable, and must be confronted on these terms. This chapter returns to the normative definition of a revolution to question the assumptive logic of progress that is not only invoked to justify its insurrectionary formation but also used to measure the evidence of its outcome. I think against the visible indicators of progress that have been taken as representative of a revolutionary event, to theorize a concept of a feminist revolution that is instead inscrutable and out of reach. The inscrutable expression of this revolution disallows it from being plotted by conventional hallmarks of feminist political progress. Its animation bears crucial witness to the insurgent histories of gendered and racialized subjectivities that, as Choi's poem reminds us, cannot and should not be contained by the existing rubric of a revolutionary movement.

In what follows, I first locate the conceptual beginnings of this phenomenon in a case study of the American feminist icon Kate Millett's 1979 trip to Iran, which was extensively documented by her, and later published, in a book-length account entitled *Going to Iran* (1982). Millett had been invited to speak at a rally at the International Women's Day celebrations on March 8, an event that for the first time would officially be realized by the state. The text offers a compelling record of Iran amid dramatic upheavals that would change its social and political landscape forever. But read from Millett's revelatory, first-person perspective, its prose is also a testament to her abrupt transplantation—as a white woman at the front lines of the women's liberation movement in the United States—into the disorienting context of Iran at its own critical revolutionary juncture. Millett harbored a resolute belief in the universal oppression of women under patriarchy, which had led her to go to Iran to build not only an "international women's movement, but a global one" that would transcend geographical and cultural boundaries.[16] In the first instance, my reading of the text is framed by Millett's utter failure to set in motion the international feminist awakening she had longed for: a failure that can largely be ascribed to her complicity with hegemonic practices of cultural imperialism that had circulated under the guise of an altruistic feminist project. More precisely, I identify an unyielding inscrutability that marked the gendered politics of the Iranian Revolution, which allowed it to escape Millett's colonizing gaze. It is in this manner that the Iranian revolution would remain out of her reach to create a cross-cultural feminist alliance. As Millett would lament during an early moment of her trip about not yet being able to convene with her fellow Iranian feminists: "*I feel I am running after feminism in Iran*; despite their invitation, I have yet to meet even one sister."[17]

I then proceed to continue theorizing an inscrutable feminist revolution as mediated through the worldmaking capacity of enchantment that extends through this book. In some sense, the incantatory force of enchantment appears to corroborate the given understanding of a revolutionary movement to overthrow an established social order, and to accordingly bring into being a new and more radical political imaginary. But this agency is exercised quite differently with a feminist revolution that is characterized by its inscrutability and its predilection for staying out of reach. It is impossible to fully discern the contours of its phenomenon, much less the resultant impact of its event, through the metrics of progressive politics that underwrite the liberal Western feminist movement. With this in mind, I turn to a reading of Ruth Ozeki's 2013 novel, *A Tale for the Time Being*, to trace the unfolding of an inscrutable feminist revolution in the space of a literary text. The literary imperative of enchantment is once more foregrounded by this move, but this time as rather paradoxically conjuring a textual lifeworld in the novel through a series of formal and thematic vanishing acts that sidestep the problem of representation. I suggest that an inscrutable feminist revolution endures in the narratives of the text: one that traverses the expansive perimeters of the transpacific and finds its temporal inception in the global anarchist uprisings at the turn of the twentieth century. But the presence of this revolution is only tangentially made known through the character of the Zen nun Jiko Yasutani, whose past inscribes a transnational history of Japanese feminism that exceeds the representational limits of the text. It is through such transitive acts of elusiveness that the novel alters the exposition and significance of a feminist revolution, thus affirming the use of inscrutability as a distinctively literary maneuver for accounting for a minoritized history of feminism.

INSCRUTABLE EXPRESSIONS
OF REVOLUTION

This chapter takes Kate Millett's fateful visit to Iran in 1979 as a point of departure for theorizing an inscrutable feminist revolution. Millett's trip offers a quintessential example of Western feminism's prescription of what a liberated female subject should look and be like, and of the incursion of hegemonic views of gender equality into the rest of the world on this same basis. To some degree, Millett's dream of an international feminist awakening was not an unexpected one; it transpired as a natural progression from the second-wave feminist movement in North America of which she had long been the face.[18] What Millett brought with her to Iran, in other words, were the residual energies of postwar rallying that included the women's rights movement emerging in the United States and beyond in the 1960s, and the women's liberation movement that followed in the latter part of the decade and into the next. Millett was heavily influenced by, and drawn to, the fantasy of a "global sisterhood" in which the women in Iran constituted her sisters in shared struggle and solidarity.[19] From her perspective, all women across the world were subjugated by an overarching structure of patriarchy that they should collectively overthrow.[20] Millett's trip was motivated by a wish of seeing her Iranian sisters released from the "universal enslavement" of patriarchy that she believed had long restricted their progress.[21] And she herself would be key to the realization of this vision. As Millett described the purpose of her visit to the immigration official overseeing her visa application: "I'm going on a mission to and for my sisters in Iran—and I want that designation."[22] These words betray the colonial sentiment that Millett had so righteously held. Indeed, she saw herself as an envoy on a mission to rescue the women in Iran so that they too might be accorded the right of liberal freedom.[23]

I bring up the case of Millett in Iran not to further critique the imperializing objective of her trip as a number of scholars have already done.[24] Rather, I am interested in the scenes of inscrutability that Millett encountered during her time there, which repeatedly forestalled her ability to comprehend the gendered uprisings that were underway at the time. Millett was of course an outsider with inadequate knowledge of the complicated histories of Iran's revolutionary struggle; in truth, she had no hope of fully grasping its social, political, or cultural significance. Millett did not even understand the Persian language, for instance, which became a huge barrier to discerning the intricate dynamics of what was happening on the ground.[25] In this sense, Negar Mottahedeh explains in her analysis of the soundscape that accompanies the historical events that much of the troubling inscrutability that Millett perceived was due to the literally untranslatable nature of the Iranian Revolution itself.[26] Listening to the tapes that Millett recorded as audio material for the book she would later write, Mottahedeh observes her to have, in more ways than one, been thoroughly "out of sync with what [was] right in front of her."[27] Millett would never end up being able to successfully align the revolutionary coordinates of the women's movement in Iran to those in the West that she had helped to spearhead. Just slightly over a week after their arrival in Iran, Millett and her partner Sophie Keir, who had travelled with her into the country, were deported by the government on March 19.

In this chapter, I focus on the way that the Iranian women, specifically, embodied a form of inscrutability that repudiated Millett's colonial urge to know. This resistant modality of inscrutability is dramatized by the full-length veil, or the chador, as the locus on which much of the Iranian women's movement would also play out. To a large extent, the women's protests that erupted during Millett's visit to Iran were precipitated by the revolutionary leader and cleric Ayatollah Ruhollah Khomeini's decree on the mandatory veiling of women that was announced on March 6.[28] These demonstrations only strengthened Millett's conviction that the women of Iran were living under a global system of patriarchal oppression, and that their veiling attested to one of its violent acts of subjection. She would thus "equate the question of veiling and the question of freedom" in her interpretation of the women's insurrectionary response, in this process restricting the ideological significance of the veil to liberal Western frameworks of feminist understanding.[29] But the history of the veil in Iran is a long and complex one that cannot be charted by this limited view. If Iran's Unveiling Act of 1936 signaled a turning point in the country's self-fashioning as a modern state, and its pandering to the more developed, Western world to this end, then the veil in fact came to acquire anti-imperialist connotations.[30] In the decades after, many women would reclaim the veil not only as a religious obligation but also as a pressing reminder of the national and cultural priorities of Iran that should not be subsumed by the encroachment of Western influence.[31] As Nima Naghibi writes, then, the veil was not simply a sign of an unthinking or passive subservience to patriarchal authority, as Millett had assumed, but rather "the site upon which issues of class, gender, and nationalism [in contemporary Iran were] continuously contested, negotiated, and rethought."[32]

As a symbol of these entangled stakes of the Iranian Revolution, the veil contained a multitude of the country's histories that would ultimately be lost to Millett. Indeed, Millett's account of the Iranian women in her book is overlaid with the exact Orientalizing stereotypes that one would expect; she is obsessed with the veil as tangible evidence of their need to be "civilized," and therefore liberated, by the Western feminist movement. Upon arrival at Mehrabad Airport in Tehran, Millett is immediately struck by the sight of the women in chador: "Like black birds," she writes, "like death, like fate, like everything alien. Foreign, dangerous, unfriendly."[33] The disturbing spectacle of these veiled women reflects a circling threat of otherness that Millett further designates as an animalistic condition of being. Individual women have blurred into a "sea of chadori . . . ancient, powerful, annihilating us," their outer appearance alluding to a more backward and primitive time.[34] The veil confirmed the "punitive, abject" existence that Millett believed these women to endure—from her perspective, they had "become prisoners [behind the veil]," which all the more warranted the intervention of the modern and progressive ideal of feminism that she, by contrast, epitomized.[35]

But the veil also presented a literal expression of inscrutability that exemplified the refusal of the Iranian women to concede to Millett's wish to know them as well as Millett's insidious demand for their control in this vein. At the scene of their encounter, Millett writes that "these women seem utterly closed to women," and that they do not respond to her efforts to establish mutual recognition.[36] For Millett, this was largely due to their wearing of the veil as a garment that covers much of the head and face. For if the veil physically obscured the presence of these women, it also made them incompatible with liberal forms of the social centered on transparency and reciprocity.[37] It is in this concrete way that the Iranian women averted Millett's projection of an international feminist revolution fueled by a regime of social and political transformation. "Look at them and they do not look back," as she would observe, "even the friendly curiosity with which women regard each other. . . . The bitterness, the driven rage behind these figures, behind these yards of black cloth. They are closed entirely."[38] Millett had gone to Iran expecting the women there to willingly partake in the feminist endeavor that had for years been fomenting in the West, and for them to collectively organize against the universal enemy of patriarchy. But the apparent opacity of these women threw into relief the impossibility of such an alliance.[39] Their outward display of the inscrutable instead emphasized the fact of their insurmountable difference that could not be overcome by any claim to a common politics.

Much has already been said about the problematic of visibility that marks the gendered and racial discourse on the veil.[40] And the veil has indeed historically symbolized a resistance to colonial forces of violence. Writing on the veiled women in Algeria, for example, Frantz Fanon argued that they challenged the penetrating gaze of the French, thus posing as a subversive threat to the colonial desire to see and know. As Fanon notes: "This woman who sees without being seen frustrates the colonizer. There is no reciprocity. She does not yield herself, does not give herself, does not offer herself."[41] In a similar way, then, the inscrutability that Millett faced in Iran—one that was inscribed on, and animated by, the surface of the veil—functioned strategically to impede her vision of including the Iranian women in her dream of a unified feminism. But the expression of inscrutability did not only act as a blunt instrument of obstruction. More overarchingly, it also served as a constant reminder to Millett that her working definition of a feminist revolution was not applicable to the context of Iran, and that the change that the Iranian women were striving toward could not be mapped by the developmental trajectory of feminist politics that was sanctioned by the West. On this account, the gendered dimensions of the revolutionary movement in Iran were unmoored from these legible bearings of progress. Millett, who was much more concerned with searching for the identifiable markers of the hegemonic feminist consciousness that she had so unquestioningly inhabited, would not be able to register the fact of this matter.

Millett would eventually acknowledge her displacement into this state of unknowing. Reflecting on her impending expulsion from the country, she lamented that "we are leaving this place, without ever having seen it, experienced it, known it, without having finished our work and our learning of it. And we can never come back."[42] But Millett's regret at not having had the time to fully understand the nuances of the Iranian Revolution belied a much plainer reality: that it would fundamentally have been impossible to do so, anyway. If the Iranian women embodied an expression of inscrutability that persistently confounded Millett's desire to know them, they also pointed to the eventual outcome of their protests as something that could not be anticipated by the past and present. It is in this regard that Mottahedeh writes that what they enunciated in their calls for revolution was "a conscious will for an as-yet unseen future."[43] This was a revolution that hinged on a distinctively speculative imperative. It gestured to a future that not only Millett but arguably also the Iranian women themselves could not grasp in the here and now, which remained elusive even to the lived realities inhabited by the latter.

A NEGATIVE ARCHIVE
OF FEMINIST HISTORY

Extrapolating from this context, the inscrutable feminist revolution that this chapter conceptualizes comes to articulate more than just an act of disavowal. It also produces a scene of endless unknowability that unfolds transformative possibilities lying in excess of dominant frameworks of thinking and knowing. In this sense, it finds affinity with an extant theory of revolution that Elizabeth Grosz has described, one that prompts "*un*predictable transformation—mutation, metamorphosis—upheaval in directions and arenas with implications or consequences that cannot be known in advance."[44] This is a conceptual model of revolution that is untethered from the obligations of progressive politics; its effects cannot be measured or regulated by pragmatic ideals. It eclipses such a prescriptive agenda in its ineluctable provocation of the new and invokes an unforeseen advent of revolutionary thought. An inscrutable feminist revolution, however, makes less of a claim to radical newness than it does an ethical commitment, once again, to marginal narratives of history that must not be coerced into essentializing paradigms of knowledge. Its inherent inscrutability does not invite an empty valorization of the unknown, but rather enacts a deliberate undoing of the principle of progress that has already determined the shape of a revolutionary future. Inscrutability invalidates the arrival at any conclusion made by predictive logic, in turn creating an opening to new and other kinds of feminist politics.

If an inscrutable feminist revolution cannot be contained by the encompassing objective of feminist political progress, then its event is one that both accounts for, and further summons into being, alternative formations of social and political life.

But these formations constitute marginal feminist histories and futures that cannot be captured by modes of knowledge production, for they seek only to constrain them to already given frames of reference. There is an impossibility that marks their representation as such, which inscrutability names and performs as its ethical premise. How then might an inscrutable feminist revolution be perceived? Through which means might its necessary omission be made legible yet not fully knowable? To address these questions, I turn here toward Ruth Ozeki's 2013 novel, *A Tale for the Time Being*, as a literary text that grapples with this exact predicament through its refusal to directly represent a feminist revolution that inheres in its narratives. This is a revolution that is only obliquely made known through its character of Jiko Yasutani, whose personal history is initially supposed to be what the novel is about but is ultimately left untold. The novel opens with its young protagonist Naoko "Nao" Yasutani declaring in a journal entry that she will be penning the biography of her 104-year-old great-grandmother, the Zen Buddhist nun and radical feminist Jiko. In Nao's brief introduction, we also learn that Jiko was also "a novelist and a New Woman of the Taishō era."[45] But Jiko's life story remains almost entirely uncharted despite Nao's earlier pronouncement. Nao's incomplete assignment does not escape her. At the close of the novel, Nao tells us that she will soon be taking up her original task again: "As soon as I've finished these last pages, I'm going to buy a new blank book and keep my promise, which is to write the whole entire story of old Jiko's life."[46] And just like that, the telling of Jiko's history becomes deferred to another time, never to be completely realized in the confines of this particular text. In my reading of the novel, I am specifically interested in the ways in which the novel withholds the exhaustive representation of certain revolutionary legacies of Japanese feminism through the structuring absence of Jiko's life story. I show how the strategy of inscrutability can be rendered through literary form as both a revelation and a critique of the bounds of dominant historiographic representation.

My engagement with the literary at this juncture continues to track this book's insistence on literature's worldmaking power through the mode of enchantment. But in this chapter, the textual lifeworld that enchantment generates from the novel under analysis, which is founded on the trace of overlapping, transpacific histories of feminist revolution, is characterized instead by its constitutive disappearance. In other words, there is no immersive lifeworld for the reader to dwell in here; there is only one that at every turn discloses the epistemic limits of its very existence. Jiko's life story is not the only narrative arc that recedes into nothingness, after all—the novel as a whole is riddled with such sites of unknowability. The existence of Nao herself is shrouded in a deep mystery, for instance, even as we readers have seemingly been given access to her innermost thoughts. Soon after we encounter Nao's greeting, in which we find out that she worryingly appears to have planned her own death, the diary washes up sometime in the future on a beach in the settlement of Whaletown, in rural British Columbia. It is serendipitously retrieved by an author named Ruth, who begins to search for the whereabouts of the Japanese girl.[47] In working her way through the diary, Ruth becomes obsessed with looking for some tangible evidence of the missing person with whom she has become strangely intertwined. She is driven not only by the need to verify the authenticity of the life story that has literally come into her inexplicable possession, but also by a kind of futile desire to help the troubled teenager.[48] Ruth thus begins a process of "forensic unpeeling," which involves triangulating the clues that she scours from within the pages of the diary in hopes of confirming the fate of its writer.[49]

But Ruth never finds closure to the story of Nao's life. This is not a disappointing plot twist that the novel springs on its reader, but a logical conclusion to a sequence of events that it has presented—each scored with the same mark of willful ambiguity. All of Ruth's attempts as an amateur detective to corroborate the details that Nao records in her diary only serve to compound the uncertainty surrounding Nao's eventual disappearance. Even the found object of the diary is itself an enigma: it may have been thrown overboard a cruise ship that trawled the Alaskan channels, or perhaps cast out into the ocean from a distant shoreline in Japan like a message in a bottle. "Any of these were plausible explanations," Ruth observes in frustration, "but none of them felt right."[50] Ruth realizes that there are any number of plausible origin stories for Nao, but they all come to proliferate a growing web of conjecture that only causes the latter's opacity to become even more distinct. In her reluctant awakening in the epilogue of the novel, Ruth concedes to a modality of "not-knowing" that has thus far imbued her pursuit to find out about Nao.[51] As she muses: "I'd much rather *know*, but then again, not-knowing keeps all the possibilities open."[52] Ruth finally acknowledges that she will never be able to obtain any concrete proof of Nao's past or present existence.

In many ways, this principle of "not-knowing" is precisely what the novel is centered on.[53] Drawn from the Zen Buddhist teaching that cultivates the practice of letting go of fixed or preconceived ideas and expectations, the "unbounded nature of not knowing" is a philosophy that inflects the nebulous trajectory of its various narratives.[54] This is arguably an offshoot of Ozeki's own professed interest in agnotology, or the study of the calculated production of ignorance or doubt. Speaking about the thematic concerns of the novel, Ozeki has reflected that she is "interested in what gets left untold . . . what drops out of history, or what gets dropped. I'm interested in where the holes are."[55] The novel dramatizes this claim in its multiple loci of unknowability, which it does not sketch into view, but instead leaves them untouched in their radical incertitude. As Ozeki continues: "We can learn a lot by studying what isn't. It seems important to me to leave the gaps and holes, rather than trying to fill them in."[56]

I want to circle back to the character of Jiko, to how her character appears to likewise embody this modality of "not-knowing." Indeed, as earlier mentioned, Nao's promise to chronicle the life story of her great-grandmother is left unfulfilled up until the end of the novel. But I argue that the absence of Jiko's personal history in its pages is not merely a reflection of the state of "not-knowing" that the novel urges its readers to inhabit. It is also the consequence of Jiko's own undertaking to ensure that her identity and life story cannot be registered by dominant modes of historiographic narration. Jiko has enacted a series of vanishing acts to enable her own disappearance; in contrast to the more open-ended mystery that Nao's existence connotes, Jiko has deliberately rendered herself inscrutable. In one of the closest instances that Ruth comes to confirming that Nao and the events of her diary are not a figment of someone else's, or indeed her own, imagination, she stumbles upon an academic article on the internet that is titled "Japanese *Shishōsetsu* and the Instability of the Female 'I.'" The article outlines some brief biographical information of a writer unknown in the West, who has written a pioneering novel of *shishōsetsu*, often translated as the "I-novel"—an autobiographical literary form that flourished in the Taishō period of Japan.[57] The author of this article explicitly names a certain "Yasutani Jiko" as a female trailblazer of this way of writing, observing that her employment of its form was altogether "groundbreaking, energetic, and radical."[58] As the author continues to observe, her writing amounted to a literary praxis that was "nothing short of revolutionary."[59]

Ruth is thrilled and relieved to read the preview of this article, the rest of which is hidden behind the paywall of an academic database. She "wanted to learn everything she could about Jiko Yasutani, and not just the scraps of information that surfaced so haphazardly in her great-granddaughter's diary."[60] But Ruth's joy is short-lived—her access to the article is quite literally disrupted, first by a power outage from a brewing storm, and then later by a notification that it has been removed from the database entirely. In some sense, this is an uncanny reflection of what the article—even in its redacted form—had noted of Jiko as a prominent figure of Japanese literary history, "who has erased herself from . . ."[61] The article is cut off at this very point, and it is not clear exactly which institutions, archives, or even entire histories Jiko has elected to obliterate her identity from. Jiko's immersion in Zen Buddhist practices later in her life would perhaps have been a deciding factor for this disavowal of the self and its independent ego. But her explicit refusal to be memorialized, at least within the confines of any particular historiographic tradition, exemplifies a strategic intervention to remain inscrutable to dominant frames of knowledge and their attendant modes of interpretation.[62] What Jiko's novel and her contribution to the literary form of shishōsetsu gesture to is a negative archive of history that is made legible by her self-effacement and yet, on this same basis, not made fully known.

Jiko's classification as a female writer of shishōsetsu in the article further reveals the gendered politics of this negative archive. She is said to belong to a group of marginalized women who actively engaged with, and shaped the development of, its autobiographical form. But their work has largely been overlooked in favor of their male counterparts. In his introduction to the noteworthy writers of the Japanese literary form, Edward Fowler defends his survey for comprising only men: "The decision is in fact not as arbitrary as it might first appear, since all but a few major writers during the time of this study were men. . . . [T]he energies of prominent female writers working in the 1910s and the 1920s . . . were devoted as much to feminist causes as they were to literary production."[63] Fowler observes that there were far fewer women who were writing during the Taishō Democracy. But he then follows up with a curious observation: that those women writers whose work had indeed been published and circulated at the time were largely concerned with feminist beliefs that were supposedly antithetical to the shishōsetsu tradition. If there is a more specific interrogation to be made about the ideological relation between the political and aesthetic commitments of these women writers that Fowler makes here, it is one purportedly conducted in the academic article about Jiko that inexplicably drops out of sight. In the preview to the full text at which Ruth manages a brief glimpse, its author rejects Fowler's observation, contending that Jiko exemplified a woman writer that did in fact employ the shishōsetsu form in a manner that incorporated her radical feminist motivations.[64] At first blush, the article advances the familiar critique of the historical exclusion of women writers from various literary canons. But what if Jiko's absence from the shishōsetsu canon might also be understood as an extension of her feminist literary praxis, given the self-induced nature of her disappearance? Jiko's choice to linger in a space of gendered omission once again signals a rejection of her work being annexed by conventional, patriarchal frameworks of knowledge making; it indicates the presence of a negative archive. But what her vanishing act also comes to compel are alternative approaches of thinking and understanding the feminist histories that are held within this archive. It attunes us to a different mode of historiographic study that relies on the inscrutable as its political and ethical premise.

TRANSPACIFIC INSCRIPTIONS OUT OF REACH

Thinking through the historiographic methods of production necessitated by this negative archive, I want to outline the feminist revolutionary influences on the character of Jiko that have become similarly elusive to the narratives of the text. We come to know about these influences through Nao, who draws up her family tree in one of the entries of her diary. As Nao explains, her great-grandmother had been so enamored by two feminist revolutionaries who were active on opposite sides of the Pacific Ocean that she had named her daughters after them. Ema, Jiko's older daughter and Nao's grandmother, was named after the prominent anarchist and feminist activist Emma Goldman, who participated in the American, Russian, and European political circuits at the turn of the twentieth century. Jiko's younger daughter, Sugako, was named after Kanno Sugako, the Japanese feminist anarchist and anti-imperialist writer who was convicted of treason and executed at the age of 29.[65] To be clear, Ema and Sugako are themselves only minor characters in the novel. Nao used to regard the small black-and-white photographs of her uncle Haruki #1, Sugako, and Ema displayed on the family altar at Jiko's temple: these long-dead relatives of hers were simply "stiff, old-fashioned strangers, time beings from another world who meant nothing to me."[66] Her dismissive attitude completely transforms when she later learns of Haruki #1's tragic fate from Jiko, and from reading the letters that he wrote to her before his untimely death as a kamikaze pilot in the Pacific War. Through the harrowing narratives that scaffold the story of his life too soon extinguished, we learn of the impact that Haruki #1 had on Jiko's existence—her eventual ordination as a Buddhist nun had been a counterpoint to the bitter hatred she felt for the general of the Imperial Japanese Army at the time, Tōjō Hideki, whose war crimes on a more staggering scale had caused the death of her only son.[67] But through their christening as such, it is Ema and Sugako who offer more insight into the years preceding Jiko's turn to pacifist religion, albeit not through the kind of extensive backstory that the text accords to Haruki #1. In the novel, the two sisters remain peripheral to its sequence of events, mere secondary references to its multiple plotlines. But by designating them the namesakes of Emma Goldman and Kanno Sugako, the text orients our attention to the intimate economy of relations that existed between these two figures of historical significance, and in turn, to the wider transpacific imaginary implied as germane to Jiko's early revolutionary tendencies.

While Goldman and Kanno might never have crossed literal paths, they certainly led parallel lives as distant revolutionary allies across the Pacific. The two women were directly intertwined by the European and American influence on anarchist movements in Japan during the mid- to late nineteenth century, and decades later became even more fully enmeshed in a global anarchist network that looked to spread its reach for a worldwide social and political uprising.[68] When Kanno was sentenced to death along with eleven other revolutionaries, Goldman and her comrades organized various protests against what they believed was a wrongful persecution.[69] This was one poignant example of the interconnectedness of their lives, engendered by transcultural channels of anarchist dissent that were unrestricted by national borders. But even as we learn from Nao of Jiko's existence as having been deeply influenced by their feminist and anarchist principles, the novel does not offer further biographical detail for how this might have come to be. There is a fleeting moment in a vision nearing the end of the novel during which Ruth is flooded by fragments of Jiko's past: "spectral images, smells and sounds; the gasp of a woman hanged for treason as the noose snaps her neck."[70] It is a horrifying sequence of events that explains, through the ghostly presence of Kanno, Jiko's radicalization as a response to the violent and senseless machinery of state imperialism.[71]

But the only further context that the novel provides for how Jiko would eventually align herself with such incendiary energies is Nao's association of her with the particular feminist order of the Japanese New Woman.[72] This was a historical development that was in part fueled by the radical actions of women such as Kanno herself, who had refused to conform to patriarchal formations of the state.[73] It was also representative of numerous transpacific undercurrents of a stirring revolutionary consciousness at the time. While the term "New Woman" was coined in Europe and North America in the late nineteenth century, it started to gain traction in Japan only later in the early 1900s. Considered a controversial sign of Westernization and modernity, the Japanese New Woman presented a direct confrontation to the feminine ideal of the "good wife, wise mother" stereotype, which had in preceding decades been duly imposed on girls and women during the Meiji period. She manifested, in short, a revolutionary figure: an unsettling force of transcultural feminist awakening that served as a substantive threat to the otherwise monolithic construct of the Japanese woman.[74]

As we already know, these unspooling histories of revolution converge in the character of Jiko, who becomes a symbol of inscrutability for some of the intertwined narratives of upheaval that have structured the critical consciousness of the transpacific.[75] In line with the negative archive that she enfolds within the text, Jiko does not clarify the ideological significance of these temporal and geographical turns of event. Rather, what she constitutes is a paradoxical vanishing point for the transpacific crosscurrents of revolution that are imperceptible but that have nevertheless shaped her very being. Even as the imprint of a kind of radical feminist past has been left on Jiko's existence, it ultimately fails to be fully represented in the text. This is an extensive personal history that eludes not only Ruth and us readers, but also Nao, who ponders the sheer difficulty of putting down into writing what Jiko tells her: "The stories seem so real while she's talking, but later, when I sit down to write them, but later, they slip away and become unreal again."[76] Nao eventually comes to produce an extended narrative of her own life story, instead of Jiko's as promised. But implicit in her departure from, or at least deferral of, this original task of recounting Jiko's past lies a certain predicament of historical representation, or more to the point, a persistent interrogation of conventional forms of historiographic record that the novel enacts as a necessary condition of its negative archive. In this sense, the novel might constitute what Yunte Huang has called a "counterpoetic work" of the transpacific, one that resists the production of its social, political, and cultural imagination through homogenous accounts of modernity and progress.[77] The marginal and singular history of transpacific revolutionary feminism that Jiko embodies thus remains inscrutable to dominant methods of his-toriographic representation that have been conditioned by regimes of chronological time and topographic space. It throws into relief the multiple, contested sites of absence and unknow-ability that can never fully be mapped by the critical terrain of the transpacific.

But if the novel insists on the elusiveness of those histories such as Jiko's, it is concurrently invested in the task of construct-ing new forms of thinking and conceiving of the narratives that make up the transpacific imaginary. Instead of forsaking it as an epistemological impasse, the novel tells Jiko's feminist revo-lutionary heritage in a different way: one that employs the worldbuilding elements of fiction as the textual infrastructure for a project that reaches beyond the scope of already given real-ities. To reference Huang once more, what the novel formulates is a poetics that "hovers between the literal and the metaphoric, the historical and the mimetic"; it draws on the density of its contextual memory to recompose a modality of feminist revolu-tionary meaning in its attendant narratives of conjecture.[78] This is less a departure from the historically situated circumstances of the transpacific, and more so an expansion—through the particular capacities of literature—of the kinds of futures that might yet be envisioned from its pasts and present. As Ruth reflects on her own discomfiting experience of slipping between the multiple narrative planes of the text: "Fiction had its own time and logic. That was its power."[79] Against the coherence of temporal progression and epistemological reasoning, then, what the novel most clearly leverages is the distinct power of literary imagining to inscribe the still-emergent potentialities of an inscrutable feminist revolution.

The force of this fictional power is most clearly imbued in the worlds that both Nao and Ruth write into existence. These manifest precisely the emergent possibilities from Jiko's existence that the novel is inclined to continue weaving, once again across those discordant temporal and geographical coordinates plotted by its unfurling narratives. The speculative entanglement of Jiko, Nao, and Ruth emerging from this textual assemblage illuminates another way of narrating the transnational and transtemporal relations of solidarity that have arisen from the long onset of transpacific feminist revolution that originated some decades ago. What the novel enacts is therefore a reconstitution of the revolutionary energies originating from Jiko's existence into the making of other, possible worlds. It is Nao who first partakes in this generative endeavor by deciding to write in her diary. As we know, she is compelled by the initial desire to record the life stories of her great-grandmother, intending to delve into the interlocking histories that had precipitated their unfolding. But, instead, Nao deviates to present an adjacent account of her own existence, which comes to involve Ruth not only as a reader but also as an agent of its narrative. To be clear, Nao had always been writing with a reader in mind; this is in part how she ensures the viability of the world that she is building within the pages of the diary: "You wonder about me. I wonder about you. Who are you and what are you doing?"[80] Her direct address to this implied reader implicates them in the very construction of the narrative that she is relaying: "together we'll make magic," she declares in the opening entry, "at least for the time being."[81] Nao likens her mode of writing to an act of conjuration—a bringing into being of a world composed by words that gathers between Jiko, herself, and now also Ruth, who salvages the diary from a shoreline across the Pacific Ocean, sometime in an undisclosed future.

Calling to mind faint impressions of those transpacific histories of Jiko's several times removed, it is these divergent spatial and temporal dimensions that Nao's imagined world comes to span. Ruth's apprehension of the diary also begets her involvement in its ongoing construction. Almost reaching its end, Ruth realizes that the handwriting within begins to taper off into blank pages, words that she had earlier seen crammed until the end had vanished without a trace. "The words had been there," she insists, "and now they weren't. What had happened to them?"[82] The advancing story of Nao's life in the material scratches of her pen ink, once indicative of the cultivation of a speculative reality, has now come to a halt. Ruth is dismayed; the writing had come to an end precisely at a moment when both Nao and her father, Haruki #2, had each decided to end their lives. But at this point in the novel, Ruth enters a dreamscape that is coeval with the reality that Nao inhabits; by engaging directly with Haruki #2 in a conversation that prevents his, and by extension also Nao's, death, she shifts the course of events in that world, thus forestalling its impending dissolution.

There can be no logical explanation for this narrative maneuver, only the defiance of chronological and teleological time, and the transcendence of geographical boundaries as an emphasis on the fluid interconnectedness of the world that Nao has built. It is in this way that Ruth assumes a collaborative role as another builder of this world, reordering its inevitable trajectory in a strange, relational exercise of hers and Nao's imaginations. But to her increasing bewilderment, this in turn becomes a reflexive process that takes on a life of its own. Even in the wake of a seemingly gratifying conclusion, in which Nao arrives at Jiko's temple in time to sit vigil on her great-grandmother's deathbed, thereby also reconciling with Haruki #2, new words continue to appear in the remaining pages of the diary. As Ruth describes this inexplicable phenomenon to one of her neighbors, Muriel: "Every time I open the diary, there are more pages . . .

the end keeps receding, like an outgoing wave. Just out of reach. I can't quite catch up."[83] Even the world summoned by Nao and Ruth reveals itself, then, to also be one that cannot fully be realized, its constitutive form always exceeding—and more crucially reimagining—the bounds of the knowable present. In line with the conceptual premise of this chapter, it is a world that might likewise be considered out of reach, but in the sense that its open-ended potentialities are interminable and thus cannot be captured by dominant modes of knowledge. Not unlike Jiko's deliberate and radical obviation of her identity, Nao presents another unsettling account of the writing of collective personal histories that expands the limits of the transpacific consciousness. The inscription of this narrative—marginal and indeterminate, yet boundless in its subversive force of speculative worlding—reckons with both the epistemological universality and the inevitability of those grand narratives of historiographic representation.

Of course, there comes a point at which the words in Nao's diary must in fact end. The physical limitation of its pages limns the contours of the conjectural world invoked within, even as the very possibilities from its making continue to persist. But instead of concluding the novel this way, Ozeki introduces a theory of multiple, possible worlds in its final pages. She draws on the work of the physicist Hugh Everett to elucidate this theory, who in 1957 devised the many-worlds interpretation of quantum mechanics in response to the paradox of Erwin Schrödinger's famous thought experiment.[84] Put simply, Everett proposed the realization of all probable outcomes from a quantum experiment, each manifesting in an abundance of different and separate worlds. He accordingly raised the possibility of multiple states of being that—rather than eventually collapsing into a singular result—would endlessly proliferate at every juncture. As Ozeki explains in the novel: "Every instance of *either/or* is replaced by an *and*. And an *and*, and an *and*, and an *and*, and another *and* . . . adding up to an infinitely all-inclusive, and yet mutually unknowable, web of many worlds."[85] Everett's theory offers a useful touchstone for the close of this chapter. To consign the world that Nao and Ruth have built to that of Jiko's in the past is only to trace one tangent of descent among others that are also in existence but can never be fully perceived; it is to acknowledge the immeasurability of heterogenous worlds that will continue to be generated in due time, circulating at once in their essential unknowability. That the fate of Nao is never ultimately revealed to Ruth or the reader, as earlier mentioned, is simply indicative of this line of thinking that permeates the entirety of the novel. The worlds that the novel is in the process of constructing, and those on which this imaginative work of worlding concurrently depends, are emphasized also in their emergent potentialities that will never fully be grasped. Through such modes of poetic articulation, what it comes to illuminate is the speculative orientation of an inscrutable feminist revolution that by its very design lies out of reach—one that hinges on an elusiveness of meaning that keeps open, and affirms the irreducibility of, the parallel, unknowable lifeworlds that it will continue to engender.

4

A COMMONS BEYOND
THE HUMAN

Against the backdrop of an incoming dust storm in Alexis Wright's *The Swan Book* (2013), a solitary black swan makes an unexpected appearance at the lake settlement that is home to Oblivia Ethyl(ene), a young Aboriginal girl and the central protagonist of the novel. The novel is set in Australia around a century into the future and offers a postapocalyptic glimpse into a world blighted by the devastating effects of climate change. Its narratives accordingly open into multiple crises of the global geopolitical imagination, framed by the interminable experience of "one extinction event after another."[1] Deeply reminiscent of the Indigenous heritage of Wright's ancestral Waanyi land, the lake where Oblivia grows up is not spared the impact of these ongoing environmental disasters and governmental collapse. Its wretched condition is moreover exacerbated by the unique violence of human invasion.[2] While the freak weather that conveys unrelenting sandstorms causes the lake to degenerate into a swamp, this atmospheric misfortune pales in comparison to the sudden, unwelcome presence of the army that designates its watery perimeters to be a dumping ground for abandoned ships, and later a militarized space for target practice. By all accounts, the swamp is a thoroughly cursed place, befitting the "anti-halcyon times" that the novel dramatizes.[3] It therefore comes as no surprise that when the swan shows up without prior warning, it is seen by the locals as more of a "paragon of anxious premonitions, rather than the arrival of a miracle for saving the world."[4] Flying in ahead of a large red cloud of roiling dust, the bird comes to stand not only for its classical metaphor of extreme rarity; it also serves as an omen for yet another impending catastrophe soon to befall them.[5] This extraordinary vision of the black swan is intensified by the encounter it stages with Oblivia, who can only wonder at the occasion of their meeting: "*What kind of premonition is this?*"[6]

In many ways, the novel unfolds as a response to the above question, bringing into being an entanglement of more-than-human existence that Oblivia and a flock of swans will come to inhabit.[7] They will together enact a radical possibility of survival amid the scenes of unending calamity assembled by its narratives. It is in this sense that the unanticipated arrival of the bird can be construed as a portent for the possibilities of another, more hospitable world that can only be grasped by reaching beyond a certain scope of the already given. After all, Wright's third novel is first and foremost an indictment of settler Australia's ongoing failure to acknowledge its Indigenous histories, and the turning of its back on the social and political dispossession suffered by Aboriginals.[8] To this end, the novel compels an unflinching gaze at these atrocities, laying bare the ruins of Indigenous presence in the wake of the nation's colonizing projects. Its overture to a dystopian future is etched within the cruel confines of a past and present that are in fact already being lived by those whose stories have been rendered destitute by a national imaginary forged in the categorical erasure of its own Indigenous memory. As the supernatural sight of the swan would then suggest, the novel is also crucially invested in an exercise to reimagine these desecrations of Aboriginal life. Operating in a palpable register of the speculative, its narratives deny the inevitability that too often overshadows the fate of Indigenous peoples otherwise preordained by the legacies of settler colonialism.

But as the novel comes to reveal, the world that it summons for this intent requires less a suspension of readerly disbelief than a reflexive expansion of the kinds of knowledges and practices that have been key to the animation of its very existence. Put another way, the world that emerges in *The Swan Book* does not simply appeal to an epistemological flight of fancy, nor instigate an escape into an alternate dimension of the impossible. Rather, it takes shape in the configurations of an Indigenous Australian ontological reality that have long stressed their dissonance from dominant Western paradigms of thinking and being, or in a literary mode that the Wiradjuri writer and scholar Jeanine Leane has described more generally as "Aboriginal realism."[9] For Leane, this is a term that accounts for the indisputable realism of Indigenous stories of time and place, which disavows their frequent—and very much inaccurate—association with the realm of pure fantasy.[10] If the novel alludes to the conjectural order of a new world, in other words, then it is one given coherent meaning by the spiritual and cultural beliefs faithful to an already existent Aboriginal tradition.[11] As Wright has elsewhere explained the evocation of Aboriginal memory and time as an intrinsic part of her writing process, "The world I try to inhabit . . . is like looking at the ancestral tracks spanning our traditional country which, if I look at the land, combines all stories, all realities from the ancient to the new, and makes it one—like all the strands on a long rope."[12] Here, she emphasizes the indebtedness of the seemingly unprecedented textual events in her novel to the actualities of an Indigenous worldview, which may be perceived by a reader as wholly inexplicable and unfamiliar only insofar as they are apprehended by non-Indigenous frameworks of understanding.

I make this case not to diminish the speculative gesture of the novel, which in this closing chapter of *Feminism Enchanted* assembles a textual lifeworld steeped in the essence of Waanyi culture. But I argue that it undertakes a more significant labor of unsettling the epistemological and ontological grounds on which most of its readers have established the validity of their lived experiences and likewise taken for granted the apparent truth of their universality. In its underlying commitment to the world-making capacities of Aboriginal existence, *The Swan Book* reckons with those other knowledges that have assumed precedence as compulsory acts of the imagination. Its narratives undermine the measure of a world constructed as such; they shift its axis to revolve instead around the possibilities engendered by Indigenous ways of living and being—ones that are moreover affirmed as inherent to a tangible, material reality in the present, rather than relegated to some abstract utopian horizon. This is a line of inquiry that can further be ascribed to the more encompassing aim of the novel to envision how, and through which means exactly, the invariable course of harm and destruction wreaked on Australian Aboriginal communities might ever come to cease. To this end, it urges the approach of this revisioning to be drawn from the distinct perspectives of an Indigenous imaginary, which would effectively entail a complete upheaval of presiding settler ideals of social and political transformation. This is to say that the novel betrays mainstream ideological assumptions that have guided the semblance of a better world as themselves expedient articulations of settler conquest, as symbolic enclosures of violence which will only serve to prolong the oppression of those beings and things presumed subordinate to their singular agenda. It overturns the ethical feasibility of such a societal model, thus deeming it unworthy of aspiration. For if there is a chance for the survival, much less the flourishing, of Indigenous lives in Australia and beyond, then its accompanying outlook can no longer be devised from the avenues of reasoning that have ensured the systemic renunciation of these same communities. In short, what the novel extends is not only an invitation to reassess the structuring premise of the world at large, but also to critically rethink the strategies that can and should be employed to more profoundly alter its being.

This is an ethical refrain that I argue must be heeded at a time marked by the catastrophic repercussions of widespread social dispossession and environmental exploitation, and when calls to salvage the remains of the planet have become so pervasive in public discourse. It is a provocation to more rigorously examine the epistemological valences inflecting those governing policies, statements, and indeed also the individual concepts that have been disseminated as supposedly desirable vehicles for enabling such a revolution. For at stake in a truly ethical reimagination of this world is also the preceding selection of which interpretive methods, practices, and habits might be most commensurate with the task.

This chapter explores the limits of these claims on a term that has of late been valorized for precisely such an aim: the commons. In the process, it brings to view a more expansive use for the mode of enchantment that underpins this project, but one that continues to rely on enchantment's critical hold to compel a closer look at the very actions that we have begun to take for want of a better future. This involves a reflexive evaluation of the conditions of possibility for genuine change to occur, a questioning of our longstanding principles and beliefs on how best to assuage our rapidly depleting existence. This fourth and final chapter of *Feminism Enchanted* tests and therefore departs from the more focused approach to feminism as an intellectual object that has anchored the book so far; it moves further to expose the failures of progressive reason as it has figured in more overarching attempts to address the exigencies of this current world. By exposing current theories of the commons as having been produced and sustained by human-centered paradigms of intellectual reasoning, the chapter develops, as its title suggests, what I call a *commons beyond the human*. As I will elaborate, this is a concept that refuses the regulating logics of liberal humanism that have thus far governed the commons and its obligation to transformative politics, but one that nevertheless stays with the open-ended capacities of its eventual manifestation.

As earlier mentioned, the literary imperative of the mode of enchantment is also invoked for its incantatory power in this chapter, which unfolds a textual lifeworld in the novel that is grounded in the lived reality of Indigenous Australia. But if this is a reality that up until now is still besieged by the acts of violence perversely sanctioned by the state, then the most instructive maneuver of the literary text lies in its directive that it can only be reimagined from a perspective that will not reproduce a future of the same. Any attendant acts of social transformation, then, and the counternarrative of survival they will come to produce must be those more ethically gleaned from the Aboriginal imaginary—that is, from modes of knowledge that have been cast as marginal to the human and, by this logic, attenuated in their utility for progressive politics. In this sense, the speculative tendency that is so often identified in the novel enacts a somewhat unusual move of orienting its readers not toward worlds of an inconceivable nature, but rather ones that have long existed and in fact once thrived beyond their narrow, epistemological fields of perception. It tells a story that expands the limits of acceptable ways of thinking, living, and being, in and for the advent of a different future. And finally, if *The Swan Book* can be argued to set for us the seemingly insurmountable task of overturning whole systems of thought as the basis for its ethical claim, then its narratives also unfurl in a manner that lessens the anguish of this intellectual labor because they help us to visualize its real and tangible possibility. As Wright observes in this light, "It was strange what a view can do to how people think."[13] Her novel demonstrates that it is perhaps literature that is best placed to sketch such a view: one that reckons with the terms of the revolution we have so desired, while at the same time making legible another, alternative horizon of the otherwise unimaginable.

My analysis of *The Swan Book* will first show how a commons beyond the human might be conceived. More specifically, I advance a reading that focuses on how Oblivia and the swans—as consigned to the durational limits of human recognition in their expression of this extant concept of the commons—discompose the temporal claim to a redemptive future. The ethical exigency arising from the demand for their collective endurance as such is therefore one that necessarily exceeds settler-colonial ways of knowing and being. In the final section of this chapter, I examine how the story of this reimagined commons is told through a means of dialogical knowledge production that rests on the gendered undercurrents of the text. In the process, I consider the novel's use of the classic literary strategy of feminist revisioning as a hermeneutic practice that finds affinity with the recantatory impulse of enchantment. If the text is indelibly marked by its intertextual references to a largely Western canon of swan poetry, then to a similar effect of the workings of enchantment, it enacts a return to these forms of prior knowledge in order to imbue them with revised meaning. It is a return framed by a particular poetics of feminist resistance, one that I argue is pivotal to the storytelling impulse of the novel. More specifically, I examine the conscious rewriting of the rape of Oblivia as the narrative premise for a commons beyond the human.

CAPITALISM AND THE COMMONS

This chapter theorizes a commons beyond the human as another way to envisage the commons and its pledge to the construction of better, alternative futures. At the heart of its insistence on examining the modes of knowledge production that have given the commons its customary form, then, lies an attempt to parse the concept through a more ethical lens. As earlier mentioned, a commons beyond the human is a conceptual model that is not entirely unsympathetic to familiar meanings of the commons sutured to a more rigorous and teleological political agenda. But its critical dimensions can only be traced by actively displacing those borders surrounding the concept as we currently know it. The commons—chiefly understood as shared resources either material or immaterial—has most often been theorized in its immediate connection to capital.[14] But there has been no agreement to date on its true relationship to capitalism, much less any consensus from commons scholarship about its absolute deployment.[15] In recent years, the notion of the commons has also experienced a dramatic resurgence of interest, gaining traction as a buzzword in both scholarly circles and commercial sectors as an extrapolation, however tenuous, of its promises of collaborative thinking and living.[16]

Much of this work has attempted to prefigure the continued potential of the commons for upheaving the foundations of the capitalist regime of extractive labor and exploitation.[17] In contrast to foundational thinkers on the commons such as Garrett Hardin and Elinor Ostrom, who focused more on the introduction of corrective policies to adjudicate the fair expenditure of common-pool resources, at stake for these scholars has been a critique of the logic of enclosure perpetuated by enduring technologies of privatization and accumulation.[18] George Caffentzis and Silvia Federici, following Karl Marx, for instance, frame the rubrics of enclosure through primitive accumulation: one of the key organizational strategies of capital to which "the capitalist class always resorts in times of crisis when it needs to reassert its command over labor."[19] With the advent of neoliberalism, moreover, primitive accumulation has been "extremized, so that privatization extends to every aspect of our existence."[20] If the ideologies of neoliberal capitalism have insinuated themselves into every atomized level of contemporary life, then the commons as its historical adversary has emerged as a convincing antidote. In the same vein, the creation and reclamation of the commons involves the participation in social and cultural habits that Peter Linebaugh has termed "practices of commoning."[21] These undertakings have been perceived as tools for developing an alternative economy founded on collaborative movements of anticapitalist means of social reproduction. With its impetus for dismantling the various structural antagonisms that mark neoliberal forms of late capitalism, it comes as no surprise that the commons, in these apocalyptic times of worsening social, political, and ecological crises, has become a symbol of hope for collective survival.

But this hope is a troubled one. Although the commons concept continues to signal the possibility of mutual solidarity against the backdrop of neoliberal globalization, current debates surrounding its relevance still clearly revolve around its vexed relationship with capitalism.[22] In other words, even as the relational politics of commoning are arguably still upheld as an unequivocally positive endeavor, the commons itself has increasingly been acknowledged to be implicated in, and at times even dependent on, the very frameworks of hegemonic capital it seeks to overturn.[23] The co-optation of the commons by forces of capitalist growth is furthermore a startling trend if only in its ubiquity, evident in the proliferation of the term in areas of life that are now ranging from real estate developments to digital resource repositories, from the privatization of ecological reserves to the management of planetary resources under the beguiling designation of the "global commons." These acts of appropriation have established the commons as no longer in direct opposition to the indices of capital—as most of its advocates on the intellectual left would prefer it—but rather as worryingly tethered to the interests of its generation.[24] Whether in name or in practice, the commons can no longer provide a clear path toward the progressive politics envisioned beyond the realities of the present.

My aim here is not to discredit these approaches whether as theoretically or empirically driven. Neither is it to further question the commitment of the commons to a radically transformative political project by continuing to parse its rejection of, or collusion with, capitalist forms of thinking. Rather, I develop the notion of a commons beyond the human as a reckoning with the analytic of human exceptionalism that has thus far mandated these efforts to build a better, if still provisional, world. This is not to say that those now mobilizing the commons have not already offered critiques of the fantasies of human supremacy and the civilizational hierarchies of knowing and living that have been installed for Man's exclusive benefit. On the contrary, much of this work, having developed precisely in response to the dire effects of large-scale social and environmental devastation, has indeed reflected on the ethics of relationality not only between singular human entities, but also on the reciprocal contact of these beings with their physical environment as that which supersedes the category of the human altogether.[25] A commons beyond the human also undertakes this crucial labor by concurrently interrogating the multiple logics safeguarding some beings as more human than others. It is similarly prescient in rethinking entirely these ways of existence proving themselves to be increasingly unlivable.

A REFUSAL OF PROGRESSIVE REASON

This line of argument follows that of Mario Blaser and Marisol de la Cadena, who have pointed out the inherently recursive nature of the conceptual tools used to advance anthropological knowledge: Inasmuch "as knowledges are world-making processes, they tend to make the worlds they know."[26] Blaser and de la Cadena reveal that intellectual modes of analysis have a kind of circular, looping quality that reinstate themselves through the objects they study. This has resulted in the "epistemic or ontological invalidations—or [the] absences" of other alternative forms of knowledge that resist the capture of scholarly tools at hand.[27] Their claim is most evident in how mainstream definitions of the commons have been shaped by the paradigm of progress as both an ideological axiom and an epistemological method. These dual iterations of progress are mutually reinforcing, and moreover do not discriminate across economic leanings or political beliefs. Whether it is for or against the power relations of capital, the conceptual groundwork of the commons has largely been laid in the shadow of a teleological trajectory of progress. Of course, I do not mean to suggest that there has been a ready agreement on what exactly the allegiance to progress should bring. Progress reveals itself as a contradictory logic; it is actualized in accordance with whichever path the commons chooses to take in its long-term tarrying with the instrument of capital. On the one hand, in those instances where the commons has shown itself to be more tolerant of systems of capital, progress is quite simply coded in their lasting perpetuation. On the other hand, where the political freight of the commons has been predicated on the deracination of capitalist inequality and enclosure, its structural recuperation of various forms of imperiled life demands progressive efforts toward pragmatic political reform. The affective worlding of the commons has moreover not been spared the inflections of progress. As a means of articulating new forms of emancipatory politics, the commons is inevitably treated as a placeholder of hope for concerted struggle and change. This has amounted to the "confirming affective surplus" that Lauren Berlant has observed the commons to deliver ahead—or even in absence—of its eventual coming into being.[28]

That the commons inhabits some kind of progressive capacity may very well be crucial for its continued relevance in social and political discourse. It might even be necessary for setting into motion the revolutionary endeavor its project has come to beckon. But I take issue with the conventional wisdom of progress insofar as it has never been, and can never be, cultivated in a neutral or all-encompassing sense. As Anna Tsing writes, progress "is embedded . . . in widely accepted assumptions about what it means to be human."[29] Whether it manifests in our attendant beliefs about historical or scientific development, or elsewhere under the guise of personal improvement, the conceit of progress has only ever been legible as a story of human advancement. It is a narrative told by and for the exclusive figure of the human. And the oversubscription to this blinkered human mindset has had the consequence of effacing the perspectives of those beings long considered other than human. "As long as we imagine that humans are made through progress," Tsing argues, "nonhumans are stuck within this imaginative framework too."[30] This naturally extends to the wishful thinking that precedes the realization of a better future, which is arguably only perceived within the limits of human experience. These fictions of progress have ensconced a singularly human state of being and knowing at the expense of other ways of existence.

THEORIZING A COMMONS BEYOND THE HUMAN

A commons that claims the realm beyond the human as a zone of possibility is in dialogue with the expansive domain of posthumanism that has, for the past two decades, been rethinking various ideologies that govern the relations and interactions between human and nonhuman entities. Generally speaking, posthumanist discourse has sought to challenge the boundaries defining the category of the human, those that have established and authorized human agency and consciousness as superior to other excluded beings. With the acknowledgment of the fallibility of liberal humanism, and by extension the sustained devolution of its project, have come new forms of understanding and relating to entities considered other than human.[31] Within the broad imaginary of posthumanism, two overlapping trajectories of thought guide my inquiry into a commons beyond the human. The first, following Blaser and de la Cadena, is an attentiveness to the ethics and politics of knowledge that have produced the conceptual object currently known as the commons, and a reorientation of its analytic configuration as such.[32] Posthumanist interventions have long troubled human epistemology as a transparent and objective lens for perceiving the world. But alongside Blaser and de la Cadena, theorists such as Isabelle Stengers, Eduardo Kohn, Donna Haraway, and María Puig de la Bellacasa have more recently expressed the urgency of cultivating new critical practices that can better accommodate the shift toward more-than-human ways of thinking. As Haraway writes: "It matters what matters we use to think other matters with; it matters what stories we tell to tell other stories with; it matters what knots knot knots, what thoughts think thoughts, what descriptions describe descriptions, what ties tie ties. It matters what stories make worlds, what worlds make stories."[33] In this vein, a commons beyond the human engenders an expansion of the existing world designated by the commons; it is concurrently invested in the task of retelling those stories responsible for having first created the limited blueprint of that world.

At the same time, and even as the ideological potential of the term remains fundamental to my rethinking of the commons, I am wary of the reductive—and oftentimes epistemologically violent—allusion to "beyond the human." The second line of thought that I follow not only involves a reconsideration of what constitutes the human, but also the more explicit articulation of what is meant by the "beyond." As earlier delineated, the interrogation of the human as a privileged locus of understanding illuminates the agency of those beings excluded from its boundaries; this has immediately come to encompass nonhuman animals and, by definition, has also extended to include forms of matter and other nonliving things. But the glaring erasure of perspectives on race, sexuality, and colonialism that has occurred when this universalized figure of the human is examined in the name of posthumanism can no longer be ignored.[34] Zakiyyah Iman Jackson argues that the methodological appeal to "beyond the human" "may actually reintroduce the Eurocentric transcendentalism this movement purports to disrupt, particularly with regard to the historical and ongoing distributive ordering of race."[35] Jackson cautions against the lure of the movement "beyond," insofar as the racialized idiom of humanism has been instantiated back into such onto-epistemological paradigms of seemingly progressive thinking.

My understanding of the commons beyond the human can finally be aligned with Nadja Millner-Larsen and Gavin Butt, who have argued that the conceptual power of the commons "is orientated toward the potentiality of a future in which more might be had by the many rather than by the few."[36] I take a similar view not in spite of the implication of the commons in multiple orders of human reasoning but precisely because of this very predicament. Underlying this claim is my belief that it does less good to abolish the commons with the ideals it encapsulates, than it will to pry open the term to other, necessary meanings of what such ideals might still entail. Rather than advance yet another definition of the commons, I examine how its means of knowledge production might ensue differently, which is to say that I dislocate the concept from its existing points of epistemological orientation.[37] What might this alternative framework of thinking resemble? Through what means are we best able to ethically narrate a theory of the commons that radically alters the shape of its design, and which critical vocabularies can we draw from to facilitate this endeavor? These questions surrounding the methodological construction of the commons pivot on the task of troubling humanist hierarchies of thinking while refusing to accept this endeavor as in and of itself an altruistic one.

SPECULATIVE ETHICS IN A TIME OF EXTINCTION

To address the above questions, I turn back to *The Swan Book* to examine how the figural capacity of the literary text extends another definition of the commons—an ethical expansion of its discursive limits through the world-making propensities of literature. My reading of the novel is suggestive of how certain Aboriginal forms of knowing might inform such a conceptual reimagination of the commons.[38] I focus on the idea of time as key to Deborah Bird Rose's explication of the cultural construction of modernity that was established and glorified as a master narrative of progress during the settler conquest of Australia.[39] As Rose writes, this violent making of a new nation was predicated on "the task of erasing specific life," which demanded the literal sacrifice of "Indigenous peoples, their cultures, their practices of time, their sources of power, and their systems of ecological knowledge and responsibility."[40] The ways of living and being that Rose lists here must be seen as inextricable from an all-encompassing creation ontology that serves as the cornerstone of Aboriginal law, religion, and philosophy.[41] On this account, what might be considered as Indigenous Australian time must not be understood as an external measure of chronology, but rather a complex "quality of life."[42] This is a temporal phenomenon that does not respond to strict demarcations of the past, present, and future; it is one that instead transcends multiple continuums of time and space, and unfolds across intergenerational histories and genealogies. It has—together with more overarching Aboriginal belief systems as its ontological provenance—been marginalized and steadily eradicated by the regime of settler colonialism.[43] In the following analysis, then, and if the velocity of progressive time has served as the presiding temporal logic for liberal-humanist notions of the commons, I trace those other temporalities that abound in *The Swan Book*, ones that refuse to be sequenced by the linear time of colonial modernity. At every narrative juncture, what the novel emphasizes is the living presence of the latter times as the temporal grounds for a commons beyond the human. By centering the experience of Aboriginal memory and time this way, it once more stresses the active realism of its existing lifeworlds that cannot be committed to the mystique of a regressive, primordial past.[44]

I return to the moment of fortuitous encounter between Oblivia and the black swan in the novel. This is a convergence of lifeworlds that coalesces an entanglement of more-than-human existence, which in turn generates a powerful force of resistance that shakes up a world predicated on the locus of human exceptionalism and sovereignty.[45] That the swan has chosen this girl to behold it cannot therefore be read as a mere coincidence. Oblivia is no ordinary human being but one whose emphatic otherness dislocates her from the epistemological coordinates that have validated the liberal category of the human. If the swan, as Oblivia notes, had been displaced from the south of the country by worsening ecological hazards, then she too has lived "the experience of an exile."[46] As a victim of a brutal gang rape by a group of intoxicated Aboriginal youths, Oblivia is indelibly scarred by the trauma of this episode. She is shunned by her family for now being sexually contaminated and then regarded as forever lost by the rest of her extended community, who are too cowardly to be reminded of the residual shame surrounding the crime. Oblivia finds solace in the bowels of an ancient eucalyptus tree, where she becomes suspended in sleep. But in a curious twist of fate, she is found and rescued a decade later by the sea gypsy Aunty Bella Donna of the Champions, a white European refugee who had always sworn that her own escape to the Australian coast was guided by the migratory flight of a swan. Oblivia resurfaces from her slumber having little recollection of the past. And if she had already been persecuted by a forced exclusion from her own Aboriginal kin, Oblivia is in her reawakening dismissed even further into the peripheries of human existence. She is reviled as a specter "best suited dead," an unwelcome reminder of some heinous violence inflicted in the past and of the violations on Aboriginal populations still being perpetrated in the present.[47]

I argue that the relational dynamic between Oblivia and the flock of swans with which she will soon convene inscribes the ethical infrastructure for a commons beyond the human in a time of extinction without end. This alternative vision of the commons that Oblivia and the birds articulate is conceived not only in the radical interweaving of their more-than-human existences but also in their steadfast repudiation of progressive time as a key driver of prevailing conceptions of the commons. More to the point, with both the girl and black swans existing on planes of temporality irreducible to the chronology of progressive modernity, they insinuate a constant threat to the arc of linear time as a regulating framework of the liberal-humanist consciousness.[48] Oblivia is a survivor of the harms imposed by unresolved histories of settler colonialism and gendered violence, a stark reminder of a living temporality out of sync with the relentless passing of sequential order. And the swans are the nonhuman collateral damage of worsening climate change in the country, in search of ancient Aboriginal narratives now lost, a marker of species history and the geological epochs of deep time. What they will together articulate is an ethics answerable to the temporal modalities of an extinction event conceived not as the demise of human teleological advancement but as one that altogether exceeds it: a speculative ethics unbound by the rhetoric of progressive or prescriptive thinking.[49]

Soon after Oblivia's inaugural meeting with the black swan, thousands of its feathery kin descend on the decaying swamp settlement. The otherworldly appearance of the swans is a sight that thoroughly disturbs the swamp people. In one sense, the birds are an evil sight for the locals, "created by devils"; they are suspected of being the final radioactive weapon of mass destruction that the army has put in place for the annihilation of the settlement.[50] The swans recall the 2007 Australian governmental reform agenda launched to address the social, political, and economic disadvantage affecting the Indigenous populations in the country, more specifically known as the Closing the Gap initiative.[51] Associated with the pervasiveness of these interventionist policies, the swans' hostile reception by the swamp people exposes the government's humanitarian reasoning as a facade for abstract and insidious state-sanctioned violence. But in another sense, the birds connote an alarming presence because the locals "feared any ancient business that was not easily translatable in the local environment."[52] These displaced flocks from the south of the country are not only a literal source of ecological endangerment to the biodiversity of the other species native to the territory. They also puncture the veneer of the lives of the swamp people with their intimate but opaque connection to the "stories in the oldest Law scriptures," stories that are profoundly disconcerting insofar as they have since been lost.[53] What the swans also represent is a recessive point of cultural origin: the endless black ribbons of their flock plummeting down onto the waters are a persistent, but also inexplicable, reminder of the vestiges of nonhuman life that have long existed on a different scale of planetary time.

Unlike the rest of the settlement, Oblivia is unfazed by the swans. She follows in the footsteps of Bella Donna, who has now extended her caregiving role to the birds and their cygnets, deciding that she herself "would be fluent in swan talk."[54] As a reflection of her own search for a past she has never been able to recall, Oblivia expresses a peculiar inclination for uncovering the mysteries of the avian migratory route toward the polluted swamp. The swans have been banished into newfound territory "where they have no story line for taking them back," a thus far uncharted terrain except perhaps by their ancestors from another time now forgotten.[55] This is a story that has no beginning, and therefore a narrative that Oblivia finds a striking affinity with: she who has "disowned her people by acting as though she had bypassed human history, by being directly descended from their ancestral tree."[56] In contrast to the other well-loved children at the settlement, whose lives have developed along a predictable, and sequential, trajectory of reproductive continuity, Oblivia's unexpected return completely fractures this semblance of temporal normalcy by which the swamp people are now desperately abiding. Her presence at the settlement is a painful reminder of a spiritual rebirth cursed by the irrecoverable absence of Aboriginal origins; the sacred eucalyptus tree from which she resurfaced is eventually destroyed by the army, that leads to "a loss that was so great, it made [the swamp people] feel unhinged from their own bodies, unmoored, vulnerable, separated from eternity."[57] Oblivia is believed to have circumvented the account of human inception and advancement that the locals, by their own necessity, had internalized in the years following their invasion and occupation by armed forces of the state. Her durational existence is an ideological interference for how it "*stands still.*"[58] It cannot simply be relegated to a distant Aboriginal past, but neither can it be ascribed to the present measure of life that has been sutured to a specific definition of what counts as human. If Mark Rifkin has identified the irreconcilability of these temporal positions as the "double bind" that Native peoples occupy within dominant settler reckonings of time, then Oblivia exemplifies the marked refusal of either orientation.[59]

That white European colonizers of Australia brought with them a particular temporal frame of reference—one with a linear, progressive directive to the future as a transcendence of the past—constitutes a given knowledge that imbues the entirety of the novel. On the one hand, the ramifications of this universalizing gesture of modernity are distilled in the legal and political violence enacted on the Aboriginal people at the swamp. It is a form of control proliferated until "there was full traction over what these people believed and permeance over their ability to . . . define what it meant to be human, without somebody else making that decision for them."[60] Because of their anachronistic position in the historical trajectory now installed for the country, the swamp dwellers are condemned for their particular failure to correspond to the rubrics of settler-colonial time. But what Wright presents on the other hand—the Indigenous assimilation of the juridical apparatus of progress as illustrated by the character of Warren Finch—is an alternative consequence that proves even more insidious for the continued oppression of Aboriginal peoples. Finch belongs to the Brolga Nation, the Indigenous community set in direct opposition to that of the swamp dwellers for their embodiment of the aspirational sentiment to be "good Black people, not seen as troublemakers, radicals, or people who made Australians feel uneasy."[61] As an antithesis to the tragic fate of those "damned people" at the swamp, the Brolga Nation has readily acceded to the modes of recognition legitimized by the settler-colonial state; their upward mobility is the result of successfully modeling the dominant outlook of the country at the expense of their own vanishing history.[62] It comes as no surprise, then, that Finch is introduced as a man who "stared at the future."[63] In his compliance with a master plan for his eventual ascendancy to the highest political office in the country, Finch is a hyperbole for what Elizabeth Povinelli has called "the impossible object of authentic self-identity" in the context of Australian liberal multiculturalism.[64] He is eagerly absorbed into the national imaginary of the country as a preeminent icon of authentic Aboriginal culture, a process that disingenuously relies on the systemic renunciation of the alterity intrinsic to that culture itself.[65] It is on account of his "post-racial" or "post-Indigenous" achievement that the novel exacts a critique of the deceptively inclusive axiom of multiculturalism revered by the Brolga Nation, a discourse that exerts its pernicious logic by way of the dissolution of Aboriginal cultural difference.[66]

In some ways, Oblivia is a mere plot device for the advancement of Finch's messianic life story, long foretold by his elders—she is his "promised wife first lady" whom he abducts from the settlement, forcibly marries in a ceremony televised nationwide, and finally imprisons in his glass-enclosed apartment in the southern capital.[67] Finch proceeds to remotely detonate the swamp settlement, which compels the swans to be on the move yet again. And on this note, it has perhaps also been foreseen that the swans will come to Oblivia's rescue; they have, after all, always connoted a lifeline for her. Each time she watched the birds lift off from the polluted waters of the settlement back then, she had already felt "the miracle of leaving . . . the lightness of being airborne."[68]

Their otherworldly disposition in the narrative, as indicative of a speculative ecology of more-than-human ethics, invites the prospect of departure from the multiple forces of continued colonization that are circulating in the text. The gesture toward this alternative ideality hereby comes to be suggestive of a commons that encompasses a plurality of lifeworlds beyond the human, those same lifeworlds that have eluded the temporal grasp of colonial modernity. Accordingly, this is a commons theorized against the normative conceptual imaginary in the foreground of the text—since exposed for the hypocrisy of supposedly progressive politics—and reassessed to account for more ethical acts of world-making that most crucially involve those beings long banished to the margins of humanity. Oblivia and the swans are exactly these existents in the novel, dwelling in the antihumanist thresholds of dominant settler-colonial time and rupturing its otherwise uninterrupted flow. By staying with the temporal bearings of the commons concept reimagined as such, they refuse to be implicated in any semblance of a redemptive future. If the possibilities of another commons might be perceived in the speculative entanglement of their being, it is a vision that is—and must be—entirely incommensurate with the epistemological continuity of liberal humanism. This is to say that there is no reassuring narrative of progress that Oblivia and the flock will actualize, then, at least not one that can be subsumed by the ideologies that they seek precisely to elude. In the southern city, the swans are preparing for what will be their final migratory path up north. Oblivia senses that the birds are "in training for something even they had not quite anticipated."[69] Indeed, there is no regimen that can prepare them for what is to come. When news breaks of Finch's assassination, Oblivia and the flock embark on a long flight back to the swamp settlement. This is a journey that will result in the extinction of the black swans.

But even, or perhaps especially, in the finitude of their deaths, the swans continue to be reminiscent of a disturbance at the temporal limits of human life. The commons to which they refer is a thoroughly disconcerting concept as much as it is also a transformative possibility of survival. Worn down by an endless drought that stretches across the country, the swans eventually "stand on baked earth and hiss at the sky they cannot reach, then the time arrives when no more sound comes from their open beaks."[70] This marks a silencing of their strange swan song as extinguished by the anthropogenic hazards of the environment. If the swans have succumbed to a certain climatic threat of extinction, however, their demise refers only to a single facet of life that can be understood as the eschatological end point of humanity. The birds are in fact illustrative of a lifeworld that exceeds this restricted posture of depletion: as their "weak, feather-torn necks drop to the ground," the dying swans are now awaiting—with their wings still spread—"spirit flight."[71] They symbolize another definition of existence at this moment, in other words, one consonant with the Aboriginal imaginary that has inevitably become intertwined with, but more importantly still extends beyond, a crisis of the human condition. Both in life and now in death, the swans are impelled by a temporal orientation that will return them to their ancestral community of the land.[72] In this sense, their extinction event should be thought of less as a vanishing of an entire species than a final questioning of the idea of extinction itself, coded as yet another structuring narrative of human development.[73] The incertitude that accompanies the fate of the swans thus becomes resonant not only with the multitude of lifeworlds that it paradoxically illuminates at the point of their vanquishing. It is also reflective of the dissonance of their temporal presence with the gratifications of progress that ensconce liberal-humanist thinking up until its very end. The swans ultimately express the oftentimes unsettling effort of apprehending the commons in a different way, one that is nevertheless imperative for its ethical commitment to life beyond the human.

"ACTS OF LOVE": LESSONS FROM A FEMINIST POETICS

The epilogue of *The Swan Book* reveals Oblivia to have likewise stayed true to her existence of temporal disjuncture. If her time had once been identified by Bella Donna as one that *"stands still,"* it is a time that will never again be set in motion.[74] We learn that Oblivia has somehow made it back to the swamp settlement with a single black swan eternally grieving for the rest of its decimated flock. She wanders the devastated terrain before her just as she has done before. Those who continue to return to the area report seeing and hearing the ghostly appearance of "the girl-wife, First Lady of whatnot, Oblivia Ethyl(ene)," and that even in her spectral form, she has "always stayed like a *wulumbarra*, teenage girl."[75] It is the abject trauma of being gang-raped "physically, emotionally, psychologically, statistically, randomly, historically, so fully," that has led Oblivia's time to be perpetually stranded as such.[76] In this durational sense, she remains endlessly steadfast in her resistance against liberal-nationalist ideals of development or growth, and is emblematic of a vexed point of irresolution in the pasts, present, and futures of Indigenous life. She manifests as an ethical witness to the exigences of settler-colonial histories, their ongoing social and political dispossession as well as the racial and sexual violence enacted on Aboriginal communities in Australia. But Oblivia has also come to be perceived as a mythical figure in a land now laid waste to. Her story is one that "might be the same story about some important person carrying a swan centuries ago, and it might be the same story in centuries to come when someone will carry a swan back to this ground where its story once lived."[77] For her existence that is marked by an event of temporal arrest, then, it is also one that transcends chronological limits in its constant unfolding across time. The story of Oblivia endures as a testament to ways of knowing and living that have been relegated beyond the limits of the human. As the novel suggests, the tellings and retellings of her narrative as centered on an Indigenous lifeworld beyond the human are "acts of love"—those demanding from us the ethical work of attention and imagination in the face of their own continuous erasure.[78]

It is such an act of love that I trace as a concluding note to this chapter, which circles back to the question of whose stories must be considered in the construction of another, different world and how best they might be relayed. I argue that this is an act located in a specific mode of feminist poetics that renders the storytelling impulse of the text as a world-making process. This mode of feminist poetics moreover resonates with the recantatory force of enchantment in this book, insofar as it similarly retrieves the residues of past knowledge to instill in them new patterns of meaning in and for the present moment. To illustrate its workings, I first return to Oblivia's deep-seated trauma of gang-rape as the principal site at which its gendered undercurrents are first made explicit. As earlier noted, Oblivia's rape has been read as representative of the invasive assault on Aboriginal bodies as construed historically, culturally, spiritually, geographically, and of course, sexually. This life-altering event becomes steeped not only in the unthinkable shame that surrounds the scandal of rape itself. It is also compounded by its indication of "the eternal reality of a legacy in brokenness," the chronic and inescapable cycle of futility that has, in the wake of settler colonialism in the country, implicated the lives of its Indigenous populations.[79] That Oblivia's biological parents elect to eventually disown their own daughter after giving up the search for her missing body, then, is a heartless but derivative turn of events. It is Bella Donna who decides to intervene and to continue to look for Oblivia, "to plow the ground with her own eyes, and to be totally ignorant of the ins and outs of family histories—their ground. She went on searching for the lost girl, losing all sense of time."[80] Bella Donna is this way portrayed as an intrusive and unwelcome character, who in a show of flagrant disrespect for the Aboriginal community, forcibly exposes what they had wished so desperately to forever conceal. For her imperviousness to the lived temporalities of these people that have long been exhausted by the incursions of settler-colonial history, however, Bella Donna will discover and then come to save Oblivia, who has been asleep for ten years in the eucalyptus tree.

The incriminating parallel that is often made between the troublemaking actions of this white European auntie and that of the colonizing treatment of Indigenous peoples in Australia does not escape me here.[81] Indeed, when Oblivia is retrieved from the bowels of the tree, she has lost most of her memory of the rape and the events prior, only to have it recreated by "what the old woman had chosen to tell her."[82] But if Oblivia becomes a captive audience to Bella Donna's stories about swans from other worlds, they are those same stories from which the Aboriginal girl will later draw for her own narrative to come into being. In many ways, Bella Donna throws a lifeline to Oblivia, both in her literal rescue of the missing girl and in her final words on the matter of rape: that it was "*not your fault.*"[83] Bella Donna's assertion of her version of the truth exposes the weaponized means of sexual power and control exerted on the young girl, and furthermore impedes its exacerbation through the processes of self-blame and guilt already visible in the Aboriginal community that has renounced Oblivia for this very reason. Through these actions, Bella Donna not only displays a willful disregard of fortified patterns of history and social life. She also positions Oblivia's existence on an alternative feminist genealogy that emerges from her dislocation of the "acts of descendancy" that have been rampant at the swamp.[84] Bella Donna thus constitutes the crucial feminist nexus from which Oblivia begins to disengage from the colonial and patriarchal orders of inheritance that would otherwise have replicated her ill-fated destiny. Another kind of life begins for Oblivia from this point of genealogical fracture, realized in the illegitimate alliances fostered with her adoptive white auntie and the flock of black swans that will soon come to find her.

I stay with Bella Donna's conscious reframing of Oblivia's rape as a political endeavor that can in fact be located at a deeper level of the narrative. More precisely, what the novel dramatizes through the abundance of stories that it recounts to the reader is the articulation of a more-than-human lifeworld that does not presume the ideological innocence of a gesture seeking to move beyond existing frameworks of epistemology. Just as Bella Donna compels a non-essentialized lineage of feminist think-ing that strings together the unlikely possibility of kindred beings, she is the purveyor of a prevailing mythology of swans that Oblivia will rewrite through a feminist lens. In the early days, the old white auntie was the *"storyteller of the swans,"* and Oblivia "a shadow that listened to the stories and secrets whis-pered into swan ears, and whatever she remembered, it was mostly poetry for swans."[85] If the text depends on the more prominent folklore that Bella Donna disseminates in order for the tale of the young Aboriginal girl and her flock of black swans to come into being, however, it is also through this process that the Oblivia's existence eventually attains its own mythical quality.[86] Put simply, Bella Donna's swan stories are the source material for the reimagined narrative of Oblivia's life-world. In this sense, the novel taps directly into Adrienne Rich's foundational feminist strategy of literary revisioning, interweaving non-Indigenous and oftentimes masculine renditions of swan poetry into its narrative "not to pass on a tradition," as Rich wrote, "but to break its hold over us."[87] Rich clarifies a feminist act of poetic resistance that is especially instrumental for transforming the discursive space that Oblivia occupies in the text. It involves not only a confrontation of the undeniable atrocities of sexual and colonial subjection, but also a reconstruction—by way of the ethical insistence on telling a familiar story in a vastly different light—of a condition of possibility for an alternative mode of living and being.

For the final time in this chapter, I return to the encounter between Oblivia and the black swan, a surprise meeting that, as we now know, occasions a commons beyond the human. I want to consider its telling in accordance with the feminist poetics engendered by the novel, which involves a means of dialogical knowledge production mobilized by a specifically intertextual capacity. More specifically, I take William Butler Yeats's celebrated sonnet "Leda and the Swan" as a point of departure for narrating the story of this reimagined commons. My analysis of the poem does not advance an all-encompassing claim to the textual politics of the novel, but rather a distilled example of the feminist strategy of literary revisioning at work in the telling of a commons beyond the human. In essence, the poem is a retelling of a well-known Greek myth: Zeus, the ruler of the gods, has taken on the guise of a swan and swooped down to

earth to seduce and rape the mortal girl Leda. Leda will lay two
eggs from this union that hatch into Helen, Clytemnestra, Cas-
tor, and Pollux, each of whom will have far-reaching consequences for the historical trajectory of Western development
and progress. Like *The Swan Book*, then, Yeats's poem grapples
with the central provocation of rape.

But the differences between the two texts, especially in the
initial encounter they each stage of an unsuspecting girl with the
imposition of a swan creature, are otherwise stark. If, as we know,
a black swan unexpectedly drops down from the sky in Wright's
novel to scrutinize Oblivia as its chosen one, these already unsettling dynamics are completely skewed with the startling event of
sexual violence that occurs in the opening lines of Yeats's poem.
There, the swan-god Zeus descends upon Leda with "A sudden
blow: the great wings beating still / Above the staggering girl,
her thighs caressed."[88] This dramatic description of rape is a pernicious assault to the imagination, achieving an irresistible pull of
the reader into its enveloping scene through the portrayal of a
ruthless attack on the swan's "helpless" victim.[89] What comes to
be borne out of Leda's rape is a disastrous chain of events that
occurs on a temporal and spatial scale unthinkable within the
limits of this shocking episode. Yeats follows the moment of
Zeus's climax—"A shudder in the loins engenders there"—with a
telescoping shift in vision; he alludes to a disorienting scene of
the breach and collapse of Troy from the distant future, with
"The broken wall, the burning roof and tower / And Agamemnon dead."[90] The onslaught of these successive disasters, which
would be formative for the inception of Western civilization, has
entirely been set in motion by the portentous sexual union
between the girl and swan-god.[91]

The transgressive scene of rape can be read as simply the
fulfillment of a kind of destiny in Yeats's poem, where its

perverse repercussions can be felt throughout the new age that it ushers in. In Wright's novel, however, Oblivia's rape by the gang of Aboriginal teenagers, while nevertheless pivotal for illuminating the sexual and colonial politics that indelibly structure its narrative, is marked as an antecedent event to the meeting between her and the black swan. If the encounter between Oblivia and her avian kin is similarly framed as an imminence of things to come, it is one that instead brings into being a newfound entanglement of existence that rewrites, rather than reinforces, the multiple violations that have been cleaved into the foundations of Oblivia's lifeworld. It resists the lure of the inevitable in favor of the speculative possibility of reimagination. In one sense, this becomes exemplified in the conception of the commons that materializes beyond human ways of thinking, and made visible in the ethical modalities of affiliation established between its constituent beings. The relational dynamics in the sonnet are complicated by the dangerous pleasures of sexual domination, where Leda will arguably establish a tenuous affinity with Zeus by feeling "the strange heart beating where it lies."[92] But their contradictory relationship, which has been rendered seductive by the voyeuristic undertones of Yeats's rhetoric, will invariably be tainted by the primary act of symbolic oppression. By contrast, there is no such ambivalence present in Oblivia's connection with the black swans in the novel. During their last migration back to the north, Oblivia watches and knows that she has found her swans because they "had found each other's heartbeat, the pulse humming through the land from one to the other, like the sound of distant clap sticks beating through ceremony, connecting together with the spirits, people and place of all times into one."[93] This particular relationship of a girl with her swans is not only sustained by a more-than-human ethics that carries the potential for surpassing the immanence of their current existence. It is moreover predicated on a living current of Aboriginal tradition—converging as a synchronous experience across space and time, comprising human and nonhuman beings, ancestral spirits, land, and country—without which their connection would soon falter.

In actuality, only two lines from Yeats's "Leda and the Swan" are reproduced in *The Swan Book*. Oblivia has since been taken from the swamp and is on a journey with Finch through a deserted landscape toward the southern city. They are accompanied by his three Aboriginal bodyguards. When the bodyguards suddenly disappear one day, Bella Donna's ghost, who has, too, been shadowing Oblivia during this time, goes ballistic. She is convinced that Finch has murdered them and fears that he will go on to kill Oblivia next. In the same vein, Bella Donna refers to the hordes of missing Aboriginal women and girls left to die in the bush: "[*u*]*nwept girls, all killed by their husbands*," unearthing in her monologue the aggravated precarity that these women—which includes Oblivia as symptomatic of this trend—have faced from within their own communities.[94] This violence can often be nothing short of lethal.[95] To this end, Bella Donna quotes directly from the Yeats's sonnet: "*So mastered by the brute blood of the air. . . . Before the indifferent beak could let her drop?*" These are lines that convey the ruthlessness of Leda's rape not only in her absolute domination by Zeus, but further in her inherent disposability once the misdeed is finished.[96] By reading this incomplete final stanza included as such in the novel, Leda can simply be presumed to be forsaken; she is underscored in her wretched powerlessness, in which her merciless "drop" by the swan-god lends a profound sense of foreboding for the future that awaits Oblivia's arranged marriage to Finch.

But what Wright has deliberately chosen to redact from Bella Donna's tirade is to me the most compelling line in Yeats's original poem, that even, and especially, in its very absence inscribes an "act of love" imperative to the operations of a feminist poetics. This is in fact a line that the only other two she includes straddle, which reads: "Did she put on his knowledge with his power."[97] Here, Yeats invites us to consider the agency accorded to Leda from her violent intercourse with the swangod, an appeal to the reader that instigates a tilt in the balance of power so deeply entrenched by its opening sequence. While it does suggest a recalibration of the positions assumed by Leda and Zeus in her purported theft of his almighty power and knowledge, the question that Yeats poses ultimately remains unanswered by the poem itself. It is instead taken up directly by the novel. Not by the character of Bella Donna, of course, who at that moment, remains understandably distraught by Finch's capture of Oblivia and the genuine possibility of the girl's death that she can no longer avert like before, but by Oblivia herself, who will live on to write her own story into being. In short, the story of the young Aboriginal girl and her flock of black swans that emerges to tell of their commons of collective existence is the affirmative response to Yeats's inquiry. This is to say that the missing line of his poem crystallizes in the novel as such a precise act of ethical world-making predicated on Indigenous histories and cultures. Its stakes have since shifted to attend to the abiding myth that endures at—and indeed, beyond—the epilogue of the novel. Here, Oblivia has certainly acquired a form of power and knowledge. It is a transformative force that does not merely invert the binaries of dominant thinking, but rather, in its specific debt to the strategy of feminist revisioning, encompasses the capacity to reimagine the plurality of narratives that have calcified around those beings and things categorized into subgenres of humanity.

CODA

Textual Power and Transformative Poetics

Feminism Enchanted has sought to reveal the value of literary inquiry for practicing feminist critique today. The measure of this value is imaginative rather than instrumental, which is to say that the literary mode of enchantment that this book has proposed and deployed is one that compels us to think more expansively but one that stops short of telling us what to do. This is a way of reading that, in its encompassing refusal to be guided by the logic of progress, does not ultimately prescribe any course of political action. Instead, the dynamic of enchantment has simply reckoned with the fact that our interpretive frameworks might never rise to the occasion of progressive politics. In so doing, it has transformed how we inhabit the structure of an encounter with the intellectual project of feminism. And this alone is enough, at least in the context of this book—for us to be given pause to more reflexively consider what we want from the methods we use to make sense of the world, especially when the knowledge they uncover about the world has the tendency to betray our hopes of ushering it into a better future.

Throughout this book, my intention has not been to decry the agency of feminist critical practice. To the contrary, I have aimed to demonstrate its newfound vitality when it is aligned

with the potential of literature at this time. Indeed, it is literature and literary criticism that have shown feminist critique
that there are other forms that it might assume, other paths that
it might pursue, or other reasons for its existence that are not
predicated on the immediacy of producing concrete material
change in the world. And the itinerary of textual lifeworlds
that this book has charted in its chapters has reflected just
this: that the very experience of inhabiting a realm of a different
time and space, each constitutive of its own unfamiliar—and
sometimes impossible—coordinates of belonging, counts, too, as
a viable alternative for understanding not only feminism but also
the world around us. For what these discursive worlds run up
against are the limits of our own; they render fraught the purpose
and meaning of our lives as so profoundly shaped by governing
ideologies that we would not have otherwise come to question.

In the introduction of this book, I gestured toward a radical
horizon of feminist politics that enchantment makes visible,
which follows from my quest for a more capacious definition of
feminism. Despite my insistence that feminist critique should
not be bound to the necessity of political progress, then, my
contention has not been that our critical methods cannot, or
should not, act in this world. Rather, it has been to advocate for
a particular mode of reading and writing that is propelled by
the force of poetic expression, a force that operates unexpectedly in and on the world. This does not just refer to any form of
textual practice, therefore, but one that must enlist the unique
ability of the literary to break open the world as we know it. In
this sense, the literary has unlocked a different register for theorizing feminism, which does not merely perform the rhetorical
move of reproducing what we already know. Instead, it draws
on the vocabulary of a poetic language that is inexplicable, otherworldly, and strange; it seethes with a vital and resistant

power that shifts the parameters of our existing reality. It is this other kind of power that the literary mode of enchantment has unleashed in this book, thus modeling an example that future approaches of feminist critique might aspire to follow.

This question of power has been thoroughly inscribed in the political, aesthetic, and methodological stakes of *Feminism Enchanted* and deserves a final unpacking at the close of the book. I want to do this through a brief reading of Audre Lorde's famous, harrowing poem "Power," in which she begins with a provocation about the distinction between rhetoric and poetry: "The difference between poetry and rhetoric / is being ready to kill / yourself / instead of your children."[1] Lorde's poem was written as a response to the 1973 acquittal of a white police officer of the murder of a ten-year-old Black boy named Clifford Glover.[2] Taken in this context, the poem fundamentally rejects the idea that art might exist outside of the actual world, that it might be exempt from responding to the unspeakable violence and suffering that mark our current reality. After all, the basic premise of the poem concerns a matter of life and death—the unending assault of police brutality on Black lives, which has only ever resulted in the blatant injustice of impunity and lack of accountability. Several decades after its publication, Lorde's poem invokes a regrettably timely, and ostensibly timeless, protest against this relentless history that continues to unfold in the present.

This recursive event of racial violence returns us to the scene of the poem's initial positioning of poetry against rhetoric; in many ways, its repetitive nature can be argued to compose the very reason for Lorde's privileging of the former over the latter. The poem underscores a danger to the utilitarian function of rhetoric that resides in its manipulation of language to argue and to persuade others, that inheres in its twisting of fact and logic to better serve its purposes. In this vein, we are alerted to the instance of the lone Black woman who had served on the jury at the trial of the aforementioned policeman, who said of the eleven other white male jurors, "'They convinced me' meaning / they had dragged her 4'10" black Woman's frame / over the hot coals / of four centuries of white male approval / until she let go / the first real power she ever had."[3] In these lines, the poem demonstrates how a Black woman is made to concede to a perspective of white supremacy; this is an effort facilitated by a rhetorical sleight of hand that masks its insidious line of reasoning. Rhetoric cannot simply be construed as a seductive vehicle for language, then, but rather poses a circling threat in its ready distortion and weaponization by perverse logics of violence. What the poem therefore suggests is that any project of transformative justice must not rely on rhetoric to defend itself, because rhetoric can so easily be emptied of its original meaning and then co-opted by the status quo. Its use carries the risk of reproducing the same oppression that such a project might seek to overcome. And therein also lies the reason behind history repeating itself. For to engage in rhetoric is to be trapped in a discursive paradigm of violence, of which—to refer back to the opening stanza of the poem here—literal children have been the collateral damage. There is no justice that might be served by the employment of rhetoric, only the perpetuation of bloodshed.

It is against this backdrop that the poem presents its case for the use of poetry. Throughout the poem, the speaker expresses their incandescent rage for the atrocities that have been committed. This explains their initial attempt to "make power out of hatred and destruction."[4] But the speaker comes to the realization that such a power only transacts in the language of rhetoric, one that—as we already know—only manifests as a force for further wreckage. The poem in fact stages the disturbing consequence of this in its final stanza, where its speaker imagines themself raping and murdering an elderly white woman. As the speaker admits, then: "But unless I learn to use / the difference between poetry and rhetoric / my power too will run corrupt as poisonous mold / or lie limp and useless as an unconnected wire."[5] With these lines we return to the question of power, which must be channeled through the circuits of poetry if it is to be considered a source of freedom and emancipation at all. Of course, what underpins this claim are the intrinsic properties of poetic language—a language that does not merely reflect reality but prompts us to go beyond it; a language that does not merely convey meaning but rather embodies meaning in its very form; a language that must be experienced even before it might make sense. In these ways, and as opposed to rhetoric, poetry cannot be exploited by violent apparatuses of extraction or appropriation. But as the poem has also warned us, the radical power of poetic language demands the high-stakes risk of abandoning all established norms of knowing and being as its conditions of possibility; it warrants assuming the almost unthinkable stance of "being ready to kill / yourself."[6] Poetry requires us to give up all that we know, including the habits of thought that we have developed not only to perceive, but also to be able to live in, this world.

As feminist theorists, what are we ready to give up for the sake of a different future? How might the critical methods that we create and mobilize in the name of feminism be those imbued with a power that does not simply enact a repetition of the same? In her influential call for dominant accounts of feminism to be told differently, Clare Hemmings writes that feminist theorists must pay closer attention to the "amenability of our own stories, narrative constructs, and grammatical forms to discursive uses of gender and feminism we might otherwise wish to disentangle ourselves from if history is not simply to repeat itself."[7] Hemmings points out that much of the rhetoric that we have used to understand and to define feminism has now calcified into standard patterns of knowledge, and in the process become too easily co-opted by emerging antifeminist regimes.[8] In the face of this reality, the task now for feminist theorists is therefore to cultivate sharper and more agile tactics that might still uphold feminism's testament to social justice. *Feminism Enchanted* has proposed a turning to the possibilities of poetic language as one such way forward, an embrace of its difficult but necessary power.

NOTES

INTRODUCTION: A LITERARY MODE OF ENCHANTMENT

1. Although my project focuses primarily on enchantment in relation to literary texts, it makes no claim for their exceptionalism as artistic objects that arouse enchantment. For discussions on other aesthetic media such as film and other forms of visual art that are just as likely to foster a state of enchantment, see for example Rita Felski, "Enchantment," in *Uses of Literature* (Malden, MA: Blackwell Publishing, 2008), 51–76; and David Morgan, *Images at Work: The Material Culture of Enchantment* (Oxford: Oxford University Press, 2018).

2. This story of feminism's divergence from literature as a key framework of feminist knowledge production has been documented by several scholars. See Susan Gubar, "What Ails Feminist Criticism?," *Critical Inquiry* 24, no. 4 (Summer 1998): 878–902; Sinead McDermott, "Notes on the Afterlife of Feminist Criticism," *PMLA* 121, no. 5 (October 2006): 1729–34; Toril Moi, "'I Am Not a Woman Writer': About Women, Literature, and Feminist Theory Today," *Feminist Theory* 9, no. 3 (2008): 259–71; and Naomi Schor, "Preface," in *Bad Objects: Essays Popular and Unpopular* (Durham, NC: Duke University Press, 1995), iv–xvi.

3. For more on how the narrative of progress has become such a structuring framework for feminist theory, see in particular Clare Hemmings, *Why Stories Matter: The Political Grammar of Feminist Theory*

(Durham, NC, Duke University Press, 2011); and Robyn Wiegman, *Object Lessons* (Durham, NC: Duke University Press, 2012).

4. See, for example, Hemmings, *Why Stories Matter*; Jennifer Nash, *Black Feminism Reimagined: After Intersectionality* (Durham, NC: Duke University Press, 2019); and Wiegman, *Object Lessons*. More specifically, this tendency is what Robyn Wiegman would more broadly call the "field imaginary" of feminist studies, its psychic life as shaped by the crosscurrents of political desire. To define this term, she draws on Donald E. Pease, who uses what he calls a "field-Imaginary" to designate a disciplinary unconscious; see, respectively, Wiegman, *Object Lessons*, 12, and Pease, "New Americanists: Revisionist Interventions into the Canon," *boundary 2* 17, no. 1 (Spring 1990): 1–37.

5. Barbara Johnson, *The Feminist Difference: Literature, Psychoanalysis, Race, and Gender* (Cambridge, MA: Harvard University Press, 1998), 13.

6. *Oxford English Dictionary*, s.v. "enchant, v., sense 2.a," July 2023, https://doi.org/10.1093/OED/9235991177.

7. My thinking on enchantment here, on its affective force that holds a distinctively ethical potential, is influenced by the work of Jane Bennett, who has argued that the mood of enchantment is "valuable for ethical life"; Bennett, *The Enchantment of Modern Life: Attachments, Crossings, and Ethics* (Princeton, NJ: Princeton University Press, 2001), 3.

8. In many ways, this claim takes its cue from Robyn Wiegman's call for a greater attentiveness to the rift between the ways we seek to transform this world and the methods we have formulated to think it, insofar as "objects and analytic categories are always incommensurate with the political desire invested in them"; Wiegman, *Object Lessons*, 42.

9. Wiegman, *Object Lessons*, 35. Robyn Wiegman elsewhere discusses the possibility of inhabiting feminism as a living thing complete with its own vitality; see Wiegman, "The Intimacy of Critique: Ruminations on Feminism as a Living Thing," *Feminist Theory* 11, no. 1 (2010): 79–84.

10. *Oxford English Dictionary*, s.v. "charm, n.1, Etymology," July 2023, https://doi.org/10.1093/OED/5242650674.

11. For further explorations on the relation between charm and poetry, see Northrop Frye, *Anatomy of Criticism: Four Essays* (1957; Princeton, NJ: Princeton University Press, 2000), and *Spiritus Mundi: Essays on*

Literature, Myth, and Society (Bloomington: Indiana University Press, 1976); Herbert F. Tucker, "After Magic: Modern Charm in History, Theory, and Practice," *New Literary History* 48, no. 1 (Winter 2017): 103–22; and Andrew Welsh, *Roots of Lyric: Primitive Poetry and Modern Poetics* (Princeton, NJ: Princeton University Press, 1978). On the sonic properties of enchantment, see Laura Zebuhr, "Sound Enchantment: The Case of Henry David Thoreau," *New Literary History* 48, no. 3 (2017): 581–603.

12. Frye, *Anatomy of Criticism*, 271. Northrop Frye makes a distinction between this manifestation of rhythm—one that he identifies in the connection between "charm" and *melos* (music)—from those that can be found in meter or in prose.

13. Frye, *Spiritus Mundi*, 124–26. Northrop Frye presents the lullaby as a kind of charm poetry that causes one to fall asleep, and the more sinister example of the siren song through which the loss of free will precedes a certain death.

14. See the third-century BCE poet Theocritus's *Idyll II* for an early literary testament to this, in which the goddess Hecate is invoked for her magical power. Theocritus, *The Greek Bucolic Poets*, trans. J. M. Edmonds (Cambridge, MA: Harvard University Press, 1991).

15. On the recursive use of old or long-dismissed ideas to think the feminist present, see Lucy Nicholas and Shelley Budgeon, "Introduction: 'Remembering Feminist Theory Forward,'" *Feminist Theory* 22, no. 2 (2021): 159–64. The dynamic of repetition is also resonant with the feminist methodology of "re-turning" to create new forms of knowledge; see Christina Hughes and Celia Lury, "Re-Turning Feminist Methodologies: From a Social to an Ecological Epistemology," *Gender and Education* 25, no. 6 (2013): 786–99.

16. For the definition of the operative term *recant* in the latter statement I make here, see *Oxford English Dictionary*, s.v. "recant (v.1), sense I.1.a," December 2023, https://doi.org/10.1093/OED/1405722181.

17. In a sense, this recalls Judith Butler's foundational claim about performativity and its operative condition of repetition. With the crucial factor of difference as incrementally introduced, performativity comes to constitute a strategic form of feminist resistance; see Butler, "Performative Acts and Gender Constitution: An Essay in Phenomenology

and Feminist Theory," *Theatre Journal* 40, no. 4 (1988): 519–31, and *Gender Trouble: Feminism and the Subversion of Identity* (New York: Routledge, 1990).

18. Sara Ahmed, *Living a Feminist Life* (Durham, NC: Duke University Press, 2017), 12.

19. This is a method that is in fact consistent across many of Sara Ahmed's works, as she herself points to her earlier considerations of terms like *will* and *happiness*; see Ahmed, *The Promise of Happiness* (Durham, NC: Duke University Press, 2010), and *Willful Subjects* (Durham, NC: Duke University Press, 2014).

20. In this sense, my use of "infrastructure" can be said to be loosely based on Lauren Berlant's conceptual understanding of the term, in which infrastructure is "not identical to system or structure," but rather defined by the "movement or patterning of social form . . . the living mediation of what organizes life: the lifeworld of structure" (393); Berlant, "The Commons: Infrastructures for Troubling Times," *Environment and Planning D: Society and Space* 34, no. 3 (2016): 393–419. See also Berlant, *On the Inconvenience of Other People* (Durham, NC: Duke University Press, 2022), 19–26.

21. Homer, *The Odyssey*, trans. Emily Wilson (New York: Norton, 2017), 12.38–39.

22. Homer, 12.45–46.

23. It is worth noting that the portrayal of the Sirens in modern and contemporary forms of media and culture has rather inaccurately taken on a sexually seductive quality, especially in the conflation of the Siren with the iconography of the mermaid that became ubiquitous in the sixteenth and seventeenth centuries and beyond. See the *OED* on this confusion: *Oxford English Dictionary*, s.v. "siren, n., sense 2," September 2023, https://doi.org/10.1093/OED/1076664955. See also Emily Wilson's introduction to her translation of *The Odyssey*, in which she suggests that enchantment—here understood to be analogous to deceit—is not necessarily presented as an inherently feminine practice, nor even a detrimental one.

24. The idea of monstrosity has a long history in feminist thought, with many feminist scholars having theorized its significance along psychoanalytic lines of inquiry. See, as key examples, Rosi Braidotti,

"Mothers, Monsters, and Machines," in *Nomadic Subjects: Embodiment and Sexual Difference in Contemporary Feminist Theory*, 2nd ed. (New York: Columbia University Press, 2011), 213–44; Barbara Creed, *The Monstrous-Feminine: Film, Feminism, Psychoanalysis* (New York: Routledge, 1993); and Mary Russo, *The Female Grotesque: Risk, Excess, Modernity* (New York: Routledge, 1995), as well as Julia Kristeva, *The Powers of Horror: An Essay on Abjection*, trans. Leon S. Roudiez (New York: Columbia University Press, 1980) as a notable reference. On the more recent designation of "trans species," see Harlan Weaver, "Trans Species," *TSQ: Transgender Studies Quarterly*, special issue "Postposttranssexual: Key Concepts for a Twenty-First-Century Transgender Studies," ed. Paisley Currah and Susan Stryker, 1, nos. 1–2 (2014): 253–54.

25. By characterizing female sexuality as such, I allude to Carole Vance and her landmark edited collection on the same topic; see Vance, ed., *Pleasure and Danger: Exploring Female Sexuality* (New York: Routledge and Kegan Paul, 1984).

26. Max Weber, *From Max Weber: Essays in Sociology*, trans. and ed. H. H. Gerth and C. Wright Mills (New York: Oxford University Press, 1946), 155.

27. For a succinct definition of Weberian disenchantment, see Ernest Gellner, *Culture, Identity, and Politics* (Cambridge: Cambridge University Press, 1987), 153, which describes it as "the Faustian purchase of cognitive, technological, and administrative power, by the surrender of our previous meaningful, humanly suffused, humanly responsive, if often also menacing or capricious world."

28. See Max Weber, *The Protestant Ethic and the Spirit of Capitalism*, trans. Talcott Parsons (1930; New York: Routledge, 1992).

29. As representative of this, see Bennett, *Enchantment of Modern Life*; Bruno Bettelheim, *The Uses of Enchantment: The Meaning and Importance of Fairy Tales* (London: Thames and Hudson, 1976); Morris Berman, *The Reenchantment of the World* (Ithaca, NY: Cornell University Press, 1981); Ann Burlein and Jackie Orr, "Introduction: The Practice of Enchantment: Strange Allures," *WSQ: Women's Studies Quarterly* 40, nos. 3–4 (2012): 13–23; Jason Crawford, *Allegory and Enchantment: An Early Modern Poetics* (Oxford: Oxford University Press, 2017); Saurabh

Dube, ed., *Enchantments of Modernity: Empire, Nation, Globalization* (New York: Routledge, 2008); Simon During, *Modern Enchantments: The Cultural Power of Secular Magic* (Cambridge, MA: Harvard University Press, 2002); Gordon Graham, *The Re-Enchantment of the World: Art Versus Religion* (Oxford: Oxford University Press, 2007); Max Horkheimer and Theodore W. Adorno, *Dialectic of Enlightenment*, trans. Edmund Jephcott and ed. Gunzelin Schmid Noeri (1944; Stanford, CA: Stanford University Press, 2002); Joshua Landy and Michael Saler, eds., *The Re-Enchantment of the World: Secular Magic in a Rational Age* (Stanford, CA: Stanford University Press, 2009); George Levine, *Darwin Loves You: Natural Selection and the Re-Enchantment of the World* (Princeton, NJ: Princeton University Press, 2008); David Morgan, "Enchantment, Disenchantment, Re-Enchantment," in *Re-Enchantment*, ed. James Elkins and David Morgan (New York: Routledge, 2009), 3–22; Michael Saler, *As If: Modern Enchantment and the Literary Pre-History of Virtual Reality* (Oxford: Oxford University Press, 2012); Mark A. Schneider, *Culture and Enchantment* (Chicago: University of Chicago Press, 1993); Michelle Sizemore, *American Enchantment: Rituals of the People in the Post-Revolutionary World* (Oxford: Oxford University Press, 2018); and Bernard Stiegler, *The Re-Enchantment of the World: The Value of Spirit Against Industrial Populism*, trans. Trevor Arthur (London: Bloomsbury Academic, 2014). For an extensive historiographic overview of modernity and enchantment, see also Michael Saler, "Modernity and Enchantment: A Historiographic Review," *American Historical Review* III, no. 3 (2006): 692–716.

30. For a foundational overview, see Mary Daly, *Gyn/Ecology: The Metaethics of Radical Feminism* (Boston: Beacon Press, 1987).

31. For a brief explanation of the phenomenon of witch-hunting being the result of a fear of witches *as* women, see Silvia Federici, *Witches, Witch-Hunting, and Women* (Oakland, CA: PM Press, 2018).

32. Following work in the 1970s by socialist feminists such as Mariarosa Dalla Costa and Selma James, Silvia Federici focuses on the gendered division of labor, especially as underscored in the realm of social reproduction, as a key factor that contributed to the rise of the capitalist order. See also Federici, *Revolution at Point Zero: Housework, Reproduction, and Feminist Struggle* (Oakland, CA: PM Press, 2012).

33. Silvia Federici, *Caliban and the Witch: Women, the Body, and Primitive Accumulation* (New York: Autonomedia, 2004), 11.

34. On the epistemic complexities of narrating history in the wake of this universalizing gesture of humanistic thinking, see Dipesh Chakrabarty, *Provincializing Europe: Postcolonial Thought and Historical Difference* (Princeton, NJ: Princeton University Press, 2000).

35. On this contested relationship between modernity and colonialism, see, especially, Chakrabarty, *Provincializing Europe*; Saurabh Dube, ed., *Enchantments of Modernity: Empire, Nation, Globalization* (New York: Routledge, 2008); and Saurabh Dube and Ishita Banerjee-Dube, eds., *Unbecoming Modern: Colonialism, Modernity, Colonial Modernities* (New York: Routledge, 2019).

36. David Scott makes this very point in his suggestion that "the birth of humanism . . . is simultaneously the initiation of Europe's colonial project"; Scott, "The Re-Enchantment of Humanism: An Interview with Sylvia Wynter," *small axe* 4, no. 2 (2000): 119–20.

37. Sylvia Wynter, "Unsettling the Coloniality of Being/Power/Truth/Freedom: Towards the Human, After Man, Its Overrepresentation—An Argument," *CR: The New Centennial Review* 3, no. 3 (2003): 264. Wynter more broadly argues here that the epistemological ruptures marking Renaissance and Enlightenment thinking can be attributed to their projects of colonialism.

38. Weber, *Essays in Sociology*, 139.

39. There has moreover been a recent return to the idea of enchantment through the earlier work of scholars such as Jane Bennett. See, for example, Stine Krøijer and Cecilie Rubow, "Introduction: Enchanted Ecologies and Ethics of Care," *Environmental Humanities* 14, no. 2 (July 2022): 375–84. And in a related sense the rhetoric of "re-enchantment" has gained traction, as evidenced by the work of Silvia Federici, *Re-Enchanting the World: Feminism and the Politics of the Commons* (New York: PM Press, 2018); Maria Sachiko Cecire, *Re-Enchanted: The Rise of Children's Fantasy Literature in the Twentieth Century* (Minneapolis: University of Minnesota Press, 2019); Mayfair Yang, *Re-Enchanting Modernity: Ritual Economy and Society in Wenzhou, China* (Durham, NC: Duke University Press, 2020).

40. This is a claim that broadly reflects the work of scholars who have written about enchantment in its potential for developing more ethical attachments to the world, and as a way of countering the general attitude of disenchantment that has permeated the dominant critical habits of the twentieth century. See, in this regard, Bennett, *Enchantment of Modern Life*; Akeel Bilgrami, *Secularism, Identity, and Enchantment* (Cambridge, MA: Harvard University Press, 2014); and Felski, *Uses of Literature*.

41. For some scholarship on the encompassing notion of wonder, see Lorraine Daston and Katherine Park, *Wonders and the Order of Nature, 1150–1750* (New York: Zone Books, 1998); Philip Fisher, *Wonder, the Rainbow, and the Aesthetics of Rare Experiences* (Cambridge, MA: Harvard University Press, 1998); and more recently, Genevieve Lloyd, *Reclaiming Wonder: After the Sublime* (Edinburgh: Edinburgh University Press, 2018), and Tulasi Srinivas, *The Cow in the Elevator: An Anthropology of Wonder* (Durham, NC: Duke University Press, 2018).

42. In this sense, my definition of *enchantment* differs from Jane Bennett's, who conflates both terms in her claim that enchantment "entails a state of wonder"; Bennett, *Enchantment of Modern Life*, 3.

43. That said, it is worth noting that wonder has in fact been a guiding disposition for the exploration and therefore domination of otherness, especially in the Renaissance era and beyond. For a brief overview, see Laura Ogden, *Loss and Wonder at the World's End* (Durham, NC: Duke University Press, 2021).

44. *Oxford English Dictionary*, s.v. "wonder (*n.*), sense II.7.a," December 2023, https://doi.org/10.1093/OED/9995260026.

45. Katherine McKittrick, *Demonic Grounds: Black Women and the Cartographies of Struggle* (Minneapolis: University of Minnesota Press, 2006), 94.

46. Katherine McKittrick also writes elsewhere on the open-ended possibilities of a Black and anticolonial method of study that is invariably sustained by wonder; see McKittrick, *Dear Science and Other Stories* (Durham, NC: Duke University Press, 2021).

47. Broadly speaking, Sara Ahmed theorizes emotions in their capacity for shaping wider social and political collectives of existence. See

also Ahmed, "Affective Economies," *Social Text* 22, no. 2 (2004): 117–39.

48. Sara Ahmed predicates her initial conception of wonder on one of René Descartes's passions.

49. Sara Ahmed, *The Cultural Politics of Emotion* (New York: Routledge, 2004), 182.

50. Ahmed, *Cultural Politics of Emotion*, 182.

51. Jennifer Nash, *Black Feminism Reimagined: After Intersectionality* (Durham, NC: Duke University Press, 2019), 12. Nash points out that the introspective turn in feminism can in fact be traced further back to several now-canonical reflections on the historical formation of women's studies as an academic institution. These collections have focused on the complex political, ethical, and ideological ramifications for feminist critique that have occurred as a result. See Elizabeth Lapovsky Kennedy and Agatha Meryl Beins, eds., *Women's Studies for the Future: Foundations, Interrogations, Politics* (New Brunswick, NJ: Rutgers University Press, 2005); Joan Wallach Scott, ed., *Women's Studies on the Edge* (Durham, NC: Duke University Press, 2008); and Robyn Wiegman, ed., *Women's Studies on Its Own: A Next Wave Reader in Institutional Change* (Durham, NC: Duke University Press, 2002).

52. For a notable example in feminist philosophy, see Sarah Tyson, *Where Are the Women? Why Expanding the Archive Makes Philosophy Better* (New York: Columbia University Press, 2018). Tyson reflects that many of the prevailing feminist strategies of reclaiming philosophy are insufficient for transforming the structures of existing philosophical practices, insofar as they often come to reproduce the same forms of exclusionary violence.

53. Hemmings, *Why Stories Matter*, 2.

54. Wiegman, *Object Lessons*, 21.

55. This framework is in line with Clare Hemmings's notable invitation to feminist theorists to experiment with "how we might tell stories differently." See Hemmings, *Why Stories Matter*, 16.

56. Felski, *Uses of Literature*, 19.

57. Felski, 6.

58. For work that has been representative of the postcritical turn, see Elizabeth S. Anker and Rita Felski, eds., *Critique and Postcritique*

(Durham, NC: Duke University Press, 2017); Stephen Best and Sharon Marcus, "Surface Reading: An Introduction," *Representations* 108, no. 1 (2009): 1–21; Rita Felski, *The Limits of Critique* (Chicago: University of Chicago Press, 2015); Heather Love, "Close but Not Deep: Literary Ethics and the Descriptive Turn," *New Literary History* 41, no. 2 (2010): 371–91; and Paul Saint-Amour, "Weak Theory, Weak Modernism," *Modernism/modernity* 25 no. 3 (2018): 437–59.

59. Along these lines, this is a stance that has often been cited as finding its origins in Paul Riceour's exposition of the "hermeneutics of suspicion" or Eve Kosofsky Sedgwick's diagnosis of "paranoid reading."

60. Since then, various critics have debated the usefulness of postcritical approaches and more, in what Rita Felski has elsewhere called the "method wars"; see Felski, "Introduction," *New Literary History*, special issue, ed. Rita Felski, 45, no. 2 (2014): v–xi.

61. Recalling the affective investments of various modes of postcritique, David Kurnick has argued that these debates on literary method have offered, at the end of the day, "not new ways to interpret texts but new ways to feel about ourselves when we do"; see Kurnick, "A Few Lies: Queer Theory and Our Method Melodramas," *ELH* 87, no. 2 (2020): 351.

62. More recently, the debates over method in literary studies have moved into thinking about what exactly is meant by close reading as a practice of literary study. See, for example, Elaine Auyong, "Becoming Sensitive: Literary Study and Learning to Notice," *PMLA* 138, no. 1 (2023): 158–64; and Jonathan Kramnick, "Criticism and Truth," *Critical Inquiry* 47, no. 2 (2021): 218–40.

63. Gubar, "What Ails Feminist Criticism?," 880.

64. For Robyn Wiegman's powerful response to Gubar's contentions, see Wiegman, "What Ails Feminist Criticism? A Second Opinion," *Critical Inquiry* 25, no. 2 (1999): 362–79.

65. Naomi Schor adopts a contrarian perspective by claiming her interest in critical objects that have circulated within the "carefully policed precincts of the academy." For her, these objects include terms such as *essentialism, universalism*, and more; see Schor, *Bad Objects* (Durham, NC: Duke University Press, 1995), xv. See also a special issue on the

"bad object" of literariness, in *differences: A Journal of Feminist Cultural Studies* 28, no. 1 (2017): iii–iv.

66. To this end, there is a dwelling with and a repurposing of these bad feelings here, with the assumption that they might constitute a site of transformative possibility. In a related vein, see Hil Malatino, *Side Affects: On Being Trans and Feeling Bad* (Minneapolis: University of Minnesota Press, 2022), on such a reclamation of the bad feelings intrinsic to trans experience.

67. Here I echo Barbara Christian's decades-old insistence on training our focus on Black feminist literary and cultural production as a strategic undertaking against totalizing formations of academic knowledge. Through its focus on the literary, this book contends that Christian's claim is one that has gained new and urgent meaning in the context of contemporary feminist scholarship. See Christian, "The Race for Theory," *Cultural Critique* 6 (1987): 51–63.

68. Schor, *Bad Objects*, xiv; emphasis in original.

69. Of course, my use of "use" in this statement is a reference to Rita Felski's exploration of the uses of literature and literary criticism; see Felski, *Uses of Literature*, and "Introduction." But it is also a nod to Sara Ahmed's suggestion of "queer use," insofar as it subverts and radically expands the narrower, original "use" of literature in feminist studies to something that actively makes visible marginalized lifeworlds of race, gender, and sexuality; see Ahmed, *What's the Use? On the Uses of Use* (Durham, NC: Duke University Press, 2019).

70. Paul Ricoeur, *Hermeneutics and the Human Sciences: Essays on Language, Action and Interpretation*, ed., trans., and intro. John B. Thompson (Cambridge: Cambridge University Press, 1981), 104, emphasis in original. More precisely, Ricoeur's theory of interpretation is shaped by a Heideggerian definition of a structure of being-in-the-world that is projected by the text.

71. Ricoeur, *Hermeneutics*, 104.

72. Ricoeur, 104. Once again, Paul Ricoeur borrows from Martin Heidegger to formulate the state of being-in-the-world in this context.

73. Paul Ricoeur writes that everyday reality thus becomes "metamorphised by what could be called the imaginative variations which literature carries out on the real"; see Ricoeur, *Hermeneutics*, 104.

74. Robyn Wiegman writes about textual inhabitation as an expression of feminist critique; see Wiegman, "Intimacy of Critique," 83. Here, I imbue this term with a specifically literary connotation.

I. UNDERWATER WITH THE FEMINIST WAVES

1. William Shakespeare, *The Tempest*, ed. Peter Hulme and William H. Sherman (New York: Norton, 2019), 2.1.374–75.
2. Shakespeare, 2.1.395–400.
3. Much has been said about the spell-like form and structure of Ariel's song. See, for example, John Tyree Fain, "Some Notes on Ariel's Song," *Shakespeare Quarterly* 19, no. 4 (1968): 329–32; and Andrew Welsh, *Roots of Lyric: Primitive Poetry and Modern Poetics* (Princeton, NJ: Princeton University Press, 1978), 155–56.
4. For a brilliant reading of how Ariel's description of Alonso's body offers a starting point for thinking about a minoritarian and anticolonial conception of human agency in the eighteenth- and nineteenth-century American tropics, see Monique Allewaert, *Ariel's Ecology: Plantations, Personhood, and Colonialism in the American Tropics* (Minneapolis: University of Minnesota Press, 2013).
5. Shakespeare, *Tempest*, 2.1.399–400.
6. By focusing on the physical conditions of the ocean as a starting point for another way of knowing, I am in direct conversation with Melody Jue, who develops a methodology of "conceptual displacement" that is brought about by the material environment of the sea. I will continue to engage Jue's work in the later parts of this chapter. See Jue, *Wild Blue Media: Thinking Through Seawater* (Durham, NC: Duke University Press, 2020).
7. Shakespeare, *Tempest*, 2.1.395.
8. For an approach to thinking with the sea in all its material and phenomenological specificity, see Philip Steinberg and Kimberly Peters, "Wet Ontologies, Fluid Spaces: Giving Depth to Volume Through Oceanic Thinking," *Environment and Planning D: Society and Space* 33, no. 2 (2015): 247–64.
9. Shakespeare, *Tempest*, 2.1.398.
10. For a historical examination of how the wave metaphor has come to be a figure for thinking about more encompassing phenomena of social

change, see Stefan Helmreich, "Wave Theory ~ Social Theory," *Public Culture* 32, no. 2 (2020): 287–326.

11. For some recent works that have discussed the relevance of the wave metaphor for thinking feminism, see Aalya Ahmad, "Feminism Beyond the Waves," *Briarpatch Magazine*, June 30, 2015, https://briarpatchmagazine.com/articles/view/feminism-beyond-the-waves/; Hokulani K. Aikau et al., eds., *Feminist Waves, Feminist Generations: Life Stories from the Academy* (Minneapolis: University of Minnesota Press, 2007); Stacy Gillis et al., eds., *Third Wave Feminism: A Critical Exploration* (Basingstoke, UK: Palgrave Macmillan, 2007); Stefan Helmreich, "The Genders of Waves," *Women's Studies Quarterly* 45, nos. 1–2 (2017): 29–51; Nancy A. Hewitt, ed., *No Permanent Waves: Recasting Histories of U.S. Feminism* (New Brunswick, NJ: Rutgers University Press, 2010); Nancy A. Hewitt, "Feminist Frequencies: Regenerating the Wave Metaphor," *Feminist Studies* 38, no. 3 (2012): 658–80; Kathleen A. Laughlin et al., "Is It Time to Jump Ship? Historians Rethink the Waves Metaphor," *Feminist Formations* 22 no. 1 (2010): 76–135; Dawn Llewelyn, *Reading, Feminism, and Spirituality: Troubling the Waves* (Basingstoke, UK: Palgrave Macmillan, 2015); Linda Nicholson, "Feminism in 'Waves': Useful Metaphor or Not?," *New Politics* 12, no. 4 (2010): 34–39; Jo Reger, "Finding a Place in History: The Discursive Legacy of the Wave Metaphor and Contemporary Feminism," *Feminist Studies* 43, no. 1 (2017): 193–221; and Jo Reger, ed. *Different Wavelengths: Studies of the Contemporary Women's Movement* (New York: Routledge, 2005).

12. Reger, "Finding a Place in History," 194.

13. See Joshua Bennett, "'Beyond the Vomiting Dark': Toward a Black Hydropoetics," in *Ecopoetics: Essays in the Field*, ed. Angela Hume and Gillian Osborne (Iowa City: University of Iowa Press, 2018), 102–17. Drawing on the work of Marcus Rediker, Bennett confronts what has largely been a tetracentric view of history and seeks to challenge its dominance by turning toward the sea.

14. These waves are also known as internal gravity waves, or deep-sea underwater waves. They exist as a complementary phenomenon to the more familiar surface gravity waves that break on the shore. See Matthew H. Alford et al., "The Formation and Fate of Internal Waves in the South China Sea," *Nature* 521 (2015): 65–69; L. Pomar et al.,

"Internal Waves, an Under-Explored Source of Turbulence Events in the Sedimentary Record," *Earth-Science Reviews* III, nos. 1–2 (2012): 56–81; Bruce R. Sutherland, *Internal Gravity Waves* (Cambridge: Cambridge University Press, 2014).

15. See Andrew J. Lucas and Robert Pinkel, "Observations of Coherent Transverse Wakes in Shoaling Nonlinear Internal Waves," *Journal of Physical Oceanography* 52, no. 6 (2022): 1277–93. Internal waves are also present in the atmosphere, formed by interactions between air masses of different densities and moisture contents. But in line with the concerns of this chapter, I focus only on internal waves that propagate within the medium of seawater.

16. Hewitt, "Feminist Frequencies," 661.

17. See, for instance, Nancy MacLean, who has put into conversation labor history and the women's movement to highlight working-class women's contributions to the development of modern feminism; Ula Y. Taylor, who has plotted an alternative account of Black feminisms that, in its resonance with the histories of the abolitionist and civil rights movements, simply cannot be contained by the white, middle-class agenda of the hegemonic wave narrative; and Becky Thompson, who has narrated a multiracial story of second-wave feminism that centers the standpoints of both women of color and white anti-racist women. See, respectively, MacLean, "The Hidden History of Affirmative Action: Working Women's Struggles in the 1970s and the Gender of Class," *Feminist Studies* 25, no. 1 (1999): 43–78; Taylor, "Making Waves: The Theory and Practice of Black Feminism," *Black Scholar* 28, no. 2 (1998): 18–28; and Thompson, "Multiracial Feminism: Recasting the Chronology of Second Wave Feminism," *Feminist Studies* 28, no. 2 (2002): 337–60.

18. To be clear, I rewrite the story in part as a shared critique of the social, political, and historical deficiencies of the wave as a governing framework of analysis. But even as the ethical oversights of the preceding wave narrative have informed this revision, it is the reflexive means of its disclosure that most explicitly clarifies the stakes of this chapter.

19. Christina Sharpe, *In the Wake: On Blackness and Being* (Durham, NC: Duke University Press, 2016), 18.

20. Saidiya Hartman, "Venus in Two Acts," *small axe* 12, no. 2 (2008): 2.

21. Saidiya Hartman writes from—and out of—the archive of Atlantic slavery, more specifically, to tell the impossible story of an enslaved "dead girl" named Venus, who was documented to be on board the slave ship *Recovery*, in 1792. In this context, the systemic violence of enslavement is one reproduced by the practices of archival documentation. It is a story, Hartman writes, that is therefore "predicated upon impossibility." See Hartman, "Venus in Two Acts," 2.

22. Patrice D. "Douglass, "Black Feminist Theory for the Dead and Dying," *Theory and Event* 21, no. 1 (2018): 115.

23. For early definitions of Afrofuturism, see Mark Dery, "Black to the Future: Interviews with Samuel R. Delany, Greg Tate, and Tricia Rose," in *Flame Wars: The Discourse of Cyberculture*, ed. Mark Dery (Durham, NC: Duke University Press, 1994), 179–222; and Kodwo Eshun, *More Brilliant Than the Sun: Adventures in Sonic Fiction* (London: Quartet Books, 1998). More key works in the field of Afrofuturism also include Mark Bould, "The Ships Landed Long Ago: Afrofuturism and Black SF," *Science Fiction Studies* 34, no. 2 (2007): 177–86; Kodwo Eshun, "Further Considerations on Afrofuturism," *CR: The New Centennial Review* 3, no. 2 (2003): 287–302; Isiah Lavender III, *Afrofuturism Rising: The Literary Prehistory of a Movement* (Columbus: Ohio State University Press, 2019); Isiah Lavender III and Lisa Yaszek, eds. *Literary Afrofuturism in the Twenty-First Century* (Columbus: Ohio State University Press, 2020); Alondra Nelson, "Introduction: Future Texts," *Social Text* 20, no. 2 (2002): 1–15; and Ytasha Womack, *Afrofuturism: The World of Black Sci-Fi and Fantasy Culture* (Chicago: Lawrence Hill Books, 2013).

24. Eshun, "Further Considerations," 292.

25. See Ednie Kaeh Garrison, "Are We on a Wavelength Yet? On Feminist Oceanography, Radios, and Third Wave Feminism," in *Different Wavelengths: Studies of the Contemporary Women's Movement*, ed. Jo Reger (New York: Routledge, 2005), 237–56; and Hewitt, "Feminist Frequencies," which has reassessed the metaphor to refer to that of a radio wave. See also Helmreich, "Genders of Waves," which explores the mobility of the metaphor to allude to a permanent wave hairstyle popular among women in the early twentieth century.

26. My question is a riff on one that Robyn Wiegman poses in her study of the progress narrative, in which she argues that the term *gender* has

become an idealized referent in the wake of *women*. Specifically, she asks: "*What would it mean if we resisted the disciplinary narrative to 'move on'?*" See Wiegman, *Object Lessons*, 53; emphasis in original.

27. Sharpe, *In the Wake*, 18.

28. Christina Sharpe builds on what Saidiya Hartman has diagnosed as the "afterlife of slavery": the systematic oppression and devaluation of Black life that persists in the present. See Hartman, *Lose Your Mother: A Journey Along the Atlantic Slave Route* (New York: Farrar, Straus and Giroux, 2007), 6.

29. Katherine McKittrick, *Dear Science and Other Stories* (Durham, NC: Duke University Press, 2021), 7. McKittrick refers more specifically to how a story-text might prompt other ways of living and knowing differently, especially in a world that so vehemently denies Black existence.

30. This is not to say that scholars have failed to employ vocabularies marked by the sea, but rather that their engagement with the onto-logical specificity of the ocean is often missing despite doing so. See Deborah L. Siegal for her use of feminist oceanography, for example: Siegal, "The Legacy of the Personal: Generating Theory in Femi-nism's Third Wave," *Hypatia* 12, no. 3 (1997): 46–75.

31. Jue, *Wild Blue Media*, 9.

32. I use this term as loosely interchangeable with *the ocean humanities*, *the oceanic turn*, or *the blue humanities*, as they have emerged from the interdisciplinary field of environmental studies. Among others contributing to this growing field, see Stacy Alaimo, "States of Sus-pension: Trans-Corporeality at Sea," *Interdisciplinary Studies in Lit-erature and Environment* 19, no. 3 (2012): 476–93; Hester Blum, "The Prospect of Oceanic Studies," *PMLA* 125, no. 3 (2010): 670–771; Cecilia Chen et al., ed., *Thinking with Water* (Montreal: McGill-Queen's University Press, 2013); Elizabeth DeLoughrey, *Routes and Roots: Navigating Caribbean and Pacific Island Literatures* (Hono-lulu: University of Hawaiʻi Press, 2007); Elizabeth DeLoughrey, "Heavy Waters: Waste and Atlantic Modernity," *PMLA* 125, no. 3 (2010): 703–12; Elizabeth DeLoughrey, "Ordinary Futures: Inter-species Worldings in the Anthropocene," in *Global Ecologies and the Environmental Humanities: Postcolonial Approaches*, ed. Elizabeth

DeLoughrey et al. (New York: Routledge, 2015): 352–72; Elizabeth DeLoughrey, "Submarine Futures of the Anthropocene," *Comparative Literature* 69, no. 1 (2017): 32–44; Elizabeth DeLoughrey, "Toward a Critical Ocean Studies for the Anthropocene," *English Language Notes* 57, no 1 (2019): 21–36; Eva Hayward, "More Lessons from a Starfish: Prefixial Flesh and Transspeciated Selves," *Women's Studies Quarterly* 36, nos. 3–4 (2008): 64–85; Eva Hayward, "FINGERY-EYES: Impressions of Cup Corals," *Cultural Anthropology* 25, no. 4 (2010): 577–99; Stefan Helmreich, *Alien Ocean: Anthropological Voyages in Microbial Seas* (Berkeley: University of California Press, 2009), *Sounding the Limits of Life: Essays in the Anthropology of Biology and Beyond* (Princeton, NJ: Princeton University Press, 2015); Stefanie Hessler, ed. *Tidalectics: Imagining an Oceanic Worldview Through Art and Science* (Cambridge, MA: MIT Press 2018); Karin E. Ingersoll, *Waves of Knowing: A Seascape Epistemology* (Durham, NC: Duke University Press, 2016); Jue, *Wild Blue Media*; Astrida Neimanis, "feminist subjectivity, watered," *Feminist Review* 103 (2013): 23–41; Astrida Neimanis, *Bodies of Water: Posthuman Feminist Phenomenology* (London: Bloomsbury, 2017); Astrida Neimanis, "The Weather Underwater: Blackness, White Feminism, and the Breathless Sea," *Australian Feminist Studies* 34, no. 102 (2019) 490–508; Astrida Neimanis, "The Sea and the Breathing," *e-flux Journal*, May 2020, http://www.e-flux.com/architecture/oceans/331869/the-sea-and-the-breathing/; Zoe Todd, "Fish Pluralities: Human-Animal Relations and Sites of Engagement in Paulatuuq, Arctic Canada," *Etudes/Inuit/Studies* 38, nos. 1–2 (2014): 217–38; and Laura Winkiel, "Introduction," *English Language Notes*, special issue "Hydro-Criticism," 57, no. 1 (2019): 1–10.

33. In particular, see Antonio Benítez-Rojo, *The Repeating Island: The Caribbean and the Postmodern Perspective* (Durham, NC: Duke University Press, 1992); and Paul Gilroy, *The Black Atlantic: Modernity and Double Consciousness* (Cambridge, MA: Harvard University Press, 1993).

34. Steinberg and Peters, "Wet Ontologies, Fluid Spaces," 248.

35. The methodological propensity to "think through" seawater, by way of "milieu-specific analysis" such that terrestrial biases of knowing become exposed and troubled, is one that Melody Jue pursues in

Wild Blue Media, 3. See also Helmreich, *Alien Ocean*, which has theorized the otherness of the ocean precisely through the figure of the alien.

36. Jue, *Wild Blue Media*, 16–17. In her conception of the ocean as such, Melody Jue cites Stefan Helmreich as one who has posited water as a medium "through which living and knowing happens"; see Helmreich, *Sounding the Limits of Life*, 186.

37. Jue, *Wild Blue Media*, 6.

38. Melody Jue's exact question is: "*How would ways of speaking about (x) change if you were to displace or transport it to a different environmental context, like the ocean?*" See Jue, *Wild Blue Media*, 6; emphasis in original.

39. Omise'eke Natasha Tinsley, "Black Atlantic, Queer Atlantic: Queer Imaginings of the Middle Passage," *GLQ: A Journal of Lesbian and Gay Studies* 14, no. 2 (2008): 191–215. In particular, the oceanic metaphors used by Paul Gilroy and Antonio Benítez-Rojo are the subject of Tinsley's critique.

40. As Omise'eke Natasha Tinsley observes, however, this is not to say that such material experiences are not also concrete and painful, even as they offer a liberatory gesture; see Tinsley "Black Atlantic, Queer Atlantic," 192–93.

41. Tinsley, 212.

42. For an engagement of the Atlantic through a specifically transgender lens, see Dora Silva Santana, "Transitionings and Returnings: Experiments with the Poetics of Transatlantic Water," *TSQ: Transgender Studies Quarterly* 4, no. 2 (2017): 181–90.

43. In more specific terms, the density of the ocean is affected by salinity and temperature; see Walter Munk, "Internal Waves and Small-Scale Processes," in *Evolution of Physical Oceanography: Scientific Surveys in Honor of Henry Stommel*, ed. Bruce A. Warren and Carl Wunsch (Cambridge, MA: MIT Press, 1980), 264–91.

44. Due to its specific geographical characteristics, some of the most powerful instances of the internal wave are generated in the Luzon Strait, near the South China Sea. This area is what many oceanographic studies of the internal wave have focused on over the last decade. See Alford, "Formation and Fate of Internal Waves"; Shuqun Cai et al.,

"An Overview of Internal Solitary Waves in the South China Sea," *Surveys in Geophysics* 33, no. 5 (2012): 927–43; David M. Farmer et al., "From Luzon Strait to Dongsha Plateau: Stages in the Life of an Internal Wave," *Oceanography* 24, no. 4 (2011): 64–77; and Matthieu J. Mercier et al., "Large-Scale, Realistic Laboratory Modeling of M2 Internal Tide Generation at the Luzon Strait," *Geophysical Research Letters* 40, no. 21 (2013): 5704–9. By invoking the phenomenon of the internal wave in this essay, I am less interested in parsing the different geographical regions that are more or less conducive to their propagation than in extending the conceptual potential of their key characteristics as such.

45. The presence of internal waves has been known for more than a century, with the earliest observation in the Arctic Ocean often attributed to the Norwegian explorer Fridtjof Nansen. But, more recently, oceanographers have been better able to understand the phenomenon due to improvements in satellite imagery.

46. Quoted in David L. Chandler, "The Ocean's Hidden Waves Show Their Power," *MIT News*, January 8, 2014, https://news.mit.edu/2013 /the-oceans-hidden-waves-show-their-power-0108/.

47. See Jessica C. Garwood et al., "Life in Internal Waves," *Oceanography* 33, no. 3 (2020): 38–49; and Yu-Huai Wang et al., "Physical and Ecological Processes of Internal Waves on an Isolated Reef Ecosystem in the South China Sea," *Geophysical Research Letters* 34, no. 18 (2007): 1–7.

48. See Sue E. Moore and Ren-Chieh Lien, "Pilot Whales Follow Internal Solitary Waves in the South China Sea," *Marine Mammal Science* 23, no. 1 (2007): 193–96; Peter Stevick, et al., "Trophic Relationships and Oceanography on and Around a Small Offshore Bank," *Marine Ecology Progress Series* 363 (2008): 15–28; and Jesús Pineda et al., "Whales and Waves: Humpback Whale Foraging Response and the Shoaling of Internal Waves at Stellwagen Bank," *Journal of Geophysical Research: Oceans* 120 (2015): 2555–70.

49. Drexciya, *The Quest*, liner notes (Submerge Recordings, 1997), CD.

50. For further analyses of the sonic properties of Drecxiya, see Kodwo Eshun, "Drexciya: Fear of a Wet Planet," *Wire*, January 1998; Eshun, *More Brilliant Than the Sun*; Nettrice R. Gaskins, "Deep Sea Dwellers:

Drexciya and the Sonic Third Space," *Shima* 10, no. 2 (2016): 68–80; Ruth Mayer, "'Africa as an Alien Future': The Middle Passage, Afrofuturism, and Postcolonial Waterworlds," *Amerikastudien/American Studies* 45, no. 4 (2000): 555–66; and Ben Williams, "Black Secret Technology: Detroit Techno and the Information Age," in *Technicolor: Race, Technology and Everyday Life*, ed. Alondra Nelson et al. (New York: NYU Press, 2001): 154–76.

51. The legend of the Drexciyans has since inspired an eclectic range of multimodal interpretations; see, for example, Ellen Gallagher, *Watery Ecstatic*, 2001, watercolor, ink, oil, plasticine, graphite, and cut paper on paper, 27 3/4 × 39 7/16 in (70.5 × 100.2 cm), Whitney Museum of American Art, New York, https://whitney.org/collection/works/18622; clipping., "The Deep," track 1 from *The Deep*, Sub Pop Records, 2019; and Abdul Qadim Haqq and Dai Satō, *The Book of Drexciya*, vol. 1 (Berlin: Tresor, 2020) and vol. 2 (Berlin: Tresor, 2023). The single by clipping., originally commissioned by the podcast *This American Life*, has directly influenced the writing of Rivers Solomon's text, in which three members of the band have been credited as collaborators: Rivers Solomon, with Daveed Diggs, William Hutson, and Jonathan Snipes, *The Deep* (New York: Saga Press, 2019).

52. Solomon et al., *Deep*, 42.

53. Solomon et al., 38.

54. Solomon et al., 8.

55. This recalls what Christina Sharpe has called "residence time," which she uses to think through the fate of the enslaved Africans thrown overboard from slave ships. Not long after the incident of these massacres, the elemental makeup of these fallen bodies begins to enter the hydrological cycle of the ocean. As Sharpe writes, "This is what we know about those Africans thrown, jumped, dumped overboard in Middle Passage; they are with us still, in the time of the wake, known as residence time"; Sharpe, *In the Wake*, 19.

56. For some work on the ocean as a space for Afroruturism, see Melody Jue, "Intimate Objectivity: On Nnedi Okorafor's Oceanic Afrofuturism," *Women's Studies Quarterly* 45, nos. 1–2 (2017): 171–88; and Mayer, "'Africa as an Alien Future.'"

57. Solomon et al., *Deep*, 2.

58. By referencing the totality of anti-Blackness here, I am alluding to Christina Sharpe's articulation of the weather, in which "antiblackness is pervasive *as* climate." See Sharpe, *In the Wake*, 106. For an extension of Sharpe's concept of the weather underwater, see also Neimanis, "Weather Underwater," and "Sea and the Breathing."

59. Jacqui M. Alexander, *Pedagogies of Crossing: Meditations on Feminism, Sexual Politics, Memory, and the Sacred* (Durham, NC: Duke University Press, 2005), 289, 290. Alexander's claim here resonates with Gaston Bachelard's on water as an "*element* which remembers the dead"; see Bachelard, *Water and Dreams: An Essay on the Imagination of Matter*, trans. Edith R. Farrell (Dallas: Dallas Institute of Humanities and Culture, 1999), 56; emphasis in original.

60. Solomon et al., *Deep*, 73.

61. Solomon et al., 71.

62. Solomon et al., 71.

63. Solomon et al., 77, emphasis mine.

64. Solomon et al., 83.

65. Hortense Spillers, "Mama's Baby, Papa's Maybe: An American Grammar Book," *Diacritics* 17, no. 2 (1987): 72.

66. Sigmund Freud examines the psychological origins of this feeling as aligned with a pre-Oedipal state of being.

67. Spillers, "Mama's Baby, Papa's Maybe," 72; emphasis in original.

68. Spillers, 72.

69. For a reading of Hortense Spillers's invocation of the oceanic as a critical framework for formations of Black age, see Habiba Ibrahim, *Black Age: Oceanic Lifespans and the Time of Black Life* (New York: NYU Press, 2021).

70. My description of being oriented to certain configurations of space and time is drawn from Sara Ahmed, who asks: "What does it mean to be oriented? . . . If we know where we are when we turn this way or that way, then we are orientated. We have our bearings. We know what to do to get to this place or to that place. To be orientated is also to be turned toward certain objects, those that help us to find our way." See Ahmed, *Queer Phenomenology: Orientations, Objects, Others* (Durham, NC: Duke University Press, 2006), 1.

71. Ibrahim, *Black Age*, 3.

72. Spillers also highlights a gendered inflection to this process of unmaking, showing how the site of the Middle Passage marked the violent transformation of gendered, Black bodies into commodified flesh.

73. Rinaldo Walcott writes on what he calls the "black aquatic" in this way, a term that names "the claim that blackness itself is birthed in salt water"; see Walcott, "The Black Aquatic," *liquid blackness* 5, no. 1 (2021): 65.

74. Solomon et al., *Deep*, 60.

75. For a reading of *The Deep* along similar lines, which considers its nurturing of a queer, multispecies kinship through the question of oceanic origins, see Elizabeth DeLoughrey, "Kinship in the Abyss, Submerging with *The Deep*," *Atlantic Studies* 20, no. 2 (2022): 348–60.

76. This conception of transcorporeality, as specifically extended through the sea, is drawn from Stacy Alaimo, "States of Suspension."

77. Solomon et al., *Deep*, 144.

78. Rachel Carson, *The Sea Around Us* (1951; Oxford: Oxford University Press, 2018), 3.

79. Carson, *Sea Around Us*, 7.

80. Carson, 13.

81. Carson, 14.

82. I am also guided by the work of Astrida Neimanis and her thinking of the human body along these same lines. See Neimanis, "feminist subjectivity, watered," and *Bodies of Water*.

83. Solomon et al., *Deep*, 84.

84. Solomon et al., 42.

85. Solomon et al., 43.

86. The term *queer ecology* has wide-reaching origins across the interdisciplinary fields of queer theory, environmental studies, feminist science studies, and more. For an indicative overview, see Catriona Mortimer-Sandilands and Bruce Erickson, eds., *Queer Ecologies: Sex, Nature, Politics, Desire* (Bloomington: Indiana University Press, 2010); and Catriona Sandilands, "Queer Ecology," in *Keywords for Environmental Studies*, ed. Joni Adamson, William A. Gleason, and

David Pellow (New York: NYU Press, 2016), 169–71, and also available at https://keywords.nyupress.org/environmental-studies/essay/queer-ecology/.

87. If Rachel Carson's oceanic origin story continues to be followed, then whales—as aquatic mammals adapted to life in the sea—might themselves be considered a reorientation of a certain trajectory of evolution, insofar as they "abandoned a land life for the ocean." See Carson, *Sea Around Us*, 14.

88. Solomon et al., *Deep*, 46.

89. Solomon et al., 51.

90. Solomon et al., 51.

91. Solomon et al., 52.

92. Solomon et al., 53.

93. Alexis Pauline Gumbs, *Undrowned: Black Feminist Lessons from Marine Mammals* (Chico, CA: AK Press, 2020), 48.

94. Alexis Pauline Gumbs refers to M. NourbeSe Philip to make this point about water as an enduring container for sound.

95. Gumbs, *Undrowned*, 49.

2. A DEMONIC AFTERLIFE OF SEXUAL DIFFERENCE

1. Ann Rosalind Jones, "Writing the Body: Toward an Understanding of 'L'Écriture Féminine',"" *Feminist Studies* 7, no. 2 (1981): 247–63. For how the term *French feminism* can largely be perceived as an American invention in academic feminist thought, see Christine Delphy, "The Invention of French Feminism: An Essential Move," *Yale French Studies* 87 (1995): 190–221; and Claire Moses, "Made in America: 'French Feminism' in Academia," *Feminist Studies* 24, no. 2 (1998): 241–74. For some major works that introduced French feminism into the American academy, see Carolyn Burke, "Irigaray Through the Looking Glass," *Feminist Studies* 7, no. 2 (1981): 288–306; Isabelle de Courtivron and Elaine Marks, eds., *New French Feminisms: An Anthology* (Amherst: University of Massachusetts Press, 1980); Hester Eisenstein and Alice Jardine, *The Future of Difference* (New Brunswick, NJ: Rutgers University Press, 1980);

Shoshana Felman, "Women and Madness: The Critical Phallacy," *Diacritics* 5, no. 4 (1975): 2–10; Christiane Makward and Hélène Cixous, "Interview with Hélène Cixous," *SubStance* 5, no. 13 (1976): 19–37; a special section titled "The French Connection," in *Feminist Studies* 7, no. 2 (1981): 247–306; a special section titled "French Feminist Theory," in *Signs* 7, no. 1 (1981): 5–86; and a special section titled "Feminist Readings: French Texts/American Contexts," in *Yale French Studies* 62 (1981): 1–236.

2. For a more extensive view on this topic, see Elizabeth Abel, ed., *Writing and Sexual Difference* (Chicago: University of Chicago Press, 1982); and Nancy K. Miller, ed., *The Poetics of Gender* (New York: Columbia University Press, 1986).

3. For key works that contributed to the Anglo-American tradition of feminist criticism, see Sandra Gilbert and Susan Gubar, *The Madwoman in the Attic: The Woman Writer and the Nineteenth-Century Literary Imagination* (New Haven, CT: Yale University Press, 1979); Patricia Meyer Spacks, *The Female Imagination* (New York: Knopf, 1975); Elaine Showalter, *A Literature of Their Own: British Women Novelists from Brontë to Lessing* (Princeton: NJ: Princeton University Press, 1977); Elaine Showalter, "Feminist Criticism in the Wilderness," *Critical Inquiry* 8, no. 2 (1981): 179–205; and Elaine Showalter, "Toward A Feminist Poetics," in *The New Feminist Criticism: Essays on Women, Literature, and Theory*, ed. Elaine Showalter. (New York: Pantheon, 1985), 125–48; Showalter coined the term *gynocriticism* in her essay "Toward a Feminist Poetics," and this Anglo-American approach to women's writing, as a rewriting of the male-centered canon, can broadly be termed as such.

4. Jones, "Writing the Body," 248. For Rosalind Jones, Hélène Cixous and Luce Irigaray were especially at fault in their problematic invocation of "women's physiology and bodily instincts" for this purpose.

5. It is important to situate Rosalind Jones's critique in the larger historical context of feminist studies in the 1980s, which had begun to pay closer attention to racial, cultural, and class differences between *women*, as opposed to making a claim for the universal construct of "Woman." See also Gayatri Chakravorty Spivak, who critiques the essentializing tendency of French feminism by taking Julia Kristeva's

1977 book *About Chinese Women* as an example of how the latter advances a homogenizing vision of so-called Third World Women; see Spivak, "French Feminism in an International Frame," *Yale French Studies* 62 (1981): 154–84.

6. Jones, "Writing the Body," 255.

7. This claim resonates, of course, with the observation in the introduction of *Feminism Enchanted* on the affective and discursive politics animating the constitution of the academic field of feminist studies as a whole.

8. See Clare Hemmings, who points out that the work of Hélène Cixous and Luce Irigaray—as closely associated with the historical troubles of French feminism—continues to remain "steeped in institutional and political anxiety" until today. Hemmings observes that even as the wider field of feminist studies has demonstrated materialist returns to the body in recent years, for instance, scholars have studiously avoided thinking through these earlier writings for their latent potential; see Hemmings, *Why Stories Matter*, 86.

9. For some intellectual advocates of French feminism, who believed in the antiessentialist possibilities that it radically opened for feminist criticism, see Carolyn Burke, "Introduction to Luce Irigaray's 'When Our Lips Speak Together,'" *Signs* 6 no. 1 (1980): 66–8; Diana Fuss, *Essentially Speaking: Feminism, Nature and Difference* (New York: Routledge, 1989); Jane Gallop, "'Quand nos lèvres s'écrivent': Irigaray's Body Politic," *Romanic Review* 74, no. 1 (1983): 77–83; Toril Moi, *Sexual/Textual Politics: Feminist Literary Theory* (New York: Methuen, 1985); Naomi Schor, "This Essentialism Which Is Not One," in *Engaging with Irigaray*, ed. Carolyn Burke et al. (New York: Columbia University Press, 1994): 57–78; and Margaret Whitford, "Luce Irigaray and the Female Imaginary: Speaking as a Woman," *Radical Philosophy* no. 43 (1986): 3–8.

10. For a similar approach of revisiting French feminism—in particular Luce Irigaray's essay "When Our Lips Speak Together" (1976)—and situating its writing and publication in the material and historical context of activist groups in 1970s Brussels, see Amanda Grimsbo Roswall, "Collectivity and Feminist History: Situating Luce Irigaray," *Signs: Journal of Women in Culture and Society* 49 no. 4 (2024): 887–911.

11. To be clear, there have been several attempts to reclaim sexual difference from the residues of its essentialist past, which have provided a more layered archive of the concept. See, for instance, Ranjana Khanna, who offers the examples of Hélène Cixous and Barbara Johnson as those who read the concept differently; see Khanna, "On the Name, Ideation, and Sexual Difference," *differences: A Journal of Feminist Cultural Studies* 27, no. 2 (2016): 62–78. As Khanna suggests, however, these efforts continue to be clouded by the overwhelming—and not untrue—sense that feminism has historically colluded with racist and colonial ideologies. She writes that "these neglected instantiations of sexual difference . . . are often forgotten in the moment that we make the more obvious point—that feminism has often been entirely complicit with colonial gestures and racism and that it continues to be" (68). See also Katherine A. Costello, "Inventing 'French Feminism,'" which argues that French feminism was in fact taken up by postcolonial theorists such as Trinh T. Minh-ha to think through racial difference between women.

12. Luce Irigaray provides a shift in terminology to "*sexuate* difference" after expressing her preference for this term to avoid confusion with theorizations of sexuality and queerness, and to distinguish this concept from the more narrowly defined biological sex differences; see Irigaray, *Luce Irigaray: Key Writings*, ed. Luce Irigaray (London: Continuum, 2004): vii–xv. That being said, I will be retaining the term *sexual difference* for the sake of consistency with the majority of scholarship in this area, as well as to emphasize the affiliation of my own reading of sexual difference with Irigaray's earlier, rather than later, definitions of the term. Irigaray comments directly on the consecutive phases of her thinking on sexual difference in an interview with Elizabeth Hirsh and Gary A. Olson; see Irigaray, "'Je—Luce Irigaray': A Meeting with Luce Irigaray," trans. Elizabeth Hirsh and Gaëtan Brulotte, *Hypatia* 10, no. 2 (1995): 93–114. For a review of the multiple—and at times contradictory—readings of the Irigarayan concept of sexual difference, see Rebecca Hill, "The Multiple Readings of Sexual Difference," *Philosophy Compass* 11, no. 7 (2016): 390–401.

13. For scholarly work that has engaged with Luce Irigaray's writing in this vein, see Elizabeth Grosz, *Sexual Subversions: Three French*

Feminists (Sydney: Allen and Unwin, 1989); and Margaret Whitford, *Luce Irigaray: Philosophy in the Feminine* (New York: Routledge, 1991).

14. Luce Irigaray, *This Sex Which Is Not One*, trans. Carolyn Burke and Catherine Porter (Ithaca, NY: Cornell University Press, 1985b), 159.

15. Irigaray, *This Sex*, 69; emphasis in original.

16. Irigaray, *An Ethics of Sexual Difference*, trans. Carolyn Burke and Gillian C. Gill (Ithaca, NY: Cornell University Press, 1993), 6; emphasis in original.

17. Irigaray, *Ethics*, 6.

18. Judith Butler, *Undoing Gender* (New York: Routledge, 2004), 178; emphasis in original.

19. Butler, *Undoing Gender*, 177; emphasis mine.

20. Irigaray, *Ethics*, 19.

21. Elizabeth Grosz, *Time Travels: Feminism, Nature, Power* (Durham, NC: Duke University Press), 176.

22. This is a conversation that was largely intertwined with discussions over the unruly temporalities of feminism, which followed from a general resistance to linear and chronological continuity, and a questioning in turn of the epistemic centrality of feminism's genealogical and generational organization of its histories. In many ways, these debates can be seen as adjacent to the "introspective turn" in women's studies that I referred to in the introduction of this book, with similarly reflexive concerns about feminist historiography.

23. Grosz, *Time Travels*, 182. For a similar insistence on thinking the new, see Elizabeth Grosz, "Thinking the New: Of Futures Yet Unthought," *Symplokē* 6, nos. 1–2 (1998): 38–55.

24. Robyn Wiegman, "Feminism's Apocalyptic Futures," *New Literary History* 31, no. 4 (2000): 822.

25. I see this counternarrative as existing in tandem with what Jack Halberstam has termed a "shadow feminism," which is marked by its antisocial, self-destructive, and antihumanist tendencies, which stand in opposition to conventional assumptions about what feminism should be or do. See Jack Halberstam, *The Queer Art of Failure* (Durham, NC: Duke University Press, 2011), 124–6.

26. Organizing her study under the framework of the apocalyptic, Robyn Wiegman similarly writes of an anxiety over feminism's failure of the

future as one that is profoundly productive, insofar as it might serve as a springboard for thinking beyond the limitations of present time; see Wiegman "Feminism's Apocalyptic Futures," 815.

27. In similar affective terms, Clare Hemmings has attributed the emotional appeal of certain feminist narratives either to a teller who is positioned as triumphant or to the feminist subject of the story who emerges as triumphant; see Hemmings, *Why Stories Matter.*

28. Sara Ahmed, "This Other and Other Others," *Economy and Society* 13, no. 4 (2002): 559.

29. Ahmed, "This Other and Other Others," 559.

30. Ahmed, "This Other and Other Others," 559.

31. Butler, *Undoing Gender,* 177.

32. See René Descartes, *The Passions of the Soul and Other Late Philosophical Writings,* trans. Michael Moriarty (Oxford: University Press, 2015).

33. Irigaray, *Ethics,* 13.

34. In more specific terms, Elizabeth Grosz writes that Luce Irigaray attributes wonder to sexual difference because the latter concept is "entirely of the order of the surprise, the encounter with the new"; see Grosz, *Time Travels,* 176.

35. In many ways, this invocation of wonder finds much affinity with my overview of the same term that I earlier provided in the introduction of this book. Here, I am guided especially by Sara Ahmed's suggestion that wonder "allows us to see the surfaces of the world *as made,* and as such wonder opens up rather than suspends historicity"; see Ahmed, *Cultural Politics of Emotion,* 179; emphasis in original.

36. Sylvia Wynter insists that the wonder evoked by literary texts must be explored rather than simply expressed, insofar as these texts are always and in the first instance enclosed by particular cultural contexts that enable their reception (and therefore, the evocation of wonder) as such; see Wynter, "But What Does 'Wonder' Do? Meanings, Canons, Too? On Literary Texts, Cultural Contexts, and What It's Like to Be One/Not One of Us," *Stanford Humanities Review* 4, no. 1 (1994): 124–29.

37. Wynter, "Unsettling the Coloniality of Being," 262. Sylvia Wynter borrows the term from Gregory Bateson, for whom a descriptive statement denotes the maintenance of the status quo. To be more specific

with her conception of Man, Wynter delineates the transition from the separate, but accretive, inventions of what she calls Man1 (a rational, secularized form of the human that was initiated from the European Renaissance up until the eighteenth century) and Man2 (an imperializing, liberal conception of the human from the nineteenth century up until today) that became reified as a universal representation. In addition, David Scott, writes that this story of Western liberal humanism—its proverbial coming-of-age narrative—is predicated on the colonial relegation of other modes of being human; see Scott, "The Re-Enchantment of Humanism: An Interview with Sylvia Wynter," *small axe: A Caribbean Journal of Criticism* 4, no. 2 (2000): 119–207.

38. Wynter, "Unsettling the Coloniality of Being," 260.

39. Sylvia Wynter also discusses the term *genre* in relation to gender and race. She suggests that, rather than understanding gender and race as distinct categories of analysis and therefore oppression, they be understood as connected functions of a genre of the human. It therefore is insufficient to separately tackle either "gender" or "race"; rather, an entire overhaul of the dominant genre of Man is necessary for a truly transformative intellectual and political project. See Wynter, "Proud-Flesh Inter/Views: Sylvia Wynter," *ProudFlesh: New Afrikan Journal of Culture Politics and Consciousness* 4 (2006): 1–35. Alexander G. Weheliye touches on these concerns; see Weheliye, "After Man," *American Literary History* 20, nos. 1–2 (2008): 321–36, and *Habeas Viscus: Racializing Assemblages, Biopolitics, and Black Feminist Theories of the Human* (Durham, NC: Duke University Press, 2014).

40. Katherine McKittrick writes in this regard that "Wynter demonstrates the ways in which a new, revalorized perspective emerges from the ex-slave archipelago and that this worldview, engendered both across and outside a colonial frame, holds in it the possibility of undoing and unsettling—*not replacing or occupying*—Western conceptions of what it means to be human"; see McKittrick, ed., *Sylvia Wynter: On Being Human as Praxis* (Durham, NC: Duke University Press, 2015), 2; emphasis in original.

41. McKittrick, *On Being Human as Praxis*, 9.

42. As previously mentioned, my assignment of wonder to Sylvia Wynter's endeavor is guided by Katherine McKittrick's engagement with

her work; see McKittrick, *Demonic Grounds: Black Women and the Cartographies of Struggle* (Minneapolis: University of Minnesota Press, 2006); McKittrick, ed., *Sylvia Wynter: On Being Human as Praxis* (Durham, NC: Duke University Press, 2015); McKittrick, "Black Human Geographies," in *Posthumanism in Art and Science: A Reader*, ed. Susan McHugh and Giovanni Aloi (New York: Columbia University Press, 2021): 249–55; and McKittrick, *Dear Science and Other Stories* (Durham, NC: Duke University Press, 2021).

43. Sylvia Wynter, "Afterword: Beyond Miranda's Meanings: Un/ Silencing the 'Demonic Ground' of Caliban's 'Woman,'" in *Out of the Kumbla: Caribbean Women and Literature*, ed. Carole Boyce Davies and Elaine Savory Fido (Trenton, NJ: Africa World Press, 1990), 366.

44. By designating the demonic as such, I am guided by Katherine McKittrick's suggestion that Sylvia Wynter "gives us a new place to go"; see McKittrick, *Demonic Grounds*, xxvi.

45. Wynter, "Beyond Miranda's Meanings," 356.

46. Wynter, 361. As indicated in the title of her essay that cites the character of Caliban in Shakespeare's *The Tempest*, Sylvia Wynter offers an analysis of the play to posit this claim. It is the glaring absence of Caliban's "woman" in the narrative, what Wynter designates as "Caliban's physiognomically complementary mate," that comes to signal the demonic presence of a racial and sexual index of meaning. Or to put it another way, Caliban's mate is missing in the play because she represents a position of Black womanhood that cannot be grasped by Western systems of understanding, and is therefore beyond the bounds of such knowledge. See Wynter, "Beyond Miranda's Meanings," 360. For more extensive overviews of this issue, see Carole Boyce-Davies, "Occupying the Terrain: Reengaging 'Beyond Miranda's Meanings: Un/Silencing the "Demonic Ground" of Caliban's Woman,'" *American Quarterly* 70, no. 4 (2018): 837–45; and Habiba Ibrahim, "Caliban, His Woman, and the Gendered (In)Humanism of *Wild Seed*," *Anthropology and Humanism* 48, no. 1 (2022): 174–87; and McKittrick, *Demonic Grounds*.

47. It is in fact Luce Irigaray's *Speculum of the Other Woman*, which Sylvia Wynter claims to rest on a "purely Western assumption of a universal

category, 'Woman,'" that composes part of the ideological backdrop against the latter's definition of the demonic ground developed in the essay; see Wynter, "Beyond Miranda's Meanings," 355. On what she calls an "autonomous feminism," one that will transcend Marxist and liberal logics of meaning, see Wynter, "Beyond Liberal and Marxist Leninist Feminisms: Towards an Autonomous Frame of Reference," *CLR James Journal* 24, nos. 1–2 (2018): 31–56.

48. Wynter, "Beyond Miranda's Meanings," 364. See also Alex Comfort, whose work Sylvia Wynter also engages in her essay, on a demonic model of evolutionary biology as extrapolated from its use in quantum mechanics; Comfort, "Demonic and Historical Models in Biology," *Journal of Social and Biological Structures* 3, no. 2 (1980): 207–15.

49. Wynter, "Beyond Miranda's Meanings," 365; emphasis mine.

50. Along these lines, see Alexander G. Weheliye on how the human has productively been transformed into a heuristic model in the field of Black studies, instead of simply standing as an ontological given, in Weheliye, "After Man," and *Habeas Viscus*.

51. Gloria E. Anzaldúa, *Light in the Dark/Luz en Lo Oscuro: Rewriting Identity, Spirituality, Reality*, ed. Analouise Keating (Durham, NC: Duke University Press, 2015), 45. There is a decolonizing function to Anzaldúa's proposal of a new perspective, insofar as it troubles the dominant Western construct of reality.

52. Given the preceding concerns of this chapter, it is also worth mentioning that the question of literature—or at least more generally that of the aesthetic domain—has been raised in a specific Irigarayan context. Drucilla Cornell argues that the evocation of an unknowable future as such demands an aesthetic dimension of inquiry, insofar as the latter offers a more expansive space for the imagination of what otherwise cannot be perceived in the present; see Cornell, *Beyond Accommodation: Ethical Feminism, Deconstruction, and The Law* (New York: Routledge, 1991). See also my analysis elsewhere of Luce Irigaray and Cornell in this vein: Er, "Anticipations, Afterlives: On the Temporal and Affective Reorientations of Sexual Difference," *Feminist Theory* 19, no. 3 (2018): 369–86.

53. Daniel Wright, *The Grounds of the Novel* (Stanford, CA: Stanford University Press, 2024), 143.

54. Wright, *Grounds of the Novel*, 144. Daniel Wright more accurately uses the metaphor of plural meeting grounds to describe the latter arrangement.

55. It is worth noting that Daniel Wright thus reads Akwaeke Emezi's *Freshwater* as embodying the metaphor of the meeting ground in both of the ways he has defined it. Drawing on Emezi's own reflections on their writing of *Freshwater*, Wright points out that Emezi emphasizes writing the self into the fictional realm of the novel, alongside their centering of Igbo ontology as a disruption of Western frameworks of knowledge. See also Akwaeke Emezi, *Dear Senthuran: A Black Spirit Memoir* (London: Faber and Faber, 2021).

56. Akwaeke Emezi, "I'd Read Everything—Even the Cereal Box," interview with Arifa Akbar, *Guardian*, October 20, 2018, www.theguardian .com/books/2018/oct/20/akwaeke-emezi-interview-freshwater.

57. Akwaeke Emezi, *Freshwater* (London: Faber and Faber, 2018), 27.

58. For some key writings on the *ogbanje*, see Christie C. Achebe, *The World of the Ogbanje* (Enugu, Nigeria: Fourth Dimension Publishers, 1986); Christie C. Achebe, "Literary Insights into the Ogbanje Phenomenon," *Journal of African Studies* 7, no. 1 (1980): 31–8; Misty Bastian, "Irregular Visitors: Narratives About Ogbaanje (Spirit Children) in Southern Nigerian Popular Writing," in *Readings in African Popular Fiction*, ed. Stephanie Newell (Bloomington: Indiana University Press, 2002), 59–67; Misty Bastian, "Married in the Water: Spirit Kin and Other Afflictions of Modernity in Southeastern Nigeria," *Journal of Religion in Africa* 27, no. 2 (1997): 116–34; Sunday T. C. Ilechukwu, "*Ogbanje/Abiku* and Cultural Conceptualizations of Psychopathology in Nigeria." *Mental Health, Religion and Culture* 10, no. 3 (2007): 239–55; Esther Nzewi, "Malevolent *Ogbanje*: Recurrent Reincarnation or Sickle Cell Disease?" *Social Science and Medicine* 59, no. 9 (2001): 1403–16; Christopher Okonkwo, *A Spirit of Dialogue: Incarnations of Ogbanje, the Born-to-Die, in African American Literature* (Knoxville: University of Tennessee Press, 2008); and Bertram I. N. Osuagwu, *The Igbos and Their Traditions*, trans. Frances W. Pritchett, 1979, http://www .columbia.edu/itc/mealac/pritchett/00fwp/igbo/secondary/txt _traditions_0105.pdf. See also John S. Mbiti for his description of spiritual beings and the "living-dead," a category under which the

ogbanje might be placed, in *African Religions and Philosophy* (Portsmouth, NH: Heinemann, 1990). Okonkwo also provides an overview of the cultural and spiritual differences between *ogbanje* and a parallel but distinct figure in Yoruba cosmology: the *abiku*, which directly translates to "born to die," in *A Spirit of Dialogue.*

59. Achebe, "Literary Insights," 33. John A. Noon defines the *ogbanje* as "repeater-children," and Bertram I. N. Osuagwu terms an *ogbanje* as "one who travels back and forth"; see, respectively, Noon, "A Preliminary Examination of the Death Concepts of the Ibo," *American Anthropologist* 44, no. 4 (1942): 638–54, and Osuagwu, *Igbos and Their Traditions.*

60. It is crucial to note that the Igbo belief in reincarnation cannot easily be conflated with a Western definition. Rather, it is better understood as *ilo/ino uwa*, or to "come back to the world" through the impression of the identities of departed ancestors on the corporeal existence of the living. For a more extensive explanation, see Anthony Ekwunife, *Meaning and Function of "Ino Uwa" (Reincarnation) in Igbo Traditional Religious Culture* (Onitsha, Nigeria: Spiritan, 2000).

61. Akwaeke Emezi elsewhere designates *ogbanje* as "unwelcome deviations," or "intruders," in the cycle of Igbo reincarnation; See Emezi, *Dear Senthuran*, 12.

62. Achebe, "Literary Insights," 33.

63. Other notable literary texts that have invoked the figure of the *ogbanje* include Chinua Achebe's *Things Fall Apart* (1958), Octavia Butler's *Kindred* (1979), Toni Morrison's *Sula* (1973) and *Beloved* (1981), and Ben Okri's *The Famished Road* (1991). For a more extensive overview of the phenomenon in African American literature, see Okonkwo, *Spirit of Dialogue.*

64. Emezi, *Freshwater*, 3.

65. Emezi, 5; emphasis in original.

66. Emezi, 41.

67. Emezi, 34; 35.

68. Emezi, 27.

69. Emezi, 140.

70. As Christie C. Achebe writes, the *ogbanje* phenomenon "defies categorization in the strict western psychological sense," and therefore

cannot be diagnosed by the explanatory frameworks of Western mental health; see Achebe, "Literary Insights," 32.

71. Emezi, *Freshwater*, 41.

72. Emezi, 207.

73. Akwaeke Emezi describes their lived reality as a "metaphysical dysphoria"; see Emezi, *Dear Senthuran*, 16.

74. Emezi, *Freshwater*, 123.

75. Emezi, 123.

76. Emezi, 186. See Emezi, *Dear Senthuran*, especially the essay "Mutilation | Dear Eugene," which details their multiple surgeries along these lines.

77. Emezi, *Freshwater*, 193.

78. Emezi, 189.

79. Emezi, 189.

80. Emezi, 189.

81. Bastian, "Irregular Visitors," 59.

82. See Oyeronke Oyewumi, *The Invention of Women: Making an African Sense of Western Gender Discourses* (Minneapolis: University of Minnesota Press, 1997), x. Oyewumi examines how Western gender categories have been imposed on Yoruba discourse as a form of discursive colonization, and how an epistemological shift is required for a more accurate delineation of the latter's cultural logic. More specifically, she focuses on the problematic of "woman" as a fundamental category of Western feminist thought, but one that finds no coherent meaning in Yoruba society prior to colonization.

83. For other key works that have critiqued Western feminist inquiry as carelessly transposed onto African societies, see Ifi Amadiume, *Male Daughters, Female Husbands: Gender and Sex in an African Society* (London: Zed Books, 1987); and Nkiru Uwechia Nzegwu, *Family Matters: Feminist Concepts in African Philosophy of Culture* (New York: SUNY Press, 2006). María Lugones calls for a decolonial feminism in light of such pervasive and ongoing forms of epistemological violence; see Lugones, "Toward a Decolonial Feminism," *Hypatia* 25, no. 4 (2010): 742–59. Crucially, my point here is not to reduce the multiplicity of African societies but, rather, to emphasize the totalizing force of such practices of colonization.

84. Emezi, *Freshwater*, 87–88.

85. For some scholarship on the concept of fugitivity, particularly in Black life, see Stephen Best and Saidiya Hartman, "Fugitive Justice," *Representations* 92, no. 1 (2005): 1–15; Tina M. Campt, *Image Matters: Archive, Photography, and the African Diaspora in Europe* (Durham, NC: Duke University Press, 2012); Akwugo Emejulu, *Fugitive Feminism* (London: Silver Press, 2022); Alexis Pauline Gumbs, *Spill: Scenes of Black Feminist Fugitivity* (Durham, NC: Duke University Press, 2016); Stefano Harney and Fred Moten, *The Undercommons: Fugitive Planning and Black Study* (New York: Minor Compositions, 2013); and Fred Moten, *Stolen Life* (Durham, NC: Duke University Press, 2018).

86. Emezi, *Freshwater*, 225.

87. Emezi, 226.

88. Emezi, 38.

3. FEMINIST REVOLUTIONS: INSCRUTABLE, OUT OF REACH

1. Franny Choi, "Orientalism (Part I)," in *Floating, Brilliant, Gone* (Austin, TX: Write Bloody Publishing, 2014), ll. 1–2.

2. Choi, "Orientalism (Part I)," ll. 2–4.

3. Vivian L. Huang, *Surface Relations: Queer Forms of Asian American Inscrutability* (Durham, NC: Duke University Press, 2022), 2.

4. Choi, "Orientalism (Part I)," ll. 5–6.

5. Anne Anlin Cheng, *Ornamentalism* (Oxford: Oxford University Press, 2019), 92–4.

6. Choi, "Orientalism (Part I)," l. 5.

7. Choi, "Orientalism (Part I)," ll. 7–8.

8. Choi, "Orientalism (Part I)," l. 8.

9. See Vivian L. Huang, *Surface Relations*; Summer Kim Lee, "Staying In: Mitski, Ocean Vuong, and Asian American Asociality," *Social Text* 37, no. 1 (2019): 27–50; Sunny Xiang, *Tonal Intelligence: The Aesthetics of Asian Inscrutability During the Long Cold War* (New York: Columbia University Press, 2020); and Xine Yao, *The Cultural Politics of Unfeeling in Nineteenth-Century America* (Durham, NC: Duke University Press, 2021). See also Tina Post, *Deadpan: The Aesthetics of*

Black Inexpression (New York: NYU Press, 2022), for a similar approach that has been taken in the context of Black studies.

10. In the context of Latinx studies, Christina A. León has similarly written about opacity as an "aesthetic and ethico-political response to the demands for transparency"; see León, "Forms of Opacity: Roaches, Blood, and Being Stuck in Xandra Ibarra's Corpus," *ASAP/Journal* 2, no. 2 (2017): 378. León's use of the strategy of opacity is informed by the work of Édouard Glissant.

11. Although transnational feminism also refers to, and is inextricable from, a movement of feminist political activism, I refer more precisely to its theoretical underpinnings in this chapter. Defined in this way, transnational feminism emerged as an intellectual movement in the US academic context in the 1990s. Although the parameters of the field are expansive, for two of the most foundational books that marked its inception, see Jacqui M. Alexander and Chandra Talpade Mohanty, eds., *Feminist Genealogies, Colonial Legacies, Democratic Futures* (New York: Routledge, 1997); and Inderpal Grewal and Caren Kaplan, eds., *Scattered Hegemonies: Postmodernity and Transnational Feminist Practices* (Minneapolis: University of Minnesota Press, 1994). See also Chandra Talpade Mohanty, "Under Western Eyes: Feminist Scholarship and Colonial Discourses," *boundary 2*, nos. 12–13 (1984): 333–58, for the influence of her theorizing of "Third World" feminisms on the developmental arc of transnational feminist thinking. Other significant works that have focused on the transnational as an operative term of description and analysis include Inderpal Grewal and Caren Kaplan, "Global Identities: Theorizing Transnational Studies of Sexualities," *GLQ: A Journal of Lesbian and Gay Studies* 7, no. 4 (2001): 663–79; Chandra Talpade Mohanty, *Feminism Without Borders: Decolonizing Theory, Practicing Solidarity* (Durham, NC: Duke University Press, 2003); Valentine M. Moghadam, *Globalizing Women: Transnational Feminist Networks* (Baltimore: Johns Hopkins University Press, 2005); Amanda Lock Swarr and Richi Nagar, ed., *Critical Transnational Feminist Praxis* (New York: SUNY Press, 2010); and, more recently, Ashwini Tambe and Millie Thayer, eds., *Transnational Feminist Itineraries: Situating Theory and Activist Practice* (Durham, NC: Duke University Press, 2021).

12. Alexander and Mohanty, "Introduction: Genealogies, Legacies, Movements," in *Feminist Genealogies, Colonial Legacies, Democratic Futures*, xviii.

13. To be clear, the *transnational* does not necessarily denote a radical or transformative feminist praxis. In fact, and to the contrary as Grewal and Kaplan have pointed out, the term *transnational* "has become so ubiquitous in cultural, literary, and critical studies that much of its political valence seems to have become evacuated"; see Grewal and Kaplan, "Global Identities," 664.

14. For more materialist takes on comparative feminist revolutions, see Rutvica Andrijasevic et al., "re-imagining revolutions," *Feminist Review* 106 (2014): 1–8; and Brenna Bhandar and Rafeef Ziadah, eds., *Revolutionary Feminisms: Conversations on Collective Action and Radical Thought* (London: Verso, 2020).

15. Here, Karl Marx's paradigmatic declaration that revolutions are the "locomotives of history" comes to mind as a testimony to the instrumental part they have played in driving the advancement of human societies; see Marx, *The Class Struggles in France, 1848–1850*, trans. Henry Kuhn (New York: New York Labor News, 1924), 165. Of course, Marx's claim must be situated historically—that is, in the specific European context of class struggle that he diagnoses. But his general vision of revolution as progressive is nevertheless helpful in tracing some of the deeply entrenched presumptions that have led to how it is still defined today.

16. Kate Millett, *Going to Iran* (New York: Coward, McCann, and Geoghegan, 1982), 164.

17. Millett, *Going to Iran*, 68; emphasis mine.

18. Following the publication of her book *Sexual Politics* (1970), Millett would grace the cover of *Time* magazine in the same year, which proclaimed her as one of the leaders of the second wave feminist movement.

19. See Robin Morgan, *Sisterhood Is Global* (New York: Feminist Press at CUNY, 1984). It is key to note that Morgan was one of Millett's contemporaries of second wave feminism. While Morgan's work consolidated this vision of a global sisterhood, this view had been circulating amongst Western feminists for many decades prior and gave rise to

what was known as the approach of "international" feminism. For a critique of the idea of global sisterhood in the specific context of Iran, see Nima Naghibi, *Rethinking Global Sisterhood: Western Feminism and Iran* (Minneapolis: University of Minnesota Press, 2007).

20. For a critique of the reductive assumption held by certain bourgeois white feminists of the 1970s women's liberation movement that a "common oppression" united the suffering of all women, see bell hooks, "Sisterhood: Political Solidarity between Women," *Feminist Review* 23, no. 1 (1986): 127.

21. Millett, *Going to Iran*, 125.

22. Millett, 39.

23. In this vein, a key text that exposes the Western feminist project's desire to save Muslim women from their supposed cultural and religious oppression is Lila Abu-Lughod's *Do Muslim Women Need Saving* (Cambridge, MA: Harvard University Press, 2015).

24. See, for example, Behrooz Ghamari-Tabrizi, *Foucault in Iran: Islamic Revolution after the Enlightenment* (Minneapolis: University of Minnesota Press, 2016); and Naghibi, *Rethinking Global Sisterhood*. Patricia J. Higgins has also revealed that Millett's book is one riddled with numerous factual inaccuracies; see Higgins, Review of *Going to Iran*, by Kate Millett, *Signs: Journal of Women in Culture and Society* 9, no. 1 (1983): 154–56.

25. As Kate Millett herself reflects, "Much of what follows is lost to me through language," though she hoped to be able to decipher this by listening to her recordings; see Millet, *Going to Iran*, 125.

26. See Negar Mottahedeh, *Whisper Tapes: Kate Millett in Iran* (Stanford, CA: Stanford University Press, 2019).

27. Mottahedeh, *Whisper Tapes*, 17.

28. The law prohibiting women from being unveiled in public would come into effect in 1983.

29. Mottahedeh, *Whisper Tapes*, 26. Negar Mottahedeh reveals how Kate Millett's prescriptive view led her to miss the contextual significance of the Persian word *azadi*, or freedom, as the rallying cry of the women's protests in Iran.

30. For a more detailed timeline of the history of the veil in Iran, see Haideh Moghissi, *Populism and Feminism in Iran: Women's Struggle in*

a Male-Defined Revolutionary Movement (London: Palgrave Macmillan, 1996); and Ashraf Zahedi, "Contested Meaning of the Veil and Political Ideologies of Iranian Regimes," *Journal of Middle East Women's Studies* 3, no. 3 (2007): 75–98. See also Leila Ahmed, *Women and Gender in Islam: Historical Roots of a Modern Debate* (New Haven, CT: Yale University Press, 1992), on the veil as a custom that articulated a means of resistance to Western domination.

31. The veil would also come to represent a class divide amongst Iranian women, thus further rendering the freedom of choice somewhat of a conceit. On this issue of class, see Homa Hoodfar, "The Veil in Their Minds and on Our Heads: Veiling Practices and Muslim Women," in *The Politics of Culture in the Shadow of Capital*, ed. Lisa Lowe and David Lloyd (Durham, NC: Duke University Press, 1997): 248–79; Naghibi, *Rethinking Global Sisterhood*; and Zahedi, "Contested Meaning of the Veil."

32. Naghibi, *Rethinking Global Sisterhood*, 65.

33. Millett, *Going to Iran*, 49.

34. Millett, 49.

35. Millett, 49; 50.

36. Millett, 49.

37. For a more specific consideration of the veil and the politics of transparency in the context of liberal society, see Falguni A. Sheth, "The Veil, Transparency, and the Deceptive Conceit of Liberalism," *philoSOPHIA* 9, no. 1 (2019): 53–72.

38. Millett, *Going to Iran*, 50.

39. In this vein, see Édouard Glissant on what he has termed the "right to opacity," in *Poetics of Relation*, trans. Betsy Wing (Ann Arbor: University of Michigan Press, 1997), 194. Writing in the French Caribbean, postcolonial context of Martinique, Glissant's famous call for opacity is a response to Western epistemic structures of domination that have been forged in the grammar of transparency.

40. In particular, see Meyda Yeğenoğlu, *Colonial Fantasies: Towards a Feminist Reading of Orientalism* (Cambridge: Cambridge University Press, 1998). On the racial politics of the veil in the specific context of the 1979 Iranian Women's Movement, see Sylvia Chan-Malik, "Chadors, Feminists, Terror: The Racial Politics of U.S. Media Representations of the

1979 Iranian Women's Movement," *ANNALS of the American Academy of Political and Social Science* 637, no. 1 (2011): 112–40.

41. Frantz Fanon, "Algeria Unveiled," in *A Dying Colonialism*, trans. Haakon Chevalier (1959; New York: Grove Press, 1965), 44.

42. Millett, *Going to Iran*, 306.

43. Mottahedeh, *Whisper Tapes*, 27.

44. Elizabeth Grosz, "Thinking the New: Of Futures Yet Unthought," *Symplokē* 6, nos. 1–2 (1998): 39; emphasis in original. Grosz's claim is part of her broader, longstanding efforts to think the temporality of the new in terms of duration and becoming, which draw primarily from the work of Henri Bergson and Gilles Deleuze.

45. Ruth Ozeki, *Tale for the Time Being* (New York: Penguin, 2013), 6. As the novel explicates in its own footnotes, the Japanese "New Woman" emerged as a figure in the early 1900s that was characterized by modern and progressive tendencies. The Taishō era, in addition, refers to a short-lived liberal, democratic movement in Japan that lasted from 1912 to 1926. These histories will be explored in more detail in my analysis of the novel that follows.

46. Ozeki, *Tale for the Time Being*, 389.

47. In this chapter, I refer to the author of the novel under analysis as "Ozeki" and the main character in the text as "Ruth." For a reading that points out the numerous parallels between the author and her protagonist, see Rocío G. Davis, "Fictional Transits and Ruth Ozeki's *A Tale for the Time Being*," *Biography* 38, no. 1 (2015): 87–103. For Ozeki's own comments on the matter, see Alison Glassie, "Ruth Ozeki's Floating World: *A Tale for the Time Being*'s Spiritual Oceanography," *Novel: A Forum on Fiction* 53, no. 3 (2020): 452–70.

48. For a critique of the unequal valence of this relationship, which positions figures of Japan as "presumed objects of rescue," see Guy Beauregard, "On Not Knowing: *A Tale for the Time Being* and the Politics of Imagining Lives After March 11," *Canadian Literature* 227 (2015): 99.

49. Ozeki, *Tale for the Time Being*, 9.

50. Ozeki, 119.

51. Ozeki, 402.

52. Ozeki, 402; emphasis in original.

53. Various scholars have since taken up the analytic of "not-knowing" as the basis for their readings of the novel, especially with regard to its depiction of an abundance of disasters both natural and manmade. These range from the 2011 Tōhoku earthquake and tsunami to World War II to the 9/11 attacks in the United States, and more. Much of this work involves an examination of the capacity of literature to bear witness to these unspeakable crises, of which existing frameworks of representation will inevitably fall short. For example, see Beauregard, "On Not Knowing"; Glassie, "Ruth Ozeki's Floating World"; and Claire Gullander-Drolet, "Translational Form in Ruth Ozeki's *A Tale for the Time Being*," *Journal of Transnational American Studies* 9, no. 1 (2018): 293–314.

54. Ozeki, *Tale for the Time Being*, 409.

55. Ruth Ozeki, "A Conversation with Ruth Ozeki," ruth ozeki's web world, 2013, https://www.ruthozeki.com/writing-film/time-being /read/.

56. Ozeki, "Conversation with Ruth Ozeki."

57. Ozeki, *Tale for the Time Being*, 149. For a formative overview of the genre, see Edward Fowler, *The Rhetoric of Confession: Shishōsetsu in Early Twentieth-Century Japanese Fiction* (Berkeley: University of California Press, 1988). As I will follow up, however, Fowler does not cover any female writers in his study. On how the I-novel was formative of a wider historical and cultural paradigm in Japan, see Tomi Suzuki, *Narrating the Self: Fictions of Japanese Modernity* (Stanford, CA: Stanford University Press, 1996).

58. Ozeki, *Tale for the Time Being*, 149.

59. Ozeki, 149.

60. Ozeki, 150.

61. Ozeki, 150.

62. In various interviews, Ruth Ozeki has connected Jiko's missing narrative to a larger trajectory of forgotten women's histories. My argument, however, is predicated on the political and ethical stakes of their deliberate concealment.

63. Fowler, *Rhetoric of Confession*, xxix.

64. In this vein, a poem by the prominent feminist writer and activist Yosano Akiko titled "Rambling Thoughts" is appended in *A Tale for*

the Time Being. Yosano is listed by Fowler as actively writing during the Taishō era of Japan, but is excluded from his study presumably for her feminist inclinations that he believes to be ideologically oppositional to the autobiographical genre of *shishōsetsu.* The novel includes Yosano's poem as a work that arguably refutes his claims. It reads: "If I could but write entirely in the first person, / I, who am a woman. / If I could write entirely in the first person, / I, I." In these very lines, the poem reveals Yosano's engagement with autobiographical undercurrents characteristic of the *shishōsetsu* tradition, thus refuting Edward Fowler's claims.

65. Following Japanese naming conventions, I refer to the character in the novel as "Sugako" and to her historical anarchist namesake as "Kanno."

66. Ozeki, *Tale for the Time Being,* 216. For context, Haruki #1 was drafted into the Japanese army as a kamikaze pilot during World War II. Haruki #2 is Nao's father, whose mother Ema names after her brother who perished in the war. Ruth Ozeki refers to the two characters as such throughout the novel.

67. For a reading that tracks a line of trauma and suffering through Nao's family tree, see Andrew Kim, "Japanese Melancholy and the Ethics of Concealment in Ruth Ozeki's *A Tale for the Time Being*," *Mosaic: an interdisciplinary critical journal* 52, no. 4 (2019): 73–90.

68. Scholars have extensively documented the transnational relations that compose the intellectual history of anarchism in Japan. See, for example, John Crump, *The Origins of Socialist Thought in Japan* (New York: St. Martin's Press, 1983); and for a more recent study, Sho Konishi, *Anarchist Modernity: Cooperatism and Japanese-Russian Intellectual Relations in Modern Japan* (Cambridge, MA: Harvard University Press, 2013).

69. The anarchist magazine *Mother Earth* that Goldman founded would later publish tributes to the executed Japanese activists; see Havel Hyppolyte, "Long Live Anarchy!," *Mother Earth* 5, no. 12 (February 1911): 375–9.

70. Ozeki, *Tale for the Time Being,* 348.

71. The other images that Ruth is assaulted with include the torture and eventual death of Jiko's son Haruki #1 and the bombings of Hiroshima and Nagasaki during World War II.

72. For key scholarly works on the Japanese New Woman, see Jan Bards-
ley, *The Bluestockings of Japan: New Woman Essays and Fiction from
Seitō, 1911–16* (Ann Arbor: University of Michigan Press, 2007); Dina
Lowy, *The Japanese "New Woman": Images of Gender and Modernity*
(New Brunswick, NJ: Rutgers University Press, 2007); and Barbara
Sato, *The New Japanese Woman: Modernity, Media, and Women in
Interwar Japan* (Durham, NC: Duke University Press, 2003). For a
reading of the novel that also touches on Jiko's history as a Japanese
New Woman, see Marlo Starr, "Beyond Machine Dreams: Zen,
Cyber-, and Transnational Feminisms in Ruth Ozeki's *A Tale for the
Time Being*," *Meridians: feminism, race, transnationalism* 13, no. 2
(2016): 99–122.

73. In her study, Dina Lowy considers these radical activists to be "fore-
mothers of Japan's New Woman"; see Lowy, *Japanese "New Woman,"* 8.

74. For a more comprehensive historical overview of the Japanese New
Woman figure, which covers its emergence from various negotiations
with paradigms of Western modernity, see Lowy, *Japanese "New
Woman."*

75. A key reading of the novel that makes use of an explicitly transpacific
frame of inquiry is Michelle N. Huang, "Ecologies of Entanglement in
the Great Pacific Garbage Patch," *Journal of Asian American Studies*,
special issue "Transpacific Overtures," 20, no. 1 (2017): 95–117. For some
recent works that have established the field of transpacific studies, see
Yunte Huang, *Transpacific Imaginations: History, Literature, Counterpoetics* (Cambridge, MA: Harvard University Press, 2008); Christine
Mok and Aimee Bahng, "Transpacific Overtures: An Introduction,"
Journal of Asian American Studies 20 no. 1 (2017): 1–9; Viet Thanh
Nguyen and Janet Hoskins, eds., *Transpacific Studies: Critical Perspec-
tives on an Emerging Field* (Honolulu: University of Hawai'i Press,
2014); Erin Suzuki, "Transpacific," in *The Routledge Companion to Asian
American and Pacific Island Literatures*, ed. Rachel Lee (New York:
Routledge, 2014), 352–64; and Lisa Yonenama, "Toward a Decolonial
Genealogy of the Transpacific," *American Quarterly* 69, no. 3 (2017):
471–82.

76. Ozeki, *Tale for the Time Being*, 97.

77. Huang, *Transpacific Imaginations*, 8. Huang specifically refers to the nationalist and imperialist visions of the transpacific that have structured its imaginary as such, and for counterpoetic works to serve as a form of resistance to these dominant paradigms of knowledge.

78. Huang, *Transpacific Imaginations*, 4.

79. Ozeki, *Tale for the Time Being*, 314.

80. Ozeki, 3.

81. Ozeki, 5.

82. Ozeki, 343.

83. Ozeki, 376.

84. In short, Erwin Schrödinger's conceptual experiment—which was used to illustrate the wave function of particles—involved a cat sealed in a box together with a radioactive substance that will decay at complete random. At this point, the fate of the cat remains unknown, and it is considered to occupy a "superposition" of both states of being alive and dead. But once the box is opened and the cat can be observed, this "superposition" of knowledge must collapse into one. For more sustained engagements with quantum mechanics in their readings of the novel, see Kandice Chuh, *The Difference Aesthetics Makes: On the Humanities "After Man"* (Durham, NC: Duke University Press, 2019); and Hsiu-chuan Lee, "Sharing Worlds through Words: Minor Cosmopolitics in Ruth Ozeki's *A Tale for the Time Being*," *ariel: A Review of International English Literature* 49, no. 1 (2018): 27–52.

85. Ozeki, *Tale for the Time Being*, 415; emphasis in original. Ruth Ozeki also links this to the Zen moment as one that infinitely proliferates.

4. A COMMONS BEYOND THE HUMAN

1. Alexis Wright, *The Swan Book* (New York: Washington Square Press, 2013), 6.

2. Alexis Wright's depiction of the swamp settlement and its tragic circumstances recalls the 2007 Northern Territory National Emergency Response that was enacted by the Australian government. "The Intervention," as it is now more colloquially known, involved the deployment of the military to enforce a series of highly controversial

measures that actively legalized the discrimination of Aboriginal people and undermined their rights to land and property.

3. Wright, *Swan Book*, 10.

4. Wright, 12.

5. The earliest reference to the black swan as a thing of perceived impossibility (*OED* 2020) has more recently been refashioned in Nicholas Nassim Taleb, *The Black Swan: The Impact of the Highly Improbable*, 2nd ed. (New York: Random House, 2010).

6. Wright, *Swan Book*, 13; emphasis in original.

7. In recent years, the conceptual analytic of entanglement has gained much traction in the wider domain of the environmental humanities. For the idea of "multispecies entanglements," see Thom van Dooren, *Flight Ways: Life and Loss at the Edge of Extinction* (New York: Columbia University Press, 2014). Linda Daley argues in her reading of the novel that Oblivia and the swans offer a relational identity of inhuman life; see Daley, "Fabulation: Toward Untimely and Inhuman Life in Alexis Wright's *The Swan Book*," *Australian Feminist Studies*. 31, no. 89 (2016): 305–18.

8. Alexis Wright's other novels are *Plains of Promise*, *Carpentaria*, and most recently, *Praiseworthy*.

9. Jeanine Leane, "Historyless People," in *Long History, Deep Time: Deepening Histories of Place*, ed. Ann McGrath and Mary Anne Jebb (Canberra: ANU Press, 2015), 155. This term confronts the label of "magical realism" that has often been used to classify Alexis Wright's work.

10. Jeanine Leane explains that Alexis Wright's narratives have been described as "magical" or "mythical," which has the effect of legitimating only a Western understanding of reality. For a critique in a similar vein, see also Alison Ravenscroft, "Dreaming of Others: *Carpentaria* and its Criticism," *Cultural Studies Review* 16, no. 2 (2010): 194–224.

11. For such a treatment of hope that the novel enacts, see Adelle L. Sefton-Rowston, "Hope at the End of the World: Creation Stories and Apocalypse in Alexis Wright's *Carpentaria* and *The Swan Book*," *Antipodes* 30, no. 2 (2016): 355–68.

12. Alexis Wright, "Politics of Writing," *Southerly* 62, no. 2 (2002): 20.

13. Wright, *Swan Book*, 9.

14. The term *commons* first appears in relation to land enclosures in pre-capitalist English property law. For a more extensive survey of its historical origins, see George Caffentzis, "Commons," in *Keywords for Radicals: The Contested Vocabulary of Late-Capitalist Struggle*, ed. Kelly Fritsch and Claire O'Connor (Chico, CA: AK Press, 2016): 93–101; and Peter Linebaugh, *The Magna Carta Manifesto: Liberties and Commons for All* (Berkeley: University of California Press, 2008).

15. In this vein, George Caffentzis ascribes confusion over the current definitions of the *commons* to its propensity for "metaphorical expansion"; see Caffentzis, "The Future of 'The Commons': Neoliberalism's 'Plan B' or the Original Disaccumulation of Capital?" *New Formations* 69, no. 1 (2010): 24. It is precisely this capaciousness, however, that I find productive for my own theorization of the commons.

16. For a comprehensive overview of both old and new uses of the *commons* as a term, see Dana D. Nelson, "The Enduring Appeal of the Commons," *Arizona Quarterly: A Journal of American Literature, Culture, and Theory* 75, no. 2 (2019): 1–21.

17. For example, see Caffentzis, "Future of 'The Commons'"; George Caffentzis and Silvia Federici, "Commons Against and Beyond Capitalism," *Community Development Journal* 49, Supplement 1 (2014): i92–i105; Massimo de Angelis, "Does Capital Need a Commons Fix?" *ephemera, theory and politics in organization* 13, no. 3 (2013): 603–15; Massimo de Angelis, *Omnia Sunt Communia: On the Commons and the Transformation to Postcapitalism* (London: Zed Books, 2017); Massimo de Angelis and Stavros Stavrides, "On the Commons: A Public Interview with Massimo De Angelis and Stavros Stavrides," *e-flux Journal* 17 (2010): 1–17; David Harvey, "The Future of the Commons," *Radical History Review* 109 (2011): 101–107; Silvia Federici, "Feminism and the Politics of the Commons," in The Wealth of the Commons: A World Beyond Market and State, 2012, http://www.wealthofthecommons.org/essay/feminism-and-politics-commons/; Silvia Federici, *Re-Enchanting the World: Feminism and the Politics of the Commons* (Oakland, CA: PM Press, 2018); Silvia Federici, "Women, Reproduction, and the Commons," *South Atlantic Quarterly* 118, no. 4 (2019): 711–24; Naomi Klein, "Reclaiming the Commons," *New Left Review* 9 (2001): 81–89; Peter Linebaugh, *The Magna Carta Manifesto: Liberties and Commons for All* (Berkeley:

University of California Press, 2008); Peter Linebaugh, *Stop, Thief! The Commons, Enclosures, and Resistance* (Oakland, CA: PM Press, 2014); Sandro Mezzandra, "Resonances of the Common," in *The Anomie of the Earth: Philosophy, Politics, and Autonomy in Europe and the Americas*, ed. Federico Luisetti, John Pickles, and Wilson Kaiser (Durham, NC: Duke University Press, 2015): 215–26; Herbert Reid and Betsy Taylor, *Recovering the Commons: Democracy, Place, and Global Justice* (Champaign: University of Illinois Press, 2010); and Stavros Stavrides, *Common Space: The City as Commons* (London: Zed Books, 2016).

18. See Garrett Hardin, "The Tragedy of the Commons," *Science* 162, no. 3859 (1968): 1243–48; and Elinor Ostrom, *Governing the Commons: The Evolution of Institutions for Collective Action* (Cambridge: Cambridge University Press, 1990).

19. Caffentzis and Federici, "Commons Against and Beyond Capitalism," 194. According to them, primitive accumulation signaled the beginnings of modern capitalist society in sixteenth- and seventeenth-century Europe.

20. Caffentzis and Federici, "Commons Against and Beyond Capitalism," 194.

21. See Linebaugh, *Stop, Thief!*

22. Lauren Berlant argues that the aspirational sign of the commons should itself be subjected to suspicion, insofar as it occludes the political struggle necessary for its realization; see Berlant, "The Commons: Infrastructures for Troubling Times," *Environment and Planning D: Society and Space* 34, no. 3 (2016): 393–419.

23. This ambivalent relationship between the commons and capital is further explored in de Angelis, "Does Capital Need a Commons Fix?"

24. For further examples on how the language of the commons has been appropriated by institutions and academic literature alike, see de Angelis, "Tragedy of the Capitalist Commons"; Caffentzis, "Future of 'The Commons'"; Federici, "Feminism and the Politics of the Commons"; Caffentzis and Federici, "Commons Against and Beyond Capitalism."

25. This includes existing scholarship on the multispecies or nonhuman commons, in which human and nonhuman species become entangled in ways that refuse conventional meaning. See Marcus Baynes-Rock,

"Life and Death in the Multispecies Commons," *Social Science Information* 52, no. 2 (2013): 210–27. My thinking on the commons differs from such work in its critique of the human-centered frameworks of knowledge that have secured the idea of the commons in the first place.

26. Blaser and de la Cadena, "Pluriverse: Proposals for a World of Many Worlds," in *A World of Many Worlds*, ed. Marisol de la Cadena and Mario Blaser (Durham, NC: Duke University Press, 2018), 6.

27. Blaser and de la Cadena, "Pluriverse," 6.

28. Berlant, "Commons," 395. Lauren Berlant is skeptical of this affective attachment to the utopian construct of the commons insofar as it risks the collapse of what is better into what merely *feels* better; see Berlant, 399; emphasis mine.

29. Anna Lowenhaupt Tsing, *The Mushroom at the End of the World: On the Possibilities of Life in Capitalist Ruins* (Princeton, NJ: Princeton University Press, 2015), 21.

30. Tsing, *Mushroom*, 21; emphasis in original.

31. For approaches that have run both parallel to—and in critique of—posthumanism, see Richard Grusin, *The Nonhuman Turn* (Minnesota: University of Minnesota Press, 2015); Dana Luciano and Mel Y. Chen, "Introduction: Has the Queer Ever Been Human?" *GLQ* 21, nos. 2–3 (2015): 183–207; and Julietta Singh, *Unthinking Mastery: Dehumanism and Decolonial Entanglements* (Durham, NC: Duke University Press, 2018).

32. Mario Blaser and Marisol de la Cadena have themselves proposed the making of an "uncommons"; see Blaser and de la Cadena, "Pluriverse," 4. For a similar perspective critical of the commons, see also Christian P. Haines and Peter Hitchcock, "Introduction: No Place for the Commons," *Minnesota Review* 93, no. 1 (2019): 55–61.

33. Donna Haraway, *Staying with the Trouble: Making Kin in the Chthulucene* (Durham, NC: Duke University Press, 2016), 12. Haraway extends this from Marilyn Strathern, *The Gender of the Gift: Problems with Women and Problems with Society in Melanesia* (Berkeley: University of California Press, 1988).

34. For similar critiques, see Mel Y. Chen, *Animacies: Biopolitics, Racial Mattering, and Queer Affect* (Durham, NC: Duke University Press,

2012); Zakiyyah Iman Jackson, "Animal: New Directions in the Theorization of Race and Posthumanism," *Feminist Studies* 39, no. 3 (2014):
669–85; Zakiyyah Iman Jackson, *Becoming Human: Matter and Meaning in an Antiblack World* (New York: NYU Press, 2020); Zakiyyah
Iman Jackson, "Outer Worlds: The Persistence of Race in Movement
'Beyond the Human,'" *GLQ* 21, nos. 2–3 (2015): 215–18; Juanita Sundberg, "Decolonizing Posthumanist Geographies," *Cultural Geographies*
21, no. 1 (2014): 33–47; Tavia Nyong'o, "Little Monsters: Race, Sovereignty, and Queer Inhumanism in *Beasts of the Southern Wild*," *GLQ* 12,
nos. 2–3 (2015): 249–72; Zoe Todd, "An Indigenous Feminist's Take on
the Ontological Turn: 'Ontology' Is Just Another Word for Colonialism," *Journal of Historical Sociology* 29, no. 1 (2016): 4–22.

35. Jackson, "Outer Worlds," 215. Jackson aligns this with "an attempt to
move *beyond* race, and in particular blackness"; Jackson, "Outer
Worlds," 216; emphasis in original.

36. Nadja Millner-Larson and Gavin Butt, "Introduction: The Queer
Commons," *GLQ* 24, no. 4 (2018): 402. For more speculative ideations
of the commons, see José Esteban Muñoz, "The Brown Commons,"
in *The Sense of Brown*, ed. Joshua Chambers-Letson and Tavia
Nyong'o (Durham, NC: Duke University Press, 2020), 1–7.

37. See also Fred Moten and Stefano Harney, *The Undercommons: Fugitive
Planning and Black Study* (New York: Minor Compositions, 2013) on
the dislocating effect of what they theorize as the undercommons.

38. Along these lines, recent scholarship in Indigenous studies has shown
how Aboriginal ecological knowledges in particular might be able to
articulate geographies beyond the human; see, for example, Margaret
Raven et al., "The Emu: More-than-Human and More-than-Animal
Geographies," *Antipode: A Radical Journal of Geography* 53, no. 5 (2021):
1526–45.

39. It is key to note that Australia was first established as a British penal
colony in 1788.

40. Deborah Bird Rose, *Reports from a Wild Country: Ethics for Decolonisation* (Sydney: University of New South Wales Press, 2004), 62.

41. In accordance with the multiplicity of Aboriginal languages from different regions of Australia, this creation ontology is known by names
such as Tjukurpa, Alcheringa, Ungud, and more. Although it has

most commonly been translated into English as "The Dreaming," the reduced form of this term simply cannot account for the inherent complexities of Aboriginal meaning. See Christine Judith Nicholls, "'Dreamtime' and 'The Dreaming'—An Introduction," *The Conversation*, January 22, 2014. https://theconversation.com/dreamtime-and-the-dreaming-an-introduction-20833.

42. Rose, *Reports from a Wild Country*, 54.

43. See also Mark Rifkin, *Beyond Settler Time: Temporal Sovereignty and Indigenous Self-Determination* (Durham, NC: Duke University Press, 2017). Rifkin focuses primarily on the Native American context, but his observations about the colonizing tendencies of settler time are nevertheless informative for my own arguments.

44. In this vein, Patrick Wolfe explains how the Dreamtime concept has been used especially in anthropological inquiry as a construct for symbolic, colonizing violence; see Wolfe, "On Being Woken Up: The Dreamtime in Anthropology and in Australian Settler Culture," *Comparative Studies in Society and History* 33, no. 2 (1991): 197–224.

45. On the idea of sovereignty in the novel, see Philip Mead, "The Injusticeable and the Imaginable," *Journal of the Association for the Study of Australian Literature* 16, no. 2 (2016), and "Unresolved Sovereignty and the Anthropocene Novel: Alexis Wright's *The Swan Book*," *Journal of Australian Studies* 42, no. 4 (2018): 524–38. On Indigenous sovereignty in the social and historical context of settler-colonial Australia, see Aileen Moreton-Robinson, ed., *Sovereign Subjects: Indigenous Sovereignty Matters* (Sydney: Allen and Unwin, 2007), and *The White Possessive: Property, Power, and Indigenous Sovereignty* (Minneapolis: University of Minnesota Press, 2015)

46. Wright, *Swan Book*, 12.

47. Wright, 18.

48. On temporal disorientation in the novel, see Daniel Fisher, "Untidy Times: Alexis Wright, Extinction, and the Politics of Apprehension," *Cultural Anthropology* 33, no. 2 (2018): 180–8.

49. My conceptualization of a speculative ethics is in line with María Puig de la Bellacasa, *Matters of Care: Speculative Ethics in More Than Human Worlds* (Minneapolis: University of Minnesota Press, 2017).

50. Wright, *Swan Book*, 51.

51. Wright, 42; emphasis in original. See also the Council of Australian Governments, "A New Way of Working Together," accessed February 18, 2025.

52. Wright, *Swan Book*, 59.

53. Wright, 58.

54. Wright, 60.

55. Wright, 13.

56. Wright, 10.

57. Wright, 69.

58. Wright, 72; emphasis in original.

59. Rifkin, *Beyond Settler Time*, vii.

60. Wright, *Swan Book*, 41.

61. Wright, 84.

62. Wright, 69.

63. Wright, 81.

64. Elizabeth Povinelli, *The Cunning of Recognition: Indigenous Alterities and the Making of Australian Multiculturalism* (Durham, NC: Duke University Press, 2002).

65. On the "impossible demand" placed on Indigenous people as a consequence of the convergences between liberalism and multiculturalism in Australia, see Povinelli, *Cunning of Recognition*, 8.

66. Wright, *Swan Book*, 110.

67. Wright, 204.

68. Wright, 60.

69. Wright, 237.

70. Wright, 295.

71. Wright, 295.

72. On this orientation "towards origins" rather than a future state, see Rose, *Reports from a Wild Country*, 55.

73. I am guided here by Claire Colebrook's thinking on extinction along similar lines; see Colebrook, *Death of the PostHuman: Essays on Extinction*, vol. 1 (Ann Arbor, MI: Open Humanities Press, 2014), and "Extinct Theory," in *Theory After "Theory,"* ed. Jane Elliott and Derek Attridge (New York: Routledge, 2011): 61–71.

74. Wright, *Swan Book*, 72; emphasis in original.

75. Wright, 301.

76. Wright, 72. Adeline Johns-Putra argues that Oblivia's rape can be read as a synecdoche for the multiple violations of Aboriginal country, people, and ontology; see Johns-Putra, "The Rest Is Silence: Postmodern and Postcolonial Possibilities in Climate Change Fiction," *Studies in the Novel* 50, no. 1 (2018): 26–42.

77. Wright, *Swan Book*, 301.

78. Wright, 301.

79. Wright, 75.

80. Wright, 75.

81. For a reading of Bella Donna along these lines, see Maria Kaaren Takolander, "Theorizing Irony and Trauma in Magical Realism: Junot Díaz's *The Brief Wondrous Life of Oscar Wao* and Alexis Wright's *The Swan Book*," *ariel: A Review of International English Literature* 47, no. 3 (2016): 95–122.

82. Wright, *Swan Book*, 77–78.

83. Wright, 75

84. Wright, *Swan Book*, 38. Sara Ahmed has written of the figure of the feminist auntie more extensively along these lines, which is instructive to my reading of the character of Bella Donna; see Ahmed, *Living a Feminist Life*.

85. Wright, *Swan Book*, 15; emphasis in original; 61.

86. For a reading that evaluates the postcolonial possibilities of magical realism in the novel on account of its mythological discourse, see Ben Holgate, "Unsettling Narratives: Re-Evaluating Magical Realism as Postcolonial Discourse through Alexis Wright's *Carpentaria* and *The Swan Book*," *Journal of Postcolonial Writing* 51, no. 6, (2015): 634–47.

87. Adrienne Rich, "When We Dead Awaken: Writing as Re-Vision," *College English* 34, no. 1 (1972): 19.

88. William Butler Yeats, "Leda and the Swan," in *The Collected Poems of W.B. Yeats*, ed. Richard J. Finneran, 2nd ed. (New York: Scribner, 1983), l. 1–2.

89. For a reading of W. B. Yeats's poem as an example of his broader claims about literature and its seduction of the imagination, see Geoffrey H. Hartman, *Criticism in the Wilderness: The Study of Literature Today* (New Haven, CT: Yale University Press, 1980): 21–26.

90. Yeats, "Leda and the Swan," l. 9–11.

91. Two of Leda's children from her impregnation by Zeus will cause the fall of Troy: Helen's abduction by Paris from her husband Menelaus, king of Sparta, sees the Greeks mounting the Trojan war, and later, Clytemnestra will murder her husband Agamemnon, who had commanded the Greek armed forces in this effort. W. B. Yeats elsewhere writes of imagining "the annunciation of Greece as founded to Leda"; see Yeats, *A Vision: The Revised 1937 Edition*, vol. 4 of *The Collected Works of W. B. Yeats*, ed. Margaret Mills Harper and Catherine E. Paul (New York: Scribner, 2015), 195.

92. Yeats, "Leda and the Swan," l. 8.

93. Wright, *Swan Book*, 273.

94. Wright, 182; emphasis in original.

95. The Deathscapes project (2016–2020), specifically one of its case studies "Indigenous Femicide and the Killing State," outlines ongoing research on these specific forms of violence against Indigenous women and girls that span across Australia, Canada, and the United States; see "Deathscapes: Mapping Race and Violence in Settler States," Carceral Geography, Royal Geographical Society with IBG, accessed February 21, 2025, https://carceralgeographies .co.uk/deathscapes-mapping-race-and-violence-in-settler-societies/ #:~:text=With%20the%20ultimate%20aim%20of,the%20United%20 States%20and%20Canada. This web page contains an archived link to the Deathscapes project by the National Library of Australia: https://webarchive.nla.gov.au/awa/20201103065140/http://pandora .nla.gov.au/pan/173410/20201103-1648/www.deathscapes.org/index .html.

96. Wright, *Swan Book*, 183; emphasis in original.

97. Yeats, "Leda and the Swan," l. 14.

CODA: TEXTUAL POWER AND
TRANSFORMATIVE POETICS

1. Audre Lorde, "Power," in *The Collected Poems of Audre Lorde* (New York: Norton, 1997), ll.1–4. Lorde alludes to a poetic practice of W. B. Yeats that he described as a quarrel that is staged with the self: "We make out of the quarrels with others, rhetoric, but of the quarrels with

ourselves, poetry"; Yeats, "Anima Hominis," in *Essays* (New York: Macmillan, 1924), 492.

2. Audre Lorde speaks about the inception of this poem in a 1982 interview with Claudia Tate: Tate, "Audre Lorde," in *Conversations with Audre Lorde*, ed. Joan Wylie Hall (Jackson: University Press of Mississippi, 2004), 85–100.

3. Lorde, "Power," ll. 35–40.

4. Lorde, l.18.

5. Lorde, ll. 45–48.

6. Lorde, ll. 2–3.

7. Hemmings, *Why Stories Matter*, 2; emphasis in original.

8. As a key example of this, a backlash against the term *gender ideology* rife with nationalist, misogynist, homophobic, and transphobic underpinnings is gaining ground across the world. For more on this, see Judith Butler, *Who's Afraid of Gender?* (New York: MacMillan, 2024); and Elizabeth S. Corredor, "Unpacking 'Gender Ideology' and the Global Right's Antigender Countermovement," *Signs* 44, no. 3 (2019): 613–38.

BIBLIOGRAPHY

Abel, Elizabeth, ed. *Writing and Sexual Difference*. Chicago: University of Chicago Press, 1982.

Abu-Lughod, Lila. *Do Muslim Women Need Saving?* Cambridge, MA: Harvard University Press, 2015.

Achebe, Christie C. "Literary Insights into the Ogbanje Phenomenon." *Journal of African Studies* 7, no. 1 (1980): 31–38.

———. *The World of the Ogbanje*. Enugu, Nigeria: Fourth Dimension, 1986.

Ahmad, Aalya. "Feminism Beyond the Waves." *Briarpatch Magazine*, June 30, 2015. https://briarpatchmagazine.com/articles/view/feminism -beyond-the-waves/.

Ahmed, Leila. *Women and Gender in Islam: Historical Roots of a Modern Debate*. New Haven, CT: Yale University Press, 1992.

Ahmed, Sara. "Affective Economies." *Social Text* 22, no. 2 (2004): 117–39.

———. *The Cultural Politics of Emotion*. New York: Routledge, 2004.

———. *Living a Feminist Life*. Durham, NC: Duke University Press, 2017.

———. *The Promise of Happiness*. Durham, NC: Duke University Press, 2010.

———. *Queer Phenomenology: Orientations, Objects, Others*. Durham, NC: Duke University Press, 2006.

———. "This Other and Other Others." *Economy and Society* 13, no. 4 (2002): 558–72.

———. *What's the Use? On the Uses of Use*. Durham, NC: Duke University Press, 2019.

———. *Willful Subjects*. Durham, NC: Duke University Press, 2014.

Aikau, Hokulani K., et al., eds. *Feminist Waves, Feminist Generations: Life Stories from the Academy.* Minneapolis: University of Minnesota Press, 2007.

Alaimo, Stacy. "States of Suspension: Trans-Corporeality at Sea." *Interdisciplinary Studies in Literature and Environment* 19, no. 3 (2012): 476–93.

Alexander, Jacqui M. *Pedagogies of Crossing: Meditations on Feminism, Sexual Politics, Memory, and the Sacred.* Durham, NC: Duke University Press, 2005.

Alexander, Jacqui M., and Chandra Talpade Mohanty, eds. *Feminist Genealogies, Colonial Legacies, Democratic Futures.* New York: Routledge, 1997.

Alford, Matthew H., Thomas Peacock, Jennifer A. MacKinnon, et al. "The Formation and Fate of Internal Waves in the South China Sea." *Nature* 521 (2015): 65–69.

Allewaert, Monique. *Ariel's Ecology: Plantations, Personhood, and Colonialism in the American Tropics.* Minneapolis: University of Minnesota Press, 2013.

Amadiume, Ifi. *Male Daughters, Female Husbands: Gender and Sex in an African Society.* London: Zed Books, 1987.

Andrijasevic, Rutvica, Carrie Hamilton, and Clare Hemmings. "reimagining revolutions." *Feminist Review* 106 (2014): 1–8.

Anker, Elizabeth, and Rita Felski, eds. *Critique and Postcritique.* Durham, NC: Duke University Press, 2017.

Anzaldúa, Gloria E. *Light in the Dark/Luz en Lo Oscuro: Rewriting Identity, Spirituality, Reality.* Ed. Analouise Keating. Durham, NC: Duke University Press, 2015.

Auyoung, Elaine. "Becoming Sensitive: Literary Study and Learning to Notice." *PMLA* 138, no. 1 (2023): 158–64.

Bachelard, Gaston. *Water and Dreams: An Essay on the Imagination of Matter.* Trans. Edith R. Farrell. Dallas, TX: Dallas Institute of Humanities and Culture, 1999.

Bardsley, Jan. *The Bluestockings of Japan: New Woman Essays and Fiction from Seitō, 1911–16.* Ann Arbor: University of Michigan Press, 2007.

Bastian, Misty L. "Irregular Visitors: Narratives About Ogbaanje (Spirit Children) in Southern Nigerian Popular Writing." In *Readings in*

African Popular Fiction, ed. Stephanie Newell, 59–67. Bloomington: Indiana University Press, 2002.

——. "Married in the Water: Spirit Kin and Other Afflictions of Modernity in Southeastern Nigeria." *Journal of Religion in Africa* 27, no. 2 (1997): 116–34.

Baynes-Rock, Marcus. "Life and Death in the Multispecies Commons." *Social Science Information* 52, no. 2 (2013): 210–27.

Beauregard, Guy. "On Not Knowing: *A Tale for the Time Being* and the Politics of Imagining Lives After March 11." *Canadian Literature* 227 (2015): 96–112.

Benítez-Rojo, Antonio. *The Repeating Island: The Caribbean and the Postmodern Perspective.* Durham, NC: Duke University Press, 1992.

Bennett, Jane. *The Enchantment of Modern Life: Attachments, Crossings, and Ethics.* Princeton, NJ: Princeton University Press, 2001.

Bennett, Joshua. "'Beyond the Vomiting Dark': Toward a Black Hydropoetics." In *Ecopoetics: Essays in the Field*, ed. Angela Hume and Gillian Osborne, 102–17. Iowa City: University of Iowa Press, 2018.

Berlant, Lauren. "The Commons: Infrastructures for Troubling Times." *Environment and Planning D: Society and Space* 34, no. 3 (2016): 393–419.

——. *On the Inconvenience of Other People.* Durham, NC: Duke University Press, 2022.

Berman, Morris. *The Reenchantment of the World.* Ithaca, NY: Cornell University Press, 1981.

Best, Stephen, and Saidiya Hartman. "Fugitive Justice." *Representations* 92, no. 1 (2005): 1–15.

Best, Stephen, and Sharon Marcus. "Surface Reading: An Introduction." *Representations* 108, no. 1 (2009): 1–21.

Bettelheim, Bruno. *The Uses of Enchantment: The Meaning and Importance of Fairy Tales.* London: Thames and Hudson, 1976.

Bhandar, Brenna, and Rafeef Ziadah, eds. *Revolutionary Feminisms: Conversations on Collective Action and Radical Thought.* London: Verso, 2020.

Bilgrami, Akeel. *Secularism, Identity, and Enchantment.* Cambridge, MA: Harvard University Press, 2014.

"black swan, n." OED Online, Oxford University Press, June 2020. https://www.oed.com/view/Entry/282957/.

Blaser Mario, and Marisol de la Cadena. "Pluriverse: Proposals for a World of Many Worlds." In *A World of Many Worlds*, ed. Marisol de la Cadena and Mario Blaser, 1–22. Durham, NC: Duke University Press, 2018.

Blum, Hester. "The Prospect of Oceanic Studies." *PMLA* 125, no. 3 (2010): 670–77.

Bould, Mark. "The Ships Landed Long Ago: Afrofuturism and Black SF." *Science Fiction Studies* 34, no. 2 (2007): 177–86.

Boyce-Davies, Carole. "Occupying the Terrain: Reengaging 'Beyond Miranda's Meanings: Un/Silencing the "Demonic Ground" of Caliban's Woman.'" *American Quarterly* 70, no. 4 (2018): 837–45.

Braidotti, Rosi. "Mothers, Monsters, and Machines." In *Nomadic Subjects: Embodiment and Sexual Difference in Contemporary Feminist Theory*, 213–44. 2nd ed. New York: Columbia University Press, 2011.

Burke, Carolyn. "Introduction to Luce Irigaray's 'When Our Lips Speak Together.'" *Signs: Journal of Women in Culture and Society* 6 no. 1 (1980): 66–68.

——. "Irigaray Through the Looking Glass." *Feminist Studies* 7, no. 2 (1981): 288–306.

Burlein, Ann, and Jackie Orr, "Introduction: The Practice of Enchantment: Strange Allures." *WSQ: Women's Studies Quarterly* 40, nos. 3–4 (2012): 13–23.

Butler, Judith. *Gender Trouble: Feminism and the Subversion of Identity*. New York: Routledge, 1990.

——. "Performative Acts and Gender Constitution: An Essay in Phenomenology and Feminist Theory." *Theatre Journal* 40, no. 4 (1988): 519–31.

——. *Undoing Gender*. New York: Routledge, 2004.

——. *Who's Afraid of Gender?* New York: Macmillan, 2024.

Caffentzis, George. "Commons." In *Keywords for Radicals: The Contested Vocabulary of Late-Capitalist Struggle*, ed. Kelly Fritsch and Claire O'Connor, 93–101. Chico, CA: AK Press, 2016.

Caffentzis, George. "The Future of 'The Commons': Neoliberalism's 'Plan B' or the Original Disaccumulation of Capital?" *New Formations* 69, no. 1 (2010): 23–41.

Caffentzis, George, and Silvia Federici. "Commons Against and Beyond Capitalism." *Community Development Journal* 49, Supplement 1 (2014): i92–i105.

Cai, Shuqun, Jieshuo Xie, and Jianling He. "An Overview of Internal Solitary Waves in the South China Sea." *Surveys in Geophysics* 33, no. 5 (2012): 927–43.

Campt Tina M. *Image Matters: Archive, Photography, and the African Diaspora in Europe.* Durham, NC: Duke University Press, 2012.

Carson, Rachel. *The Sea Around Us.* Oxford: Oxford University Press, 2018. First published in 1951.

Cecire, Maria Sachiko. *Re-Enchanted: The Rise of Children's Fantasy Literature in the Twentieth Century.* Minneapolis: University of Minnesota Press, 2019.

Chakrabarty, Dipesh. *Provincializing Europe: Postcolonial Thought and Historical Difference.* Princeton, NJ: Princeton University Press, 2000.

Chan-Malik, Sylvia. "Chadors, Feminists, Terror: The Racial Politics of U.S. Media Representations of the 1979 Iranian Women's Movement." *The ANNALS of the American Academy of Political and Social Science* 637, no. 1 (2011): 112–40.

Chandler, David L. "The Ocean's Hidden Waves Show Their Power." *MIT News,* January 8, 2014. http://news.mit.edu/2013/the-oceans-hidden -waves-show-their-power-0108/.

Chen, Cecilia, Janine MacLeod, and Astrida Neimanis, eds. *Thinking with Water.* Montreal: McGill-Queen's University Press, 2013.

Chen, Mel Y. *Animacies: Biopolitics, Racial Mattering, and Queer Affect.* Durham, NC: Duke University Press, 2012.

Cheng, Anne Anlin. *Ornamentalism.* Oxford: Oxford University Press, 2019.

Choi, Franny. *Floating, Brilliant, Gone.* Austin, TX: Write Bloody Publishing, 2014.

Christian, Barbara. "The Race for Theory." *Cultural Critique* 6 (1987): 51–63.

Chuh, Kandice. *The Difference Aesthetics Makes: On the Humanities "After Man."* Durham, NC: Duke University Press, 2019.

clipping. "The Deep." Track 1 of *The Deep,* Sub Pop Records, 2019.

Colebrook, Claire. *Death of the PostHuman: Essays on Extinction.* Vol. 1 of *Essays on Extinction.* Ann Arbor, MI: Open Humanities Press, 2014.

——. "Extinct Theory." In *Theory After "Theory,"* ed. Jane Elliott and Derek Attridge, 61–71. New York: Routledge, 2011.

Comfort, Alex. "Demonic and Historical Models in Biology." *Journal of Social and Biological Structures* 3, no. 2 (1980): 207–15.

Cornell, Drucilla. *Beyond Accommodation: Ethical Feminism, Deconstruction, and the Law.* New York: Routledge, 1991.

Corredor, Elizabeth S. "Unpacking 'Gender Ideology' and the Global Right's Antigender Countermovement." *Signs* 44, no. 3 (2019): 613–38.

Costello, Katherine. "Inventing 'French Feminism': A Critical History." PhD diss. Duke University, 2016.

Council of Australian Governments. "A New Way of Working Together." Accessed February 18, 2025. http://www.closingthegap.gov.au/.

Crawford, Jason. *Allegory and Enchantment: An Early Modern Poetics.* Oxford: Oxford University Press, 2017.

Creed, Barbara. *The Monstrous-Feminine: Film, Feminism, Psychoanalysis.* New York: Routledge, 1993.

Crump, John. *The Origins of Socialist Thought in Japan.* New York: St. Martin's Press, 1983.

Daley, Linda. "Fabulation: Toward Untimely and Inhuman Life in Alexis Wright's *The Swan Book.*" *Australian Feminist Studies.* 31, no. 89 (2016): 305–18.

Daly, Mary. *Gyn/Ecology: The Metaethics of Radical Feminism.* Boston: Beacon Press, 1987.

Daston Lorraine, and Katherine Park. *Wonders and the Order of Nature, 1150–1750.* New York: Zone Books, 1998.

Davis, Rocío G. "Fictional Transits and Ruth Ozeki's *A Tale for the Time Being.*" *Biography* 38, no. 1 (2015): 87–103.

de Angelis, Massimo. "Does Capital Need a Commons Fix?" *ephemera, theory and politics in organization* 13, no. 3 (2013): 603–15.

——. "The Tragedy of the Capitalist Commons [blog]." *Turbulence,* 2009. http://www.turbulence.org.uk/turbulence-5/capitalist-commons/index .html.

de Angelis, Massimo, and Stavros Stavrides. "On the Commons: A Public Interview with Massimo De Angelis and Stavros Stavrides." *e-flux Journal* 17 (2010): 1–17.

"Deathscapes: Mapping Race and Violence in Settler States." Carceral Geography, Royal Geographical Society with IBG. Accessed February 21, 2025. https://carceralgeographies.co.uk/deathscapes-mapping

-race-and-violence-in-settler-societies/#:~:text=With%20the%20ulti-mate%20aim%20of,the%20United%20States%20and%20Canada. This web page contains an archived link to the Deathscapes project by the National Library of Australia: https://webarchive.nla.gov.au/awa /20201103065140/http://pandora.nla.gov.au/pan/173410/20201103-1648 /www.deathscapes.org/index.html.

de Courtivron, Isabelle, and Elaine Marks, es. *New French Feminisms: An Anthology*. Amherst: University of Massachusetts Press, 1980.

DeLoughrey, Elizabeth. "Heavy Waters: Waste and Atlantic Modernity." *PMLA* 125, no. 3 (2010): 703–12.

——. "Kinship in the Abyss: Submerging with *The Deep.*" *Atlantic Studies* 20, no. 2 (2022): 348–60.

——. "Ordinary Futures: Interspecies Worldings in the Anthropocene." In *Global Ecologies and the Environmental Humanities: Postcolonial Approaches*, ed. Elizabeth DeLoughrey, Jill Didur, and Anthony Carrigan, 352–72. New York: Routledge, 2015.

——. *Routes and Roots: Navigating Caribbean and Pacific Island Literatures*. Honolulu: University of Hawai'i Press, 2007.

——. "Submarine Futures of the Anthropocene." *Comparative Literature* 69, no. 1 (2017): 32–44.

——. "Toward a Critical Ocean Studies for the Anthropocene." *English Language Notes* 57, no 1 (2019): 21–36.

Delphy, Christine. "The Invention of French Feminism: An Essential Move." *Yale French Studies* 87 (1995): 190–221.

Dery, Mark. "Black to the Future: Interviews with Samuel R. Delany, Greg Tate, and Tricia Rose." In *Flame Wars: The Discourse of Cyberculture*, ed. Mark Dery, 179–222. Durham, NC: Duke University Press, 1994.

Descartes, René. *The Passions of the Soul and Other Late Philosophical Writings*. Trans. Michael Moriarty. Oxford: Oxford University Press, 2015.

Douglass, Patrice D. "Black Feminist Theory for the Dead and Dying." *Theory and Event* 21, no. 1 (2018): 106–23.

Drecxiya. *The Quest*. Submerge Recordings, 1997. CD.

Dube, Saurabh, ed. *Enchantments of Modernity: Empire, Nation, Globalization*. New York: Routledge, 2008.

Dube, Saurabh, and Ishita Banerjee-Dube, eds. *Unbecoming Modern: Colonialism, Modernity, Colonial Modernitie*s. New York: Routledge, 2019.

During, Simon. *Modern Enchantments: The Cultural Power of Secular Magic.* Cambridge, MA: Harvard University Press, 2002.

Eisenstein, Hester, and Alice Jardine. *The Future of Difference.* New Brunswick, NJ: Rutgers University Press, 1980.

Ekwunife, Anthony. *Meaning and Function of "Inu Uwa" (Reincarnation) in Igbo Traditional Religious Culture.* Onitsha, Nigeria: Spiritan, 2000.

Emejulu, Akwugo. *Fugitive Feminism.* London: Silver Press, 2022.

Emezi, Akwaeke. *Dear Senthuran: A Black Spirit Memoir.* London: Faber and Faber, 2021.

——. *Freshwater.* London: Faber and Faber, 2018.

——. "I'd Read Everything—Even the Cereal Box." Interview with Arifa Akbar. *Guardian,* October 20, 2018. www.theguardian.com/books/2018/oct/20/akwaeke-emezi-interview-freshwater.

Er, Yanbing. "Anticipations, Afterlives: On the Temporal and Affective Reorientations of Sexual Difference." *Feminist Theory* 19, no. 3 (2018): 369–86.

Eshun, Kodwo. "Drexciya: Fear of a Wet Planet." *Wire,* January 1998.

——. "Further Considerations on Afrofuturism." *CR: The New Centennial Review* 3, no. 2 (2003): 287–302.

——. *More Brilliant Than the Sun: Adventures in Sonic Fiction.* London: Quartet Books, 1998.

Fain, John Tyree. "Some Notes on Ariel's Song." *Shakespeare Quarterly* 19, no. 4 (1968): 329–32.

Fanon, Frantz. "Algeria Unveiled." In *A Dying Colonialism,* trans. Haakon Chevalier, 35–67. New York: Grove Press, 1965. Book first published in 1959.

Farmer, David M., Matthew H. Alford, Ren-Chieh Lien, Yiing Jiang Yang, Ming-Huei Chang, and Qiang Li. "From Luzon Strait to Dongsha Plateau: Stages in the Life of an Internal Wave." *Oceanography* 24, no. 4 (2011): 64–77.

Federici, Silvia. *Caliban and the Witch: Women, the Body, and Primitive Accumulation.* New York: Autonomedia, 2004.

——. "Feminism and the Politics of the Commons." The Wealth of the Commons: A World Beyond Market and State. [2012.] http://www.wealthofthecommons.org/essay/feminism-and-politics-commons/.

———. *Re-Enchanting the World: Feminism and the Politics of the Commons.* New York: PM Press, 2018.

———. *Revolution at Point Zero: Housework, Reproduction, and Feminist Struggle.* Oakland, CA: PM Press, 2012.

———. *Witches, Witch-Hunting, and Women.* Oakland, CA: PM Press, 2018.

———. "Women, Reproduction, and the Commons." *South Atlantic Quarterly* 118, no. 4 (2019): 711–24.

Felman, Shoshana. "Women and Madness: The Critical Phallacy." *Diacritics* 5, no. 4 (1975): 2–10.

Felski, Rita. "Introduction." *New Literary History*, special issue "Interpretation and Its Rivals," ed. Rita Felski, 45, no. 2 (2014): v–xi.

———. "Introduction." *New Literary History*, special issue "Use," ed. Rita Felski, 44, no. 4 (2013): v–xii.

———. *The Limits of Critique.* Chicago: University of Chicago Press, 2015.

———. *Uses of Literature.* Malden, MA: Blackwell Publishing, 2008.

Fisher, Daniel. "Untidy Times: Alexis Wright, Extinction, and the Politics of Apprehension." *Cultural Anthropology* 33, no. 2 (2018): 180–88.

Fisher, Philip. *Wonder, the Rainbow, and the Aesthetics of Rare Experiences.* Cambridge, MA: Harvard University Press, 1998.

Fowler, Edward. *The Rhetoric of Confession: Shishōsetsu in Early Twentieth-Century Japanese Fiction.* Berkeley: University of California Press, 1988.

Frye, Northrop. *Anatomy of Criticism: Four Essays.* Princeton, NJ: Princeton University Press, 2000. First published in 1957.

———. *Spiritus Mundi: Essays on Literature, Myth, and Society.* Bloomington: Indiana University Press, 1976.

Fuss, Diana. *Essentially Speaking: Feminism, Nature and Difference.* New York: Routledge, 1989.

Gallagher, Ellen. *Watery Ecstatic.* 2001. Watercolor, ink, oil, plasticine, graphite, and cut paper on paper, 27 3/4 × 39 7/16 in (70.5 × 100.2 cm). Whitney Museum of American Art, New York. https://whitney.org/collection/works/18622.

Gallop, Jane. "'Quand nos lèvres s'écrivent': Irigaray's Body Politic." *Romanic Review* 74, no. 1 (1983): 77–83.

Garrison, Ednie Kaeh. "Are We on a Wavelength Yet? On Feminist Oceanography, Radios, and Third Wave Feminism." In *Different Wavelengths:*

Studies of the Contemporary Women's Movement, ed. Jo Reger, 237–56. New York: Routledge, 2005.

Garwood, Jessica, Ruth C. Musgrave, and Andrew J. Lucas. "Life in Internal Waves." *Oceanography* 33, no. 3 (2020): 38–49.

Gaskins, Nettrice R. "Deep Sea Dwellers: Drexciya and the Sonic Third Space." *Shima* 10, no. 2 (2016): 68–80.

Gellner, Ernest. *Culture, Identity, and Politics*. Cambridge: Cambridge University Press, 1987.

Ghamari-Tabrizi, Behrooz. *Foucault in Iran: Islamic Revolution after the Enlightenment*. Minneapolis: University of Minnesota Press, 2016.

Gilbert, Sandra, and Susan Gubar. *The Madwoman in the Attic: The Woman Writer and the Nineteenth-Century Literary Imagination*. New Haven, CT: Yale University Press, 1979.

Gillis, Stacy, Gillian Howie, and Rebecca Munford, eds. *Third Wave Feminism: A Critical Exploration*. Basingstoke, UK: Palgrave Macmillan, 2007.

Gilroy, Paul. *The Black Atlantic: Modernity and Double Consciousness*. Cambridge, MA: Harvard University Press, 1993.

Glassie, Alison. "Ruth Ozeki's Floating World: *A Tale for the Time Being*'s Spiritual Oceanography." *Novel: A Forum on Fiction* 53, no. 3 (2020): 452–70.

Glissant, Édouard. *Poetics of Relation*. Trans. Betsy Wing. Ann Arbor: University of Michigan Press, 1997.

Graham, Gordon. *The Re-Enchantment of the World: Art Versus Religion*. Oxford: Oxford University Press, 2007.

Grewal, Inderpal, and Caren Kaplan. "Global Identities: Theorizing Transnational Studies of Sexualities." *GLQ: A Journal of Lesbian and Gay Studies* 7, no. 4 (2001): 663–79.

——, eds. *Scattered Hegemonies: Postmodernity and Transnational Feminist Practices*. Minneapolis: University of Minnesota Press, 1994.

Grosz, Elizabeth. *Sexual Subversions: Three French Feminists*. Sydney: Allen and Unwin, 1989.

——. "Thinking the New: Of Futures Yet Unthought." *Symplokē* 6, nos. 1–2 (1998): 38–55.

——. *Time Travels: Feminism, Nature, Power*. Durham, NC: Duke University Press, 2005.

Grusin, Richard, ed. *The Nonhuman Turn*. Minneapolis: University of Minnesota Press, 2015.

Gubar, Susan. "What Ails Feminist Criticism?" *Critical Inquiry* 24, no. 4 (1998): 878–902.

Gullander-Drolet, Claire. "Translational Form in Ruth Ozeki's *A Tale for the Time Being*." *Journal of Transnational American Studies* 9, no. 1 (2018): 293–314.

Gumbs, Alexis Pauline. *Spill: Scenes of Black Feminist Fugitivity*. Durham, NC: Duke University Press, 2016.

——. *Undrowned: Black Feminist Lessons from Marine Mammals*. Chico, CA: AK Press, 2020.

Haines, Christian P., and Peter Hitchcock. "Introduction: No Place for the Commons." *Minnesota Review* 93, no. 1 (2019): 55–61.

Halberstam, Jack. *The Queer Art of Failure*. Durham, NC: Duke University Press, 2011.

Haqq, Abdul Qahim, and Dai Satō. *The Book of Drexciya*, Vol. 1. Berlin: Tresor, 2020.

——. *The Book of Drexciya*, Vol. 2. Berlin: Tresor, 2023.

Haraway, Donna. *Staying with the Trouble: Making Kin in the Chthulucene*. Durham, NC: Duke University Press, 2016.

Hardin, Garrett. "The Tragedy of the Commons." *Science* 162, no. 3859 (1968): 1243–48.

Hartman, Geoffrey H. *Criticism in the Wilderness: The Study of Literature Today*. New Haven, CT: Yale University Press, 1980.

Hartman, Saidiya. "Venus in Two Acts." *small axe* 12, no. 2 (2008): 1–14.

——. *Lose Your Mother: A Journey Along the Atlantic Slave Route*. New York: Farrar, Straus and Giroux, 2008.

Hayward, Eva. "FINGERYEYES: Impressions of Cup Corals." *Cultural Anthropology* 25, no. 4 (2010): 577–99.

——. "More Lessons from a Starfish: Prefixial Flesh and Transspeciated Selves." *Women's Studies Quarterly* 36, nos. 3–4 (2008): 64–85.

Helmreich, Stefan. *Alien Ocean: Anthropological Voyages in Microbial Seas*. Berkeley: University of California Press, 2009.

——. "The Genders of Waves." *Women's Studies Quarterly* 45, nos. 1–2 (2017): 29–51.

——. *Sounding the Limits of Life: Essays in the Anthropology of Biology and Beyond*. Princeton, NJ: Princeton University Press, 2015.

——. "Wave Theory ~ Social Theory." *Public Culture* 32, no. 2 (2020): 287–326.

Hemmings, Clare. *Why Stories Matter: The Political Grammar of Feminist Theory.* Durham, NC: Duke University Press, 2011.

Hesford, Victoria. *Feeling Women's Liberation.* Durham, NC: Duke University Press, 2013.

Hessler, Stefanie, ed. *Tidalectics: Imagining an Oceanic Worldview Through Art and Science.* Cambridge, MA: MIT Press 2018.

Hewitt, Nancy A. "Feminist Frequencies: Regenerating the Wave Metaphor." *Feminist Studies* 38, no. 3 (2012): 658–80.

——, ed. *No Permanent Waves: Recasting Histories of U.S. Feminism.* New Brunswick, NJ: Rutgers University Press, 2010.

Higgins, Patricia J. Review of *Going to Iran,* by Kate Millett. *Signs: Journal of Women in Culture and Society* 9, no. 1 (1983): 154–56.

Hill, Rebecca. "The Multiple Readings of Sexual Difference." *Philosophy Compass* 11, no. 7 (2016): 390–401.

Hirsh, Elizabeth, and Gary A. Olson, "'Je—Luce Irigaray': A Meeting with Luce Irigaray." Trans. Elizabeth Hirsh and Gaëtan Brulotte. *Hypatia* 10, no. 2 (1995): 93–114.

Holgate, Ben. "Unsettling Narratives: Re-Evaluating Magical Realism as Postcolonial Discourse through Alexis Wright's *Carpentaria* and *The Swan Book.*" *Journal of Postcolonial Writing* 51, no. 6, (2015): 634–47.

Homer. *The Odyssey.* Trans. Emily Wilson. New York: Norton, 2017.

Hoodfar, Homar. "The Veil in Their Minds and on Our Heads: Veiling Practices and Muslim Women." In *The Politics of Culture in the Shadow of Capital,* ed. Lisa Lowe and David Lloyd, 248–79. Durham, NC: Duke University Press, 1997.

hooks, bell. "Sisterhood: Political Solidarity Between Women." *Feminist Review* 23, no. 1 (1986): 125–38.

Horkheimer, Max, and Theodore W. Adorno. *Dialectic of Enlightenment.* Trans. Edmund Jephcott. Ed. Gunzelin Schmid Noeri. Stanford, CA: Stanford University Press, 2002. First published in 1944.

Huang, Michelle N. "Ecologies of Entanglement in the Great Pacific Garbage Patch." *Journal of Asian American Studies,* special issue "Transpacific Overtures," 20, no. 1 (2017): 95–117.

Huang, Vivian L. *Surface Relations: Queer Forms of Asian American Inscrutability.* Durham, NC: Duke University Press, 2022.

Huang, Yunte. *Transpacific Imaginations: History, Literature, Counterpoetics.* Cambridge, MA: Harvard University Press, 2008.

Hughes, Christina, and Celia Lury. "Re-Turning Feminist Methodologies: From a Social to an Ecological Epistemology." *Gender and Education* 25, no. 6 (2013): 786–99.

Hyppolyte, Havel. "Long Live Anarchy!" *Mother Earth* 5, no. 12 (February 1911): 375–9.

Ibrahim, Habiba. *Black Age: Oceanic Lifespans and the Time of Black Life.* New York: NYU Press, 2021.

——. "Caliban, His Woman, and the Gendered (In)Humanism of *Wild Seed.*" *Anthropology and Humanism* 48, no. 1 (2022): 174–87.

Ilechukwu, Sunday T. C. "*Ogbanje/Abiku* and Cultural Conceptualizations of Psychopathology in Nigeria." *Mental Health, Religion and Culture* 10, no. 3 (2007): 239–55.

Ingersoll, Karin E. *Waves of Knowing: A Seascape Epistemology.* Durham, NC: Duke University Press, 2016.

Irigaray, Luce. *An Ethics of Sexual Difference.* Trans. Carolyn Burke and Gillian C. Gill. Ithaca, NY: Cornell University Press, 1993.

——, ed. *Luce Irigaray: Key Writings.* London: Continuum, 2004.

——. *Speculum of the Other Woman.* Trans. Gillian C. Gill. Ithaca, NY: Cornell University Press, 1985.

——. *This Sex Which Is Not One.* Trans. Carolyn Burke and Catherine Porter. Ithaca, NY: Cornell University Press, 1985.

Jackson, Zakiyyah Iman. "Animal: New Directions in the Theorization of Race and Posthumanism." *Feminist Studies* 39, no. 3 (2014): 669–85.

——. *Becoming Human: Matter and Meaning in an Antiblack World.* New York: NYU Press, 2020.

——. "Outer Worlds: The Persistence of Race in Movement 'Beyond the Human.'" *GLQ: A Journal of Lesbian and Gay Studies* 21, nos. 2–3 (2015): 215–18.

Johns-Putra, Adeline. "The Rest Is Silence: Postmodern and Postcolonial Possibilities in Climate Change Fiction." *Studies in the Novel* 50, no. 1 (2018): 26–42.

Johnson, Barbara. *The Feminist Difference: Literature, Psychoanalysis, Race, and Gender.* Cambridge, MA: Harvard University Press, 1998.

Jones, Ann Rosalind. "Writing the Body: Toward an Understanding of 'L'Écriture Féminine.'" *Feminist Studies* 7, no. 2 (1981): 247–63.

Jue, Melody. "Intimate Objectivity: On Nnedi Okorafor's Oceanic Afrofuturism." *Women's Studies Quarterly* 45, nos. 1–2 (2017): 171–88.

——. *Wild Blue Media: Thinking Through Seawater.* Durham, NC: Duke University Press, 2020.

Kennedy, Elizabeth Lapovsky, and Agatha Meryl Beins, eds. *Women's Studies for the Future: Foundations, Interrogations, Politics.* New Brunswick, NJ: Rutgers University Press, 2005.

Khanna, Ranjana. "On the Name, Ideation, and Sexual Difference." *differences: A Journal of Feminist Cultural Studies* 27, no. 2 (2016): 62–78.

Kim, Andrew. "Japanese Melancholy and the Ethics of Concealment in Ruth Ozeki's *A Tale for the Time Being.*" *Mosaic: An Interdisciplinary Critical Journal* 52, no. 4 (2019): 73–90.

Klein, Naomi. "Reclaiming the Commons." *New Left Review* 9 (2001): 81–89.

Konishi, Sho. *Anarchist Modernity: Cooperatism and Japanese-Russian Intellectual Relations in Modern Japan.* Cambridge, MA: Harvard University Press, 2013.

Kramnick, Jonathan. "Criticism and Truth." *Critical Inquiry* 47, no. 2 (2021): 218–40.

Kristeva, Julia. *The Powers of Horror: An Essay on Abjection.* Trans. Leon S. Roudiez. New York: Columbia University Press, 1980.

Krøijer, Stine, and Cecilie Rubow, "Introduction: Enchanted Ecologies and Ethics of Care." *Environmental Humanities* 14, no. 2 (July 2022): 375–84.

Kurnick, David. "A Few Lies: Queer Theory and Our Method Melodramas." *ELH* 87, no. 2 (2020): 349–74.

Landy, Joshua, and Michael Saler, eds. *The Re-Enchantment of the World: Secular Magic in a Rational Age.* Stanford, CA: Stanford University Press, 2009.

Laughlin, Kathleen A., Julie Gallagher, Dorothy Sue Cobble, et al. "Is It Time to Jump Ship? Historians Rethink the Waves Metaphor." *Feminist Formations* 22, no. 1 (2010): 76–135.

Lavender, Isiah, III. *Afrofuturism Rising: The Literary Prehistory of a Movement.* Columbus: Ohio State University Press, 2019.

Lavender, Isiah, III, and Lisa Yaszek, eds. *Literary Afrofuturism in the Twenty-First Century*. Columbus: Ohio State University Press, 2020.

Leane, Jeanine. "Historyless People." *Long History, Deep Time: Deepening Histories of Place*, ed. Ann McGrath and Mary Anne Jebb, 151–62. Canberra: ANU Press, 2015.

Lee, Hsiu-chuan. "Sharing Worlds Through Words: Minor Cosmopolitics in Ruth Ozeki's *A Tale for the Time Being*." *ariel: A Review of International English Literature* 49, no. 1 (2018): 27–52.

Lee, Summer Kim. "Staying In: Mitski, Ocean Vuong, and Asian American Asociality." *Social Text* 37, no. 1 (2019): 27–50.

León, Christina A. "Forms of Opacity: Roaches, Blood, and Being Stuck in Xandra Ibarra's Corpus." *ASAP/Journal* 2, no. 2 (2017): 369–94.

Levine, George. *Darwin Loves You: Natural Selection and the Re-Enchantment of the World*. Princeton, NJ: Princeton University Press, 2008.

Linebaugh, Peter. *The Magna Carta Manifesto: Liberties and Commons for All*. Berkeley: University of California Press, 2008.

——. *Stop, Thief! The Commons, Enclosures, and Resistance*. Oakland, CA: PM Press, 2014.

Llewelyn, Dawn. *Reading, Feminism, and Spirituality: Troubling the Waves*. Basingstoke, UK: Palgrave Macmillan, 2015.

Lloyd, Genevieve. *Reclaiming Wonder: After the Sublime*. Edinburgh: Edinburgh University Press, 2018.

Lorde, Audre. *The Collected Poems of Audre Lorde*. New York: Norton, 1997.

Love, Heather. "Close but Not Deep: Literary Ethics and the Descriptive Turn." *New Literary History* 41, no. 2 (2010): 371–91.

Lowy, Dina. *The Japanese "New Woman:" Images of Gender and Modernity*. New Brunswick, NJ: Rutgers University Press, 2007.

Lucas, Andrew J., and Robert Pinkel. "Observations of Coherent Transverse Wakes in Shoaling Nonlinear Internal Waves." *Journal of Physical Oceanography* 52, no. 6 (2022): 1277–93.

Luciano, Dana, and Mel Y. Chen. "Introduction: Has the Queer Ever Been Human?" *GLQ: A Journal of Lesbian and Gay Studies* 21, nos. 2–3 (2015): 183–207.

Lugones, María. "Toward a Decolonial Feminism." *Hypatia* 25, no. 4 (2010): 742–59.

MacLean, Nancy. "The Hidden History of Affirmative Action: Working Women's Struggles in the 1970s and the Gender of Class." *Feminist Studies* 25, no. 1 (1999): 43–78.

Makward, Christiane, and Hélène Cixous. "Interview with Hélène Cixous." *SubStance* 5, no. 13 (1976): 19–37.

Malatino, Hil. *Side Affects: On Being Trans and Feeling Bad*. Minneapolis: University of Minnesota Press, 2022.

Marx, Karl. *The Class Struggles in France, 1848–1850*. Trans. Henry Kuhn. New York: New York Labor News, 1924.

Mayer, Ruth. "'Africa as an Alien Future': The Middle Passage, Afrofuturism, and Postcolonial Waterworlds." *Amerikastudien/American Studies* 45, no. 4 (2000): 555–66.

Mbiti, John S. *African Religions and Philosophy*. Portsmouth, NH: Heinemann, 1990.

McDermott, Sinead. "Notes on the Afterlife of Feminist Criticism." *PMLA* 121, no. 5 (2006): 1729–34.

McKittrick, Katherine. "Black Human Geographies." *In Posthumanism in Art and Science: A Reader*, ed. Susan McHugh and Giovanni Aloi, 249–55. New York: Columbia University Press, 2021.

——. *Dear Science and Other Stories*. Durham, NC: Duke University Press, 2021.

——. *Demonic Grounds: Black Women and the Cartographies of Struggle*. Minneapolis: University of Minnesota Press, 2006.

——, ed. *Sylvia Wynter: On Being Human as Praxis*. Durham, NC: Duke University Press, 2015.

Mead, Philip. "The Injusticeable and the Imaginable." *Journal of the Association for the Study of Australian Literature* 16, no. 2 (2016). https://openjournals.library.sydney.edu.au/index.php/JASAL/article/view/11400/.

——. "Unresolved Sovereignty and the Anthropocene Novel: Alexis Wright's *The Swan Book*." *Journal of Australian Studies* 42, no. 4 (2018): 524–38.

Mercier, Matthieu J., Louis Gostiaux, Karl Helfrich, Joel Sommeria, et al. "Large-Scale, Realistic Laboratory Modeling of M2 Internal Tide Generation at the Luzon Strait." *Geophysical Research Letters* 40, no. 21 (2013): 5704–09.

Mezzandra, Sandro. "Resonances of the Common." In *The Anomie of the Earth: Philosophy, Politics, and Autonomy in Europe and the Americas*, ed. Federico Luisetti, John Pickles, and Wilson Kaiser, 215–26. Durham, NC: Duke University Press, 2015.

Miller, Nancy K. ed. *The Poetics of Gender*. New York: Columbia University Press, 1986.

Millett, Kate. *Going to Iran*. New York: Coward, McCann, and Geoghegan, 1982.

Millner-Larson, Nadja, and Gavin Butt. "Introduction: The Queer Commons." *GLQ: A Journal of Lesbian and Gay Studies*, special issue "The Queer Commons," 24, no. 4 (2018): 399–419.

Moghadam, Valentine M. *Globalizing Women: Transnational Feminist Networks*. Baltimore: Johns Hopkins University Press, 2005.

Moghissi, Haideh. *Populism and Feminism in Iran: Women's Struggle in a Male-Defined Revolutionary Movement*. London: Palgrave Macmillan, 1996.

Mohanty, Chandra Talpade. *Feminism Without Borders: Decolonizing Theory, Practicing Solidarity*. Durham, NC: Duke University Press, 2003.

——. "Under Western Eyes: Feminist Scholarship and Colonial Discourses." *boundary 2*, nos. 12–13 (1984): 333–58.

Moi, Toril. "'I Am Not a Woman Writer': About Women, Literature, and Feminist Theory Today." *Feminist Theory* 9, no. 3 (2008): 259–71.

——. *Sexual/Textual Politics: Feminist Literary Theory*. New York: Methuen, 1985.

Mok, Christine, and Aimee Bahng. "Transpacific Overtures: An Introduction." *Journal of Asian American Studies* 20, no. 1 (2017): 1–9.

Moore, Sue E., and Ren-Chieh Lien. "Pilot Whales Follow Internal Solitary Waves in the South China Sea." *Marine Mammal Science* 23, no. 1 (2007): 193–96.

Moreton-Robinson, Aileen, ed. *Sovereign Subjects: Indigenous Sovereignty Matters*. Sydney: Allen and Unwin, 2007.

——. *The White Possessive: Property, Power, and Indigenous Sovereignty*. Minneapolis: University of Minnesota Press, 2015.

Morgan, David. *Images at Work: The Material Culture of Enchantment*. Oxford: Oxford University Press, 2018.

———. "Introduction: Enchantment, Disenchantment, Re-Enchantment." In *Re-Enchantment*, ed. James Elkins and David Morgan, 3–22. New York: Routledge, 2009.

Morgan, Robin. *Sisterhood Is Global*. New York: Feminist Press at CUNY, 1984.

Mortimer-Sandilands, Catriona, and Bruce Erickson, eds. *Queer Ecologies: Sex, Nature, Politics, Desire*. Bloomington: Indiana University Press, 2010.

Moses, Claire. "Made in America: 'French Feminism' in Academia." *Feminist Studies* 24, no. 2 (1998): 241–74.

Moten, Fred. *Stolen Life*. Durham, NC: Duke University Press, 2018.

Moten, Fred, and Stefano Harney. *The Undercommons: Fugitive Planning and Black Study*. New York: Minor Compositions, 2013.

Mottahedeh, Negar. *Whisper Tapes: Kate Millett in Iran*. Stanford, CA: Stanford University Press, 2019.

Munk, Walter. "Internal Waves and Small-Scale Processes." In *Evolution of Physical Oceanography: Scientific Surveys in Honor of Henry Stommel*, ed. Bruce A. Warren and Carl Wunsch, 264–91. Cambridge, MA: MIT Press, 1980.

Muñoz, José Esteban. "The Brown Commons." In *The Sense of Brown*, ed. Joshua Chambers-Letson and Tavia Nyong'o, 1–7. Durham, NC: Duke University Press, 2020.

Naghibi, Nima. *Rethinking Global Sisterhood: Western Feminism and Iran*. Minneapolis: University of Minnesota Press, 2007.

Nash, Jennifer. *Black Feminism Reimagined: After Intersectionality*. Durham, NC: Duke University Press, 2019.

Neimanis, Astrida. *Bodies of Water: Posthuman Feminist Phenomenology*. London: Bloomsbury, 2017.

———. "feminist subjectivity, watered." *Feminist Review* 103 (2013): 23–41.

———. "The Sea and the Breathing." *e-flux Journal*, May 2020, http://www.e-flux.com/architecture/oceans/331869/the-sea-and-the-breathing/.

———. "The Weather Underwater: Blackness, White Feminism, and the Breathless Sea." *Australian Feminist Studies* 34, no. 102 (2019): 490–508.

Nelson, Alondra. "Introduction: Future Texts." *Social Text* 20, no. 2 (2002): 1–15.

Nelson, Dana D. "The Enduring Appeal of the Commons." *Arizona Quarterly: A Journal of American Literature, Culture, and Theory* 75, no. 2 (2019): 1–21.

Nguyen, Viet Thanh, and Janet Hoskins, eds. *Transpacific Studies: Critical Perspectives on an Emerging Field.* Honolulu: University of Hawai'i Press, 2014.

Nicholas, Lucy, and Shelley Budgeon. "Introduction: 'Remembering Feminist Theory Forward.'" *Feminist Theory* 22, no. 2 (2021): 159–64.

Nicholls, Christine Judith. "'Dreamtime' and 'The Dreaming'—An Introduction." The Conversation, January 22, 2014. https://theconversation .com/dreamtime-and-the-dreaming-an-introduction-20833.

Nicholson, Linda. "Feminism in 'Waves': Useful Metaphor or Not?" *New Politics* 12, no. 4 (2010): 34–39.

Noon, John A. "A Preliminary Examination of the Death Concepts of the Ibo." *American Anthropologist* 44, no. 4 (1942): 638–54.

Nyong'o, Tavia. "Little Monsters: Race, Sovereignty, and Queer Inhumanism in *Beasts of the Southern Wild.*" *GLQ: A Journal of Lesbian and Gay Studies* 12, nos. 2–3 (2015): 249–72.

Nzegwu, Nkiru Uwechia. *Family Matters: Feminist Concepts in African Philosophy of Culture.* New York: SUNY Press, 2006.

Nzewi, Esther. "Malevolent *Ogbanje*: Recurrent Reincarnation or Sickle Cell Disease?" *Social Science and Medicine* 59, no. 9 (2001): 1403–16.

Ogden, Laura. *Loss and Wonder at the World's End.* Durham, NC: Duke University Press, 2021.

Okonkwo, Christopher. *A Spirit of Dialogue: Incarnations of Ogbanje, the Born-to-Die, in African American Literature.* Knoxville: University of Tennessee Press, 2008.

Ostrom, Elinor. *Governing the Commons: The Evolution of Institutions for Collective Action.* Cambridge: Cambridge University Press, 1990.

Osuagwu, Bertram I. N. *The Igbos and Their Traditions.* Trans. Frances W. Pritchett, 1979. http://www.columbia.edu/itc/mealac/pritchett/00fwp /igbo/secondary/txt_traditions_0105.pdf.

Oyewumi, Oyeronke. *The Invention of Women: Making an African Sense of Western Gender Discourses.* Minneapolis: University of Minnesota Press, 1997.

Ozeki, Ruth. "A Conversation with Ruth Ozeki." ruth ozeki's web world, March 2013. https://www.ruthozeki.com/writing-film/time-being /read/.

——. *A Tale for the Time Being*. New York: Penguin, 2013.

Pease, Donald E. "New Americanists: Revisionist Interventions into the Canon." *boundary 2* 17, no. 1 (Spring 1990): 1–37.

Pineda, Jesús, Victoria Starczak, José C. B. da Silva, Karl Helfrich, Michael Thompson, and David Wiley. "Whales and Waves: Humpback Whale Foraging Response and the Shoaling of Internal Waves at Stellwagen Bank." *Journal of Geophysical Research: Oceans* 120 (2015): 2555–70.

Pomar, L., M. Morsilli, P. Hallock, and B. Bádenas. "Internal Waves, an Under-Explored Source of Turbulence Events in the Sedimentary Record." *Earth-Science Reviews* 111, nos. 1–2 (2012): 56–81.

Post, Tina. *Deadpan: The Aesthetics of Black Inexpression*. New York: NYU Press, 2022.

Povinelli, Elizabeth. *The Cunning of Recognition: Indigenous Alterities and the Making of Australian Multiculturalism*. Durham, NC: Duke University Press, 2002.

Puig de la Bellacasa, María. *Matters of Care: Speculative Ethics in More Than Human Worlds*. Minneapolis: University of Minnesota Press, 2017.

Raven, Margaret, Daniel Robinson, and John Hunter. "The Emu: More-than-Human and More-than-Animal Geographies." *Antipode: A Radical Journal of Geography* 53, no. 5 (2021): 1526–45.

Ravenscroft, Alison. "Dreaming of Others: *Carpentaria* and Its Critics." *Cultural Studies Review* 16, no. 2 (2010): 194–224.

Reger, Jo, ed. *Different Wavelengths: Studies of the Contemporary Women's Movement*. New: Routledge, 2005.

——. "Finding a Place in History: The Discursive Legacy of the Wave Metaphor and Contemporary Feminism." *Feminist Studies* 43 no. 1 (2017): 193–221.

Reid, Herbert, and Betsy Taylor. *Recovering the Commons: Democracy, Place, and Global Justice*. Champaign: University of Illinois Press, 2010.

Rich, Adrienne. "When We Dead Awaken: Writing as Re-Vision." *College English* 34, no. 1 (1972): 18–30.

Ricoeur, Paul. *Hermeneutics and the Human Sciences: Essays on Language, Action and Interpretation*. Edited, translated, and introduced by John B. Thompson. Cambridge: Cambridge University Press, 1981.

Rifkin, Mark. *Beyond Settler Time: Temporal Sovereignty and Indigenous Self-Determination*. Durham, NC: Duke University Press, 2017.

Rose, Deborah Bird. *Reports from a Wild Country: Ethics for Decolonisation*. Sydney: University of New South Wales Press, 2004.

Roswall, Amanda Grimsbo. "Collectivity and Feminist History: Situating Luce Irigaray." *Signs: Journal of Women in Culture and Society* 49, no. 4 (2024): 887–911.

Russo, Mary. *The Female Grotesque: Risk, Excess, Modernity*. New York: Routledge, 1995.

Saint-Amour, Paul. "Weak Theory, Weak Modernism." *Modernism/modernity* 25, no. 3 (2018): 437–59.

Saler, Michael. *As If: Modern Enchantment and the Literary Pre-History of Virtual Reality*. Oxford: Oxford University Press, 2012.

——. "Modernity and Enchantment: A Historiographic Review." *American Historical Review* 111, no. 3 (2006): 692–716.

Sandilands, Catriona. "Queer Ecology." In *Keywords for Environmental Studies*, ed. Joni Adamson, William A. Gleason, and David Pellow, 169–71. New York: NYU Press, 2016. Also available at https://keywords.nyupress.org/environmental-studies/essay/queer-ecology/.

Santana, Dora Silva. "Transitionings and Returnings: Experiments with the Poetics of Transatlantic Water." *TSQ: Transgender Studies Quarterly* 4, no. 2 (2017): 181–90.

Sato, Barbara. *The New Japanese Woman: Modernity, Media, and Women in Interwar Japan*. Durham, NC: Duke University Press, 2003.

Schneider, Mark A. *Culture and Enchantment*. Chicago: University of Chicago Press, 1993.

Schor, Naomi. *Bad Objects: Essays Popular and Unpopular*. Durham, NC: Duke University Press, 1995.

——. "This Essentialism Which Is Not One." In *Engaging with Irigaray*, ed. Carolyn Burke, Naomi Schor, and Margaret Whitford, 57–78. New York: Columbia University Press, 1994.

Scott, David. "The Re-Enchantment of Humanism: An Interview with Sylvia Wynter." *small axe* 4, no. 2 (2000): 119–207.

Scott, Joan Wallach, ed., *Women's Studies on the Edge*. Durham, NC: Duke University Press, 2008.

Sefton-Rowston, Adelle L. "Hope at the End of the World: Creation Stories and Apocalypse in Alexis Wright's *Carpentaria* and *The Swan Book*." *Antipodes* 30, no. 2 (2016): 355–68.

Shakespeare, William. *The Tempest*. Ed. Peter Hulme and William H. Sherman. New York: Norton, 2019.

Sharpe, Christina. *In the Wake: On Blackness and Being*. Durham, NC: Duke University Press, 2016.

Sheth, Falguni A. "The Veil, Transparency, and the Deceptive Conceit of Liberalism." *philoSOPHIA* 9, no. 1 (2019): 53–72.

Showalter, Elaine. "Feminist Criticism in the Wilderness." *Critical Inquiry* 8, no. 2 (1981): 179–205.

——. *A Literature of Their Own: British Women Novelists from Brontë to Lessing*. Princeton: NJ: Princeton University Press, 1977.

——. "Toward A Feminist Poetics." In *The New Feminist Criticism: Essays on Women, Literature, and Theory*, ed. Elaine Showalter, 125–48. New York: Pantheon, 1985.

Siegal, Deborah L. "The Legacy of the Personal: Generating Theory in Feminism's Third Wave." *Hypatia* 12, no. 3 (1997): 46–75.

Singh, Julietta. *Unthinking Mastery: Dehumanism and Decolonial Entanglements*. Durham, NC: Duke University Press, 2018.

Sizemore, Michelle. *American Enchantment: Rituals of the People in the Post-Revolutionary World*. Oxford: Oxford University Press, 2018.

Solomon, Rivers, with Daveed Diggs, William Hutson, and Jonathan Snipes. *The Deep*. New York: Saga Press, 2019.

Spacks, Patricia Meyer. *The Female Imagination*. New York: Knopf, 1975.

Spillers, Hortense. "Mama's Baby, Papa's Maybe: An American Grammar Book." *Diacritics* 17, no. 2 (1987): 65–81.

Spivak, Gayatri Chakravorty. "French Feminism in an International Frame." *Yale French Studies* 62 (1981): 154–84.

Srinivas, Tulasi. *The Cow in the Elevator: An Anthropology of Wonder*. Durham, NC: Duke University Press, 2018.

Starr, Marlo. "Beyond Machine Dreams: Zen, Cyber-, and Transnational Feminisms in Ruth Ozeki's *A Tale for the Time Being*." *Meridians: feminism, race, transnationalism* 13, no. 2 (2016): 99–122.

Stavrides, Stavros. *Common Space: The City as Commons*. London: Zed Books, 2016.

Steinberg, Philip, and Kimberly Peters. "Wet Ontologies, Fluid Spaces: Giving Depth to Volume Through Oceanic Thinking." *Environment and Planning D: Society and Space* 33, no. 2 (2015): 247–64.

Stevick, Peter, Lewis Incze, Scott D Kraus, and Shale Rosen. "Trophic Relationships and Oceanography on and Around a Small Offshore Bank." *Marine Ecology Progress Series* 363 (2008): 15–28.

Stiegler, Bernard. *The Re-Enchantment of the World: The Value of Spirit Against Industrial Populism*. Trans. Trevor Arthur. London: Bloomsbury Academic, 2014.

Strathern, Marilyn. *The Gender of the Gift: Problems with Women and Problems with Society in Melanesia*. Berkeley: University of California Press, 1988.

Sundberg, Juanita. "Decolonizing Posthumanist Geographies." *Cultural Geographies* 21, no. 1 (2014): 33–47.

Sutherland, Bruce R. *Internal Gravity Waves*. Cambridge: Cambridge University Press, 2014.

Suzuki, Erin. "Transpacific." In *The Routledge Companion to Asian American and Pacific Island Literatures*, ed. Rachel Lee, 352–64. New York: Routledge, 2014.

Suzuki, Tomi. *Narrating the Self: Fictions of Japanese Modernity*. Stanford, CA: Stanford University Press, 1996.

Swarr, Amanda Lock, and Richi Nagar, ed. *Critical Transnational Feminist Praxis*. New York: SUNY Press, 2010.

Takolander, Maria Kaaren. "Theorizing Irony and Trauma in Magical Realism: Junot Díaz's *The Brief Wondrous Life of Oscar Wao* and Alexis Wright's *The Swan Book*." *ariel: A Review of International English Literature* 47, no. 3 (2016): 95–122.

Taleb, Nicholas Nassim. *The Black Swan: The Impact of the Highly Improbable*. 2nd ed. New York: Random House, 2010.

Tambe, Ashwini, and Millie Thayer, eds. *Transnational Feminist Itineraries: Situating Theory and Activist Practice*. Durham, NC: Duke University Press, 2021.

Tate, Claudia. "Audre Lorde." In *Conversations with Audre Lorde*, ed. Joan Wylie Hall Jackson, 85–100. Jackson: University Press of Mississippi, 2004.

Taylor, Ula Y. "Making Waves: The Theory and Practice of Black Feminism." *Black Scholar* 28, no. 2 (1998): 18–28.

Theocritus. *The Greek Bucolic Poets*. Trans. J. M. Edmonds. Cambridge, MA: Harvard University Press, 1991.

Thompson, Becky. "Multiracial Feminism: Recasting the Chronology of Second Wave Feminism." *Feminist Studies* 28, no. 2 (2002): 337–60.

Tinsley, Omise'eke Natasha. "Black Atlantic, Queer Atlantic: Queer Imaginings of the Middle Passage." *GLQ: A Journal of Lesbian and Gay Studies* 14, no. 2 (2008): 191–215.

Todd, Zoe. "An Indigenous Feminist's Take on the Ontological Turn: 'Ontology' Is Just Another Word for Colonialism." *Journal of Historical Sociology* 29, no. 1 (2016): 4–22.

——. "Fish Pluralities: Human-Animal Relations and Sites of Engagement in Paulatuuq, Arctic Canada." *Etudes/Inuit/Studies* 38, nos. 1–2 (2014): 217–38.

Tsing, Anna Lowenhaupt. *The Mushroom at the End of the World: On the Possibilities of Life in Capitalist Ruins*. Princeton, NJ: Princeton University Press, 2015.

Tucker, Herbert F. "After Magic: Modern Charm in History, Theory, and Practice." *New Literary History* 48, no. 1 (2017): 103–22.

Vance, Carole S., ed. *Pleasure and Danger: Exploring Female Sexuality*. New York: Routledge and Kegan Paul, 1984.

van Dooren, Thom. *Flight Ways: Life and Loss at the Edge of Extinction*. New York: Columbia University Press, 2014.

Walcott, Rinaldo. "The Black Aquatic." *liquid blackness* 5, no. 1 (2021): 63–73.

Wang, Yu-Huai, Chang-Feng Dai, and Yang-Yih Chen. "Physical and Ecological Processes of Internal Waves on an Isolated Reef Ecosystem in the South China Sea." *Geophysical Research Letters* 34, no. 18 (2007): 1–7.

Weaver, Harlan. "Trans Species." *TSQ: Transgender Studies Quarterly*, special issue "Postposttranssexual: Key Concepts for a Twenty-First-Century Transgender Studies," ed. Paisley Currah and Susan Stryker, 1, nos. 1–2 (2014): 253–54.

Weber, Max. *From Max Weber: Essays in Sociology*. Trans. and ed. H. H. Gerth and C. Wright Mills. New York: Oxford University Press, 1946.

——. *The Protestant Ethic and the Spirit of Capitalism.* Trans. Talcott Parsons. New York: Routledge, 1992. First published in English in 1930.

Weed, Elizabeth, and Ellen Rooney, eds. "Editor's Note." *differences: A Journal of Feminist Cultural Studies* 28, vol. 1 (2017): iii–iv.

Weheliye, Alexander G. "After Man." *American Literary History* 20, nos. 1–2 (2008): 321–36.

——. *Habeas Viscus: Racializing Assemblages, Biopolitics, and Black Feminist Theories of the Human.* Durham, NC: Duke University Press, 2014.

Welsh, Andrew. *Roots of Lyric: Primitive Poetry and Modern Poetics.* Princeton, NJ: Princeton University Press, 1978.

Whitford, Margaret. *Luce Irigaray: Philosophy in the Feminine.* New York: Routledge, 1991.

——. "Luce Irigaray and the Female Imaginary: Speaking as a Woman." *Radical Philosophy* no. 43 (1986): 3–8.

Wiegman, Robyn. "Feminism's Apocalyptic Futures." *New Literary History* 31, no. 4 (2000): 805–25.

——. "The Intimacy of Critique: Ruminations on Feminism as a Living Thing." *Feminist Theory* 11, no. 1 (2010): 79–84.

——. *Object Lessons.* Durham, NC: Duke University Press, 2012.

——. "What Ails Feminist Criticism? A Second Opinion." *Critical Inquiry* 25, no. 2 (1999): 362–79.

——, ed. *Women's Studies on Its Own: A Next Wave Reader in Institutional Change.* Durham, NC: Duke University Press, 2002.

Williams, Ben. "Black Secret Technology: Detroit Techno and the Information Age." In *Technicolor: Race, Technology and Everyday Life*, ed. Alondra Nelson, Thuy Linh Nguyen Tu, and Alicia Headlam Hines, 154–76. New York: NYU Press, 2001.

Winkiel, Laura, ed. "Introduction." *English Language Notes*, special issue "Hydro-Criticism," 57, no. 1 (2019): 1–10.

Wolfe, Patrick. "On Being Woken Up: The Dreamtime in Anthropology and in Australian Settler Culture." *Comparative Studies in Society and History* 33, no. 2 (1991): 197–224.

Womack, Ytasha. *Afrofuturism: The World of Black Sci-Fi and Fantasy Culture.* Chicago: Lawrence Hill Books, 2013.

Wright, Alexis. *Carpentaria.* Sydney: Giramondo, 2006.

——. *Plains of Promise.* Brisbane: University of Queensland Press, 1997.

——. "Politics of Writing." *Southerly* 62, no. 2 (2002): 10–20.

——. *Praiseworthy*. Sydney: Giramondo, 2023.

——. *The Swan Book*. New York: Washington Square Press, 2013.

Wright, Daniel. *The Grounds of the Novel*. Stanford, CA: Stanford University Press, 2024.

Wynter, Sylvia. "Afterword: Beyond Miranda's Meanings: Un/Silencing the 'Demonic Ground' of Caliban's 'Woman.'" In *Out of the Kumbla: Caribbean Women and Literature*, ed. Carole Boyce Davies and Elaine Savory Fido, 355–72. Trenton, NJ: Africa World Press, 1990.

——. "Beyond Liberal and Marxist Leninist Feminisms: Towards an Autonomous Frame of Reference." *CLR James Journal* 24, nos. 1–2 (2018): 31–56.

——. "But What Does 'Wonder' Do? Meanings, Canons, Too? On Literary Texts, Cultural Contexts, and What It's Like to Be One/Not One of Us." *Stanford Humanities Review* 4, no. 1 (1994): 124–29.

——. "ProudFlesh Inter/Views: Sylvia Wynter." *ProudFlesh: New Afrikan Journal of Culture Politics and Consciousness* 4 (2006): 1–35.

——. "Unsettling the Coloniality of Being/Power/Truth/Freedom: Towards the Human, After Man, Its Overrepresentation—An Argument." *CR: The New Centennial Review* 3, no. 3 (2003): 257–337.

Xiang, Sunny. *Tonal Intelligence: The Aesthetics of Asian Inscrutability During the Long Cold War*. New York: Columbia University Press, 2020.

Yang, Mayfair. *Re-Enchanting Modernity: Ritual Economy and Society in Wenzhou, China*. Durham, NC, Duke University Press, 2020.

Yao, Xine. *The Cultural Politics of Unfeeling in Nineteenth-Century America*. Durham, NC: Duke University Press, 2021.

Yeats, William Butler. *Essays*. New York: Macmillan, 1924.

——. "Leda and the Swan." In *The Collected Poems of W.B. Yeats*, ed. Richard J. Finneran, 182. 2nd ed. New York: Scribner, 1983.

——. *A Vision: The Revised 1937 Edition*. Vol. 14 of *The Collected Works of W.B. Yeats*. Ed. Margaret Mills Harper and Catherine E. Paul. New York: Scribner, 2015.

Yeğenoğlu, Meyda. *Colonial Fantasies: Towards a Feminist Reading of Orientalism*. Cambridge: Cambridge University Press, 1998.

Yonenama, Lisa. "Toward a Decolonial Genealogy of the Transpacific." *American Quarterly* 69, no. 3 (2017): 471–82.

Zahedi, Ashraf. "Contested Meaning of the Veil and Political Ideologies of Iranian Regimes." *Journal of Middle East Women's Studies* 3, no. 3 (2007): 75–98.

Zebuhr, Laura. "Sound Enchantment: The Case of Henry David Thoreau." *New Literary History* 48, no. 3 (2017): 581–603.

INDEX

lifeworlds, 168n20; Black, suspended by ocean, 26, 45, 47, 53–55; competing ontologies within, 88; of feminism, 3, 39; marginal, 3, 14, 16, 23, 76, 91, 98. *See also* textual lifeworlds

Linebaugh, Peter, 133

literary criticism, 21–24, 160, 175n69; close reading, 24, 36, 66, 174n62; postcritical turn, 22, 174n61; psychoanalytical focus, 63; return to, 3–4

literature: alternative feminist uses of, 23–24; "bad object" of, 23, 174–75n65, 175n66; hermeneutic function of, 6, 25, 131, 174n59; novel as meeting ground, 81–82; speculative environment of, 9–10

Lorde, Audre, 161–63, 217–18n1

Man, 78, 192–93n37, 193n39; as central archetype of humanism, 75–76; and coloniality, 15–16; and the commons, 134; as "overrepresented," 27, 66, 76; Sirens as threat to, 12

Marx, Karl, 133, 201n15

masculinity: of discourse, 68–70, 77; enchantment as threat to, 11–12; feminine subjectivity suppressed by, 67–68

McKittrick, Katherine, 18–19, 41–42, 77, 172n46, 180n29, 193–94n42, 193n40

"meeting ground," novel as, 81–82

Millett, Kate, 101–9, 201n18, 202n25; colonial sentiment of, 104–5; deported from Iran, 105–6

Millner-Larsen, Nadja, 139

modernity: counterhistories and futures of, 54; disenchantment claimed by, 2, 12–15; Japanese New Woman, 118–19, 204n45; management of otherness, 13–14; and settler conquest of Australia, 140; underside to consolidation of, 14; as universalizing project, 15, 171n34

Mohanty, Chandra Talpade, 99

monstrosity, 12, 168–69n24

more-than-human, 28, 125; "acts of love," 150; commons beyond the human, 28, 130–42, 147–50, 153; convergence of lifeworlds, 48, 85–86, 88, 141–42, 147; ethics, 150, 155–56; human entanglement with, 57–58, 209n7, 211n25; life beyond the human, 56, 59–60; matter and nonliving things, 138; multispecies interactions, 33, 48, 55–56, 58, 186n75; queer ecology of, 58–60; underwater, 32–33, 43, 48, 55. *See also* ogbanje (Igbo spirit)

Morgan, Robin, 201n19

Mottahedeh, Negar, 104, 108

Naghibi, Nima, 105–6

Nash, Jennifer, 19–20, 173m51

neoliberalism, 133–34

GPSR Authorized Representative: Easy Access System Europe, Mustamäe tee 50, 10621 Tallinn, Estonia, gpsr.requests@easproject.com